AGING, HEALTH, AND PUBLIC POLICY: DEMOGRAPHIC AND ECONOMIC PERSPECTIVES

AGING, HEALTH, AND PUBLIC POLICY: DEMOGRAPHIC AND ECONOMIC PERSPECTIVES

Linda J. Waite

Editor

POPULATION AND DEVELOPMENT REVIEW

A Supplement to Volume 30, 2004

POPULATION COUNCIL
New York

Library of Congress Cataloging-in-Publication Data

Aging, health, and public policy: demographic and economic perspectives / Linda J. Waite, editor.

   p. cm.

   "Population and development review, a supplement to volume 30, 2004."
   Includes bibliographical references.

   ISBN 0-87834-112-9 (pbk. : alk. paper)

   1. Age distribution (Demography)--Economic aspects. 2. Older people--Health and hygiene. 3. Older people--Economic conditions. 4. Older people--Social conditions. 5. Older people--Government policy--Economic aspects. 6. Old age assistance--Forecasting. I. Waite, Linda J. II. Population and development review.

HB1531.A35 2004

305.26—dc22   2004062826

ISSN 0098-7921
ISBN 0-87834-112-9

Printed in the United States of America.

CONTENTS

III. AGING, WORK, AND PUBLIC POLICY

IV. DATA AND STATISTICS

EPILOGUE

ACKNOWLEDGMENTS

The RAND Summer Institute on the Demography, Economics, and Epidemiology of Aging annually brings together research scientists from the centers on population aging supported by the US National Institute on Aging. The tenth anniversary Summer Institute, held at Santa Monica, California, 11–12 July 2003, provided an occasion for highlighting some recent achievements of aging research in the social sciences undertaken in these centers. This volume is largely based on the papers presented at this conference. The authors and the editor express their gratitude to Bob Schoeni and Lora Myers of the Michigan Center on the Demography of Aging, and Dana Goldman and Dawn Matsui at RAND for their role in organizing the meeting. We also thank the Michigan Center for logistic support and Bob Schoeni for encouragement and advice during the production of this supplement.

Financial support for both the conference and the volume came from the Office of Behavioral and Social Research, National Institute on Aging. We wish to acknowledge in particular the instrumental role of Richard Suzman, Associate Director of the Office. Without Richard's vision, persistence, and willingness to support new directions and new ideas, the demography and economics of aging would not be the vibrant, productive, exciting research arena that it has become. Of course, Richard's vision would have come to little without the support of Richard Hodes, Director of the National Institute on Aging, and, ultimately, the support of the US National Institutes of Health.

This publication was also supported by contributions from:

—Center for the Demography and Economics of Aging at the University of California at Berkeley

—Center on the Demography and Economics of Aging at the University of Chicago

—Population Aging Center at the University of Colorado

—Center for Demographic Studies at Duke University

—Center on the Demography of Aging at the University of Michigan

—Center for Aging and Health Research, NBER

—Population Aging Research Center at the University of Pennsylvania

—Center for the Study of Aging at RAND

—Center on the Demography and Economics of Health and Aging at Stanford University

—Center on Biodemography and Population Health at USC-UCLA

—Center for Demography of Health and Aging at the University of Wisconsin-Madison

We also thank the editorial staff of *Population and Development Review* for their assistance in producing this volume.

L.J.W.

INTRODUCTION

The Demographic Faces
of the Elderly

LINDA J. WAITE

Much of the world is aging rapidly. Both the number and proportion of people aged 65 years and older are increasing, although at different rates in different parts of the world. The number of older adults has risen more than threefold since 1950, from approximately 130 million to 419 million in 2000, with the elderly share of the population increasing from 4 percent to 7 percent during that period. In the United States, those aged 65 and older currently make up about 13 percent of the population. The US Census Bureau (2004) projects that in 25 years this proportion will exceed 20 percent. Over the next 50 years the United States will undergo a profound transformation, becoming a mature nation in which one citizen in five is 65 or older. (Now, one person in eight is that old.) The dramatic increases to come in the older population will exert powerful pressures on health care delivery systems, on programs such as Social Security, Medicare, Medicaid, and Supplemental Security Income that provide financial support, and on social institutions such as the family that provide instrumental, financial, and emotional support for the elderly.

As part of the same process, the older population itself will age, with large increases in the number of people who are 85 and older. In 2004, these oldest-old Americans accounted for just over 1 percent of the population (US Census Bureau 2004), but they exert a disproportionate effect on both their families and the health care system. These oldest-old men and—more frequently—women are much more likely than the young-old to live in nursing homes, to have substantial disabilities, and to have restricted financial resources.

Both the American population and the population of the world are adding oldest-old members at a much faster rate than any other age group. This means that the numbers of very old people will increase and the proportion of the population that is very old will rise. The Census Bureau (2004) projects that the US population aged 85 and older will double from about 4.3 million today to about 7.3 million in 2020, then double again to 15 million by 2040, as members of the very large baby boom cohorts born after World War II reach these ages. If the Census Bureau is correct, by 2050 one American in 20 will be 85 years old or older, compared to one in 100 today.

Both the number of older adults in the population and their proportion within the total population are concerns. The number of older adults we can expect in the future tells us something about how many hospital beds, geriatricians, home health aides, and nursing home beds will be needed. The proportion of the population that is old, and especially oldest-old, tells us how many working-age adults will be available to provide financial support to the elderly and to work as home health aides, geriatricians, food services workers, and so on. Thus, a large number of older adults has different implications in a large overall population than in a small one.

Many parts of the world are undergoing this demographic transformation. More than 18 percent of Italians are 65 and older, with Sweden, Belgium, Greece, and Japan just slightly younger. As these figures suggest, Europe has the highest proportion elderly and will probably remain the oldest region for decades. But the rapid declines in fertility in Asia, Latin America and the Caribbean, and the Near East/North Africa, combined with increases in life expectancy, mean that the proportions elderly in these regions will more than triple by 2050 (RAND 2001).

All the men and women in the world who will be very old in 2050 are alive today. Their maximum numbers are known. But how long these men and women will work, how long they will live, and what their resources and their needs will be are not known. We know little about the risks of illness and disability that will face older adults over the next half century.

We cannot plan for population change or design appropriate and effective responses without understanding, for example, the processes that underlie increases in longevity, the mechanisms that accelerate or delay the onset of disability, the incentives that affect retirement decisions, including employment and saving for retirement, and the role of public programs and policies in all of these factors.

Given that the vast majority of those who will make up the older population in the United States in next 50 years are already born and living in the country, the size of the older population in the future depends on how long these people will live. This past century has witnessed a remarkably constant decline in age-specific death rates. During the early part of the century, declines in death rates occurred when infectious diseases were brought under control. Since 1960, death rates from cardiovascular disease have fallen sharply, lowering overall death rates. Scientists continue to debate how much room exists for further improvement in longevity, and the outcome carries far-reaching implications. For example, the actuarial balance of the Social Security Trust Fund is more sensitive to alternative assumptions about future trends in longevity than to any other factor, including disability, immigration, wage growth, or inflation (Preston 1996).

History, biology, and disease

Both Robert Fogel and James Vaupel address this controversy, from different directions but with remarkably similar conclusions. During his study of Union Army veterans in the United States, Fogel and his colleagues (Chapter 1) found that chronic disease and disability were ubiquitous in the century prior to World War II, with a sizable proportion of those in their teens and early adulthood afflicted. Since that time, the age at onset of chronic disease has risen substantially, extending the period of healthy life and lowering mortality. Fogel and colleagues found that elimination of exposure to specific infectious diseases during childhood and young adulthood contributed significantly to improving health, in part by increasing height and weight, which led to a decline in morbidity and mortality.

This evidence prompted Fogel and colleagues to develop a "theory of technophysio evolution," which points to increasing human control of the environment, including a dependable supply of food and water free of pathogens, virtual elimination of exposure to many infectious diseases in utero, infancy, and childhood, and improvements in personal hygiene, clothing, housing, medical interventions, and public health practices. This control over the environment has allowed human populations to greatly increase average body size and to substantially improve the capacity and robustness of vital organ systems, leading to an approximate doubling of life span.

The theory of technophysio evolution has testable implications, as theories should. It implies that between the mid-1800s and the present day, birth cohorts changed substantially in their stock of health capital at birth and in the rate of depreciation of that capital over time, with later cohorts having much greater health capital and much lower rates of depreciation of it. This implies that the age of onset of chronic diseases and disability will increase for later birth cohorts and that life expectancy will rise.

Perhaps the theory of technophysio evolution will replace James Fries's theory, proposed in the early 1980s, of a biologically fixed maximum human life span. James Vaupel and colleagues have developed testable implications of Fries's theory and applied data from contemporary and historical populations, from twin registries, and from Mediterranean fruitflies and other nonhuman species to test the idea that human life span is biologically fixed. Fries's theory implies that death rates at very old ages should be relatively stable, since virtually all death at advanced ages is due not to accident or unlucky chance but to the wearing out of organ systems as the maximum life span is approached. As recapitualated in Chapter 2, Vaupel found, instead, that death rates at older ages have declined substantially over the last century, as the theory of technophysio evolution would suggest; even at age 100, death rates among Swedish adults have fallen by half during the last century. Fries's theory further implies that genetically identical individuals should have identical maximum potential life spans. Vaupel's work on twin registries, however, found no evidence that Danish twins share a maximum potential life span. If life span is fixed at some maximum, which differs between species, then death rates should rise very rapidly as that maximum is approached. But Vaupel's work has shown that the reverse appears to happen, with death rates for humans, Medflies, and other species, reaching a maximum and then declining with increasing age. Vaupel has not developed a theory of human aging and life span to replace the one he has so effectively falsified. But Fogel's theory of technophysio evolution may prove a useful starting point.

Both Fogel and Vaupel conclude that we might expect further and perhaps sizable increases in life expectancy in the United States and other countries, as we reap the benefits of extensive and intensive human control of the environment, combined with what appear to be highly plastic mortality rates at older ages and consequent expansions of life span. The policy implications of these conclusions are enormous.

Clearly, disease and death are fundamentally biological processes, although it has been recognized at least since Malthus and Durkheim that they take place within a social context that profoundly influences them. The last decade has seen a burgeoning of interest within demography in the specific physiological processes underlying the relationships we study, for example the connection between socioeconomic status and health, or the causes of racial disparities in health and disease. Biology also joins with demography in Douglas Ewbank's work (Chapter 3) on the contribution of genes to differences in mortality for a specific disease and to all-cause mortality. Ewbank began by estimating the proportion of deaths in the United States that could be attributed to Alzheimer's disease. Using two different approaches, he found that only one in four Alzheimer's deaths was listed as such on death certificates, and that a more complete count would put Alzheimer's disease on a par with cerebrovascular disease as the third-leading cause of death in the United States.

Ewbank extended the methodological underpinning of this work toward "demographic synthesis," through which he combined various types of data from different studies—say, information on incidence of disease from one study with data on prevalence by age from another—to answer questions about the contribution of genotype to mortality from Alzheimer's disease. Obviously, this approach can be generalized to other chronic diseases. Less obviously, it can be generalized to studying the population-level effects of genetic variability and the development of chronic disease. Ewbank's approach allows demographers to incorporate data from clinical studies into models of population processes, arguably giving us the best of both worlds in our effort to understand health, disease, and length of life.

Why is higher socioeconomic status associated with better health?

This question has long puzzled scholars, policymakers, and members of both advantaged and less-advantaged groups; speculation abounds about the causal processes at work and the medical and policy interventions that might mitigate health disparities. We know that regardless of the measure of socioeconomic status we use, those with more of it tend to live longer, healthier lives. James Smith (Chapter 5) has found that the proportion of adults who report their health as excellent or very good is 40 percentage points greater in the highest than in the lowest income quartile (see his Figure 1). The gradient is at least as large if educational attainment is used as the measure of socioeconomic status, with the poorly educated much likelier than those with more education to suffer higher mortality from almost all causes, including diabetes, hypertension, and heart disease, and to show higher levels of disability, functional loss, and cognitive impairment (Crimmins and Seeman, Chapter 4). These differences by income and education are reflected in large health and mortality differentials by race and ethnicity in the United States, although blacks tend to be more disadvantaged and Hispanics less clearly disadvantaged relative to whites once we take education and income into account. Of course, the relationship between socioeconomic status, health, illness, disability, and mortality for blacks, whites, and Hispanics is more complicated than this broad outline suggests, as Crimmins and Seeman make clear. One of the most important research and policy questions facing demographers, epidemiologists, physicians, and health care providers focuses on the pathways through which education, income, and other measures of inequality affect health, illness, disability, and life expectancy.

Three of the chapters in this volume summarize programs of research that investigate social differentials in biological and physiological processes that affect health and illness. This research, together with that done by the larger scientific community, has begun to change, fundamentally, the way social scientists think about social inequality, the way behavioral scientists think about the role of psychosocial factors in well-being, and the way epidemiologists think about public health. It has also begun to change the way physicians, medical researchers, and biologists think about gene expression and about processes at the level of the cell, organ system, and organism. Of course, this ongoing process is encountering much resistance in both the social/behavioral and biomedical camps, at least in part because many scholars, trained in another era, have little knowledge or understanding of current approaches in unfamiliar disciplines.

Research on disparities in health has concentrated on a few key aspects of socioeconomic status—income or wealth, education, and occupation, the benefits that these bring for health, and the mechanisms through which they work. Clearly, there are incomplete overlaps between the several aspects of socioeconomic status, and they operate in very different ways in delivering health and long life. And, although low levels of income or education may lead to declines in health and the onset of illness, poor health and illness may also lead to declines in income and wealth, and, early in life, may curtail education as well. The same characteristics that lead some people to invest little in their own education may also lead them to invest little in their own health, so that socioeconomic status and well-being are linked through their shared causes but do not cause each other.

Eileen Crimmins and Teresa Seeman (Chapter 4) propose a model in which demographic characteristics affect health outcomes directly and through their effect on biological processes such as inflammation. Socioeconomic status affects health only through its effect on health behaviors, like smoking, and social psychological factors, like depression, and these affect biological process and, thus, health outcomes. In a novel approach, Crimmins, Seeman, and their colleagues show that educational disparities in health can be described by the age at which various groups experience the same rates or prevalence of health problems. Those with the lowest levels of education experience equivalent rates of disease prevalence starting 5 to 15 years earlier in life than those with a college degree, so the aging process and related health problems begin at much earlier ages for them. The physiological processes through which education affects health and functioning include, for example, markers of inflammation, which are related to cardiovascular disease and are negatively distributed by education. Crimmins, Seeman, and colleagues find that a more general measure of long-term wear and tear on physiological systems—cumulative allostatic load—is significantly higher for those with low levels of education and that differences in allostatic load mediate about a third of the educational difference in mortality at older ages.

In Chapter 5, James Smith begins to unravel the connection between income, education, and health. Looking at the consequences for older adults of the onset of a major health event, he finds a substantial impact of a decline in health on financial well-being, primarily through reduced earnings rather than through medical expenses. At younger ages, those with the lowest levels of education stand out both for their poor health and for their low level of labor force participation, which reduces earnings and household income. Smith concludes that health *causes* socioeconomic status, at least to some extent. But does socioeconomic status *cause* health? In some impressive detective work, Smith uses the exogenous increase in wealth resulting from the large stock market gains during the 1990s to examine the impact of changes in wealth on changes in health among older adults. He finds that household income *never* predicts future onset of either major or minor health conditions. So, in the short run, money does not buy health. But education does. The chances of developing a new major or minor disease fall with increases in years of schooling completed. But why and how?

Health benefits of education for the disease Smith studied, diabetes, did not come either through higher household income or through greater adherence to beneficial therapies among the well-educated. Perhaps, Smith's results suggest, education affects one's ability to think abstractly about risks and costs, allowing one to internalize the future consequences of current decisions.

Andrew Steptoe and Michael Marmot (Chapter 6) propose a different conceptual model of the relationship between socioeconomic status and disease, especially cardiovascular disease, on which they focus. They argue that the disadvantaged tend to have relatively few protective resources such as social support and effective coping responses, while they tend to face greater adversity than those of high status. The combination of high adversity and low resources to cope with it negatively affects biological responses, increasing the risk of cardiovascular disease.

Steptoe and Marmot show that many of the factors involved in vascular inflammation and processes of blood clotting are sensitive to psychosocial stress. And, although they find few differences in stress reactivity by socioeconomic status, they see significant differences in recovery following stress, with a greater likelihood of incomplete recovery in those of lower status. Thus, given stress, socioeconomic status seems to affect physiological reactions to it. Steptoe and Marmot argue that lifestyle is probably the most important pathway through which socioeconomic status affects coronary heart disease, through smoking, nutrition, alcohol consumption, and exercise. Their Whitehall II study suggests that these lifestyle choices account for about a quarter of socioeconomic differences in heart disease among civil servants in London.

Aging, work, and public policy

The vast majority of Americans aged 65 and older receive government transfers, primarily through Social Security and Medicare, and so are dependent on these programs for at least some of their support. The number and characteristics of older adults alive in the future will determine how much the government must pay in future benefits—given the current formula—and the number of working-age adults at that point will determine how many workers are potentially available to support the expected number of beneficiaries.

We can summarize the number of adults potentially available to support the older population using the old-age dependency ratio, the ratio of those aged 65 and older to those aged 20 to 64. Of course, not all older adults receive support (although 93 percent of the elderly receive Social Security benefits) and not all young adults provide it, but the ratio allows us to view the outlines of at least potential generational exchange. In the United States, old-age dependency ratios will probably *double* between now and 2050, from about 0.2 around 2000 to about 0.4 by the middle of this century (Lee, Chapter 7, Figure 6). This means that in about 50 years each working-age adult will have twice as many older adults to support as is currently the case. Because Social Security is structured as a transfer from the current working population to the current beneficiary population, the Social Security tax must rise or benefits must fall when the number of beneficiaries increases in proportion to the number of working adults paying the tax, at least in the long run. Elderly support ratios point to the coming increase in the number of beneficiaries per potential worker, and so point to the need to closely monitor the future health of financial support policies for the elderly.

Although the sheer number of older adults will have a large effect on the amount of various kinds of support that society must provide, the costs of retirement and disability programs depend on the benefits they provide and the number of people who receive them. And it is unclear what will happen to these factors in the future.

The Census Bureau's middle-series projections of the size of the older population assume that in 2050 life expectancy at birth will have risen for US males from 71.8 years today to 79.7, and for females from 78.9 years today to 85.6. But if the same gains in longevity are achieved over the next 50 years as were gained in the last century, life expectancy in 2065 would reach 86 years (Lee and Carter 1992). Substantial gains in life expectancy could lead to an American population in which almost one in four people was aged 65 and older and one in 15 was aged 85 and older. This would be a very different country, with very different demands for health care and related services and for financial support of the aged, than the one of today.

In Chapter 7, Ronald Lee describes a program of research that uses the inherent uncertainty in demographic processes to forecast population. Lee extended this approach to bracket the uncertainty about *consequences* of changes in population for public budgets. Beginning with methods for forecasting mortality, he also derived the probability distributions of age-specific death rates and life expectancy. He approached fertility in much the same way, reasoning that once the fertility transition was over, fertility could best be treated as a stochastic process; and after many attempts to develop alternatives, this is the approach he settled on. With forecasts of fertility and of mortality, one can provide a probability distribution for the forecast of any demographic quantity, so now Lee had the tools in hand. But what could he say about public policy?

Lee and his colleagues focused on the Social Security Trust Fund as a key application of stochastic forecasting methods, eventually adding stochastic forecasts of economic inputs usually viewed as uncertain, including productivity growth rates and real interest rates, to the more familiar fertility and mortality rates. This approach led Lee and colleagues to forecasts that differ in key ways from those developed by the Trustees of the Social Security Trust Fund. And these differences have critical implications for the long-run financial stability of the Fund.

The same approach, Lee has shown, can be applied to almost any other public program. He has developed stochastic forecasts of the federal budget, public spending on programs for youth and the elderly, and health care costs, disaggregated by type of expenditure. This approach and the forecasts it provides can point policymakers toward pieces of the puzzle that will determine the future course of local, state, and federal budgets, enabling them to understand and focus on those parts with the greatest uncertainty and the biggest impact.

This basic approach drove David Wise (Chapter 8) in his effort to understand the link between demography, economics, and one key government program—social security. Wise began with the observation that almost all industrialized countries have seen a notable decline in labor force participation of older adults. This has happened in the period since the adoption in these countries of both employer-provided pension plans and government-supported social security plans, both of which typically provide benefits that depend on years of employment and one's earnings history during those years. The combination of declining rates of labor force participation, longer life expectancy, and pay-as-you-go financing means that governments in virtually all industrialized countries have made promises they cannot keep. What caused the problem?

Wise and his colleague Jonathan Gruber designed a program of research to answer this question, collaborating with scholars from 12 industrialized countries, each of whom carried out identical analyses on the retirement incentives built into the various countries' social security programs. The conclusions were striking: all countries showed a marked correspondence between the age at which retirement benefits become available and workers' departure from the labor force. Social security programs provide strong incentives for labor force withdrawal at older ages, often taxing continued participation at high rates.

Next, Wise and colleagues estimated the effects of changes in plan provisions on labor force participation for each of the countries. They found that across 12 countries with very different labor market institutions and social security programs, the effects of the retirement incentives in social security programs are consistent and large: the greater the financial incentives to retire at a particular age, the higher the rate at which workers do so. The financial implications for the economies of these countries of changes in plan provisions can also be sizable. Estimated costs to governments of these benefits, offset by contributions made and taxes paid by those who continue to work, show that these also can be large. The net implications for governments depend on the extent to which current benefits are "actuarially fair," increasing with delayed retirement to reflect the smaller number of years over which the benefits are taken and the larger number of years over which contributions are made, and on the age at which benefits are first available. In Germany, for example, where the mean age at retirement for men is about age 62, the move to an actuarially fair benefit schedule would, theoretically, raise the mean retirement age to just over 65 and result in a net reduction in total government expenditures minus revenues of about 43 percent of base benefits under the current system. By any calculation, this is a huge effect. Clearly, changes in the provisions of social security programs are an essential tool for policymakers trying to bring the promises made to workers into line with the money required to fund these programs.

How do we know what we know? Innovations in data collection

The advances that we have achieved over the last several decades in our understanding of the demography and economics of aging could not have taken place without important advances in the data we use. Large-scale surveys of populations have been compared in their importance for demography to the Hubble telescope or the Human Genome Project—very complicated, very expensive, but absolutely essential resources that are available to the entire community of researchers once they have been built and are functioning well.

Two models of innovation in survey design and methodology are the Wisconsin Longitudinal Study and the Health and Retirement Study, both longitudinal, but one focused on a single birth cohort in a single state and the other representative of the US population over age 52. Large, rich surveys that follow individuals over a number of years, they allow researchers to investigate the processes which produce health, disability, poverty, death, widowhood, labor force withdrawal, dementia, grandparenthood, and the other experiences of older adults. The current generation of such surveys often includes links to administrative data, such as records of doctor visits, hospitalizations, and medical treatments, Social Security earnings records, and death records. These surveys are beginning to expand from simple answers to (often complicated) questions to direct measurement of physiological and biological processes such as immune function or inflammation. And, of course, the measurement of key variables, such as income and assets in the Health and Retirement Study or cognitive functioning in the Wisconsin Longitudinal Study, has been the focus of almost continual innovation and evaluation, generally with substantial improvements in data quality. In Chapter 9, Robert Hauser and Robert Willis argue that such data sets are an invaluable public resource, paid for with tax dollars and ultimately aimed at improving the good of the community. A system of survey data should, they argue, represent real populations, enjoy sustained institutional support, be ultimately responsible to the public, include perspectives from multiple disciplines, cover multiple domains and units of observation, and offer opportunities for flexibility, serendipity, and scientific opportunism.

Large, ongoing surveys provide natural laboratories, if used wisely, for close observation of particular populations, unusual events or characteristics, or specific parts of a process. The Health and Retirement Study, with its sample of more than 20,000 cases, has enough respondents for whom survey responses suggest mild cognitive impairment to permit an intensive study of this population using assessments generally available only in clinical settings. Ultimately this will allow the development of survey measures that discriminate more finely among levels of cognitive function, provide estimates of the prevalence of mild cognitive impairment in the general population, and allow researchers to track the development of dementia and Alzheimer's disease.

The importance of the family

The changes that we can expect in the share of the older population and its size have profound implications for families. Most older adults receive whatever care they need from relatives. Married older couples almost always live alone and almost always count on each other for help. Husbands care for wives with Alzheimer's disease, wives help husbands who need help bathing and dressing. The situation faced by older men is substantially better on this dimension than that faced by older women, because most men remain married until they die, while most women experience the death of their husband and end their lives as widows. Some 75 percent of men aged 65 and older but only 41 percent of such women are married and live with their spouse. Among those aged 85 and older, 58 percent of men and only 12 percent of women are married and living with their spouse (US Census Bureau 2003a). Marriage provides older women with financial support, which is especially important since many do not have pensions or retirement benefits on their own account. So the differences in the chances of widowhood between men and women, combined with differences in access to retirement benefits based on lifetime work, mean that older unmarried women face very high chances of financial constraint and poverty. Social Security exacerbates these problems by over-benefiting married couples (who tend to be younger) and under-benefiting survivors, who tend to be older widows (Burkhauser 1994). More than half of women aged 75 and older who live alone have incomes below $10,000 per year, and the vast majority have incomes below $20,000 per year. Even among the young-old, most women living alone have relatively modest financial resources (US Census Bureau 2003b).

Note that the rapid aging of the older population, described earlier, has important implications, since the oldest-old tend to have very different needs for health care and help from family. Half of all oldest-old adults require assistance with everyday activities such as bathing, dressing, eating, and toilet use. Only about 10 percent of those aged 65 to 75 need such help. So, as the older population ages further, the demand for assistance, which could be met by paid helpers or by family members, will greatly increase. The proportion of the elderly who are poor or nearly poor is substantially higher among the oldest-old than among the young-old. About 11 percent of those aged 65–74 are poor, compared to 20 percent of those aged 85 and older (US Census Bureau 1996). If this situation persists into the middle of the twenty-first century, the oldest-old, who are predominantly women, are very unlikely to be currently married. Thus, they must receive family help—if they receive it at all—from siblings, children, or other relatives. The result may be an increasing number of young-old daughters retiring to care for their oldest-old mothers.

The next 50 years may see sizable increases in the proportion of older men and women who lack family members to help them. More will reach older ages without ever having married, and more will spend the end of their lives having divorced and not remarried. Both of these changes will likely be more common among men. Their effects also will have larger repercussions for men, because men are much more likely than women to lose contact with their children following divorce (Lye et al. 1995). Also, baby boomers had relatively small families, giving them few children to call on for help later. On the plus side, increasing longevity will mean more older years spent married, as both men and women lose their spouse at older ages than in the past.

The family experience of the black and Hispanic elderly differs in a number of ways from that of the white elderly. Older black men and women are much less likely than either whites or Hispanics to be married; only some 25 percent of black women aged 65 and older are married, compared to 42 percent of whites and 37 percent of Hispanics. For men, the differences are even more striking: 57 percent of older black men are married, compared to 77 percent of whites and 67 percent of Hispanics (US Census

Bureau 1996). And marked declines in the proportion of black adults who are married suggest that future generations of elderly blacks will have substantially fewer family members to draw on for support than older blacks of today (Waite 1995).

Older adults most in need of help from others—either from government programs or from family or both—are those in poor health, those with few financial resources, and those with few or no family members they can call on. All of these disadvantages appear most frequently among the oldest-old, most of whom are widowed women. Health policy researchers, planners in insurance companies, social service agencies who serve the elderly, individuals and families planning for the future, and state and federal governments all need to take into account the coming changes in the makeup of the future population of aging societies. Preventive steps taken now—to improve health and functioning of individuals into the oldest ages, to ensure the health of the financial systems that support older adults, to encourage individual saving for later years, and to bring health care policies and practices into line with future constraints and demands—can avert or ameliorate a crisis later.

Advanced industrial societies face a challenge in improving health and functioning at advanced ages, supporting families who are caring for older members, helping today's workers prepare financially for their older years, and designing and implementing public policies to achieve these goals. Although many difficult issues must be addressed to reach this goal, research advances in the demography and economics of aging provide some of the tools needed to plan for this future.

Note

The preparation of this chapter was supported in part by Grant No. P20 AG12857 from the Office of the Demography of Aging, Behavioral and Social Research Program, National Institute on Aging.

References

Burkhauser, R. V. 1994. "Protecting the most vulnerable: A proposal to improve social security insurance for older women," *The Gerontologist* 34: 148–149.

Lee, R. D. and L. Carter. 1992. "Modeling and forecasting the time series of U.S. mortality," *Journal of the American Statistical Association* 87: 659–671.

Lye, D. N., D. H. Klepinger, P. D. Hyle, and A. Nelson. 1995. "Childhood living arrangements and adult children's relations with their parents," *Demography* 32(2): 261–280.

Preston, S. H. 1996. *American Longevity: Past, Present, and Future*. Policy Brief No. 7. Center for Policy Research, Syracuse University.

RAND. 2001. *Preparing for an Aging World: The Case for Cross-National Research*. Washington, DC: National Academy Press.

US Census Bureau. 1996. *65+ in the United States*. Washington, DC: U.S. Government Printing Office.

———. 2003a. "The older population in the United States: March 2002," Figures 3 and 6 «http://www.census.gov/prod/2003pubs/p20-546.pdf»

———. 2003b. "Selected characteristics of people 15 years and over by total money income in 2002, work experience in 2002, race, Hispanic origin, and sex," Table 1 «http://ferret.bls.census.gov/macro/032003/perinc/new01_019.htm»

———. 2004. "U.S. interim projections by age, race, sex, and Hispanic origin," Tables 2a and 2b «http://www.census.gov/ipc/www/usinterimproj/natprojtab02a.pdf»

Waite, L. J. 1995. "Does marriage matter?," *Demography* 32(4): 483–508.

I. HISTORY, BIOLOGY, AND DISEASE

Changes in the Process of Aging during the Twentieth Century: Findings and Procedures of the *Early Indicators* Project

ROBERT WILLIAM FOGEL

The results to date of the project called *Early Indicators of Later Work Levels, Disease and Death* have exceeded expectations expressed in 1986, when we began our work on it, because so many of the findings were unanticipated. The original aim was to create a life-cycle sample that would permit a longitudinal study of the aging of Union Army veterans of the American Civil War. Born mainly between 1830 and 1847, these veterans were the first cohort to turn age 65 during the twentieth century. It was possible to create the life-cycle sample by linking together information from about a dozen sources, including the manuscript schedules of censuses between 1850 and 1910; regimental, military, and medical records; public health records; Union Army pension records; surgeons' certificates giving the results of successive examinations of the veterans from first pension application until death; death certificates; daily military histories of each regiment in which the veterans served; and rejection records of volunteers.

The original plan was to draw a random sample of 39,300 recruits from the regular regiments of the army. Since that sample produced too few black veterans, we subsequently enlarged the sample by drawing about 6,000 veterans from the black regiments. All told, the completed sample consists of about 45,300 observations. It takes about 15,000 variables to describe the complete life-cycle history of each veteran.

The project was funded by the National Institute on Aging in 1991 and has been extended by competitive applications in 1994 and 2001, each time for five years. About 80 percent of the effort during the first two grant periods was devoted to creating the life-cycle sample and about 20 percent to analysis. Under the current award about 20 percent is for extension of the sample, 10 percent for outreach (to make this complex data set more accessible to investigators outside of the project), and about 70 percent for data analysis.

When the *Early Indicators* project began, it was led by a team of seven senior investigators and four consultants. Of these, four were primarily economists, one was a demographer, one was a specialist in biological anthropology, and five were physicians. The large number of physicians reflected the central role assigned to biomedical issues and their interaction with socioeconomic factors. The biomedical group has been headed by Nevin Scrimshaw, who was trained in biology, medicine, public health, and epidemiology. He has been the principal investigator and consultant in several major field studies concerned with the effectiveness of public health and nutritional interventions on morbidity and mortality. He not only greatly influenced our approach to biomedical issues, but profoundly influenced the entire strategy of the project. Two other physicians deeply involved in shaping the strategy were Irwin H. Rosenberg, a gastroenterologist and head of the US Department of Agriculture's Human Nutrition Center on Aging at Tufts University, and J. M. Tanner of London University, a specialist in pediatric endocrinology, human growth, and the use of anthropometric measures as indexes of nutritional status and general health.

The output of the project has been substantial. So far the project has produced more than 80 published papers, five books, and eight Ph.D. dissertations. Another six papers have been accepted for publication. Dora Costa's book, *The Evolution of Retirement: An American Economic History, 1880–1890*, won the Paul A. Samuelson prize for 1998 awarded by TIAA/CREF. Two more dissertations are in progress, and about 40 working papers have been completed or are in progress. So far 11 manuals for data users have been published and CD-ROMs containing data have been distributed.

Many of the findings of the *Early Indicators* project were unanticipated, and they significantly altered our research strategy as we proceeded. Of these unanticipated findings, perhaps the most surprising was the discovery that chronic diseases began earlier in the life cycle and were more severe at the beginning of the twentieth century than at the end of it. This finding was surprising because leading epidemiologists and demographers writing in the 1980s and early 1990s found what appeared to be credible evidence that the extension of life expectancy had brought with it worsening health (Verbrugge 1984 and 1989; Alter and Riley 1989; Riley 1989; cf. Riley 1990a and 1990b; Riley 1997; Riley and Alter 1996; Wolfe and Haveman 1990; Verbrugge and Jette 1994; Waidmann, Bound, and Schoenbaum 1995). By the early 1990s that proposition had evolved into the "Theory of the health or epidemiological transition," a gloss on an idea originally proposed by A. R. Omran, not to describe the change in the pattern of morbidity, but to describe the change in the pattern of mortality: from mainly deaths due to acute diseases to mainly deaths due to chronic diseases (Omran 1971; Murray and Chen 1992, 1993a, and 1993b).

Questions about the feasibility of the research design

At the time we began the preliminary research into constructing a longitudinal sample of aging based on Union Army veterans, there were no laptops that could be carried into archives and no commercial software for the management of databases as large as the one we contemplated, even on mainframes. There was no previous experience with creating longitudinal aging samples based on microdata constructed by linking together information on particular individuals from a dozen or more data sets covering nearly the whole life cycle of these individuals. Moreover, the desired data for our project were deposited in archives, mainly in Washington, DC and in Utah, that were not accustomed to the traffic we created.

Some of those who commented on the project found the undertaking highly dubious. They felt we were pushing computers and sampling techniques beyond their capacity, and in a sense we were. Fortunately, the advances in computer hardware and software were so rapid that we were not ahead of this technology but at its leading edge, continually modifying analytical techniques and research design to take maximum advantage of the rapidly evolving technology.

Organizing the data retrieval and processing

Still another challenge was organizational. We had to create a network of data retrievers, inputters, checkers, and programmers capable of putting the data we needed into machine-readable form accurately, efficiently, and at a low enough cost to make the enterprise viable. That organizational feat was accomplished by Larry T. Wimmer of Brigham Young University. He exploited the talent of students at his university who, because of their interest in constructing their own family genealogies, were already familiar with archival research. He created a training program to introduce successive teams of students to the specific skills needed for work in the records of the US National Archives and the microfilm holdings of the Family History Library in Salt Lake City, which is part of the Church of Jesus Christ of Latter-Day Saints (Mormons). For much of the first ten years of the project, Wimmer was supervising about 75 data retrievers, inputters, coordinators, programmers, and analysts. Because of the tightness and efficiency of the operation, Wimmer was able to keep the cost of transforming the data into machine-readable form remarkably low, thus contradicting the forecasts of those who thought that the cost of the *Early Indicators* project would exceed acceptable bounds.

Evaluating sample selection and other biases

Perhaps the most formidable obstacle to the design of the *Early Indicators* project pertained to the reliability and range of applicability of the synthetic longitudinal sample we aimed to base on the military and pension records of the Union Army. Before 1991 it was widely doubted that a useful prospective sample on aging for either an extinct or a living cohort could be created synthetically, given the numerous risks of failure. Much of the skepticism was focused on the pension records that were said to be corrupted by agents who sought pensions for bogus veterans and by pension physicians who were bribed to report nonexistent disabilities. Census records, it was said, were more reliable and preferable.

Where the quality of census and pension records can be compared, as in the case of variables that appear in both, such as name, place of birth, and age, the pension records are far superior. Census records are subject to frequent name misspellings, often because the census taker put down a variant spelling. Age and place of birth are often in error in the census because the respondent did not know the place of birth of all residents in the household, or because of spelling errors for small European principalities. Census records also suffer from age heaping and poor memory. In the pension records, by contrast, numerous documents are provided to support claims concerning name, age, and place of birth, including birth records, baptismal records, enlistment and discharge papers, marriage certificates, affidavits by neighbors and company officers, and death certificates.[1]

The contention that there would be a void of information in the Union Army and pension records between ages 25 and 65 (between discharge from the Union Army and enrollment in the pension system) also turned out to be wrong. About 80 percent of all medical examinations of the veterans pertain to those ages. There are frequent listings, by both age and date, of occupation, residence, and health conditions during these ages.[2]

Sample selection biases due to linkage failure turned out to be far less severe than some observers conjectured. Logit and OLS regressions were run to identify factors that affected the odds of linking recruits to the various censuses and military and pension records. The 11 behavioral variables used as predictors are attributes obtained from the sample of recruits. The main finding of these regressions is that being foreign born was the principal nonrandom factor accounting for the failure of linkage to the 1850 and 1860 censuses. In linking to the 1900 and 1910 censuses, being a foreigner is much less important in explaining linkage failure than in the pre–Civil War period. The discrepancy is due primarily to the fact that about two-thirds of the foreign-born recruits arrived in the United States after 1 June 1850 and about 7 percent arrived after 1 June 1860 and hence were not covered by the census.[3] In the case of the pension records, "died during the war" and being a deserter are the principal reasons for nonrandom linkage failure.[4]

The predictability of the factors that explain linkage failure indicates that biases introduced by censoring can be corrected by reweighting subsamples having the relevant characteristics (this applies to subgroups overrepresented as well as those underrepresented). However, tests revealed that reweighting had little effect on estimates of key parameters.

Several other tests of the representativeness of the linked sample were undertaken. One of these concerned the wealth distribution of all adult males (aged 20 and older) in the households to which the recruits were linked in the 1860 census. The distribution was lognormal and not significantly different from Lee Soltow's (1975) random sample of the wealth of Northern males aged 20 and older in 1860.

The most difficult problems of inference related to screening problems stem from the varying dates of entry into the pension records. The governing principle in dealing with such data is that individuals are not at risk for most purposes until they apply for a pension. Life tables constructed on this principle for the period circa 1900 are similar to the mortality schedules constructed from the death registration data but are somewhat lower, as is to be expected, since the areas covered by death registration in 1900 were still concentrated in locations where mortality rates were above the national average (Preston, Keyfitz, and Schoen 1972; Preston and Haines 1991).

The prehistory of the *Early Indicators* project

Given the widespread doubts about the feasibility of the *Early Indicators* project, it is worth considering how it ever got off the ground. The answer lies in the prehistory of this project, which covers the period between 1955 and 1985. Those three decades produced a group of economists, well trained in the new mathematical models and statistical techniques of their discipline, who were focused on the explanation for modern, long-term economic growth. These economists, who came to be called "cliometricians," sought to exploit the potentialities of the newly developed high-speed computers, typified by the IBM 650 mainframe, that were being installed at leading research universities across the country at deep discounts if the universities would agree to offer courses to students and faculty in how to use them (Ceruzzi 2003).

I took part in a one-week course in how to program the 650 at Columbia University in the spring of 1957, as did many other cliometricians about that time. Such exposure was not enough to master the art, but it awakened in us the realization that a new era was at hand, in which mountains of microdata sets that were lying unexploited in various archives could now be put to use in the quest for empirically well-founded answers to the sources of American economic growth during the previous 150 years and in the future.

In the mid-1960s, William N. Parker of Yale University and Robert A. Gallman of the University of North Carolina, with the aid of a group of their graduate students, sought to retrieve information from one of these mountains of neglected data: the "manuscript schedules" of the US decennial census of 1860. These were the original sheets of paper that the census takers carried around to each household, farm, and business together with instructions from Washington on how to fill them out. Since there were over 6 million of these schedules collected for the 1860 census, Parker and Gallman decided to draw a random sample of about 5,000 of the farm households with which they were concerned, thus encountering the problem of how to design random samples of archival data.

They encountered still another problem. The focus of their research was the institution of slavery and the comparative analysis of the operation of free farms and large slave plantations in the cotton-producing counties of the South. That objective required them to link together information from three of the six schedules that constituted the 1860 census. Other investigators sought to link plantations to the same information in both the 1850 and 1860 censuses (Menn 1964a and b; Wilcox 1992; cf. Foust 1968). Thus began the process of creating synthetic, longitudinal data sets by linking together information from several sources over space and time.[5]

Another aspect of the prehistory was the discovery of a large number of genealogies that could be used to recreate the vital statistics of the United States, going back to early colonial times. The US death registration system did not begin until 1890 and at first embraced only ten states. It did not become national until the 1930s. National trends in mortality rates before 1890 were unknown, except for the inaccurate but usable data collected by the decennial censuses between 1850 and 1900. Trends before 1850 were a void, with leading historical demographers at odds with each other's conjectures based on isolated fragments of information.

There are both published and unpublished genealogies. The published ones consist of volumes that attempt to describe all the descendants of a particular patriarch down to current times. A ten-generation book, if complete, could contain well over 50,000 individuals. Many of these volumes are on deposit in the Library of Congress, the Newberry Library in Chicago, and the Family History Library in Salt Lake City. It has been estimated that at least 60,000 of these volumes are in existence for the United States covering over 100 million individuals (Fogel et al. 1978; Fogel 1993).

There are also large numbers of unpublished genealogies, many of which exist only in the households of individual genealogists and are difficult to access. However, a large collection of these unpublished genealogies is on deposit at the Family History Library.[6]

Work with both published and unpublished genealogies demonstrated that they were representative of the living population when proper attention was given to a variety of selection biases, many of which were novel and peculiar to genealogies.[7] Moreover, the information in the genealogies made it possible not only to calculate the mean odds of dying at each stage in the life cycle for particular cohorts, but to run regressions that made the odds of dying ($_nq_x$) at any age interval, period, or cohort a function of such variables as birth order, parents' and grandparents' ages at death, ages at death of collateral kin, mother's age at birth, extent of geographic mobility, the number of generations that ancestors of the family lived within the United States, and socioeconomic status variables that could be treated both immediately and intergenerationally.[8]

Yet another aspect of the prehistory is our introduction to the uses of anthropometric data. In 1974 Stanley Engerman and I published *Time on the Cross*, in which we used data from probate records to calculate the ages of slave women at their first birth. The exercise yielded an average figure of 22 years. Since the standard sources suggested that slave women were generally fecund in their midteens, and since slaves were not using contraception, we conjectured that most slave women must have abstained from sexual intercourse for six or seven years, probably until, or in contemplation of, marriage. Our analysis was challenged by some scholars who argued that the use of probate records biased the calculated age at first birth upward by at least four years. They also argued that slaves could not have become menarcheal until at least age 18. Since (according to J. M. Tanner) Norwegian girls did not become menarcheal until age 17, it was argued that slaves in the United States could not have done so until at least a year later because their diets were far worse than the diets of Norwegian girls.[9]

Engerman and I were aware of both upward and downward biases when using probate records (which were cross-sectional) to calculate the mean age at first birth. In grappling with the issues raised by other scholars, we worked out a theoretical argument to show that upward and downward biases would tend to cancel out. We sent Ansley Coale a letter with our results, asking for his assessment. Coale passed our letter on to James Trussell, then a young assistant professor in the Office of Population Research at Princeton, who became interested in our problem. Since he would be spending 1975–76 at the London School of Hygiene and Tropical Medicine working with William Brass, a leading mathematical demographer, while I was visiting at Cambridge University, Trussell suggested that we get together after we had both settled in.

Early that fall, Trussell came up to Cambridge and gave me what I can only describe as a brilliant lecture on the singulate mean, a statistic invented by John Hajnal to eliminate types of biases that arise when using cross-sectional data to estimate the mean age at marriage in a cohort of women, which Trussell extended to the fertility schedule. Working with Richard Steckel (Trussell and Steckel 1978) and using data drawn from both probate and plantation records, Trussell estimated that the mean age at marriage of female slaves was about 21 years.

When Trussell reported the good news, he added that there was a problem because the age of menarche was still open, but that it could be estimated from information on weight by age or height by age. Engerman and I had collected thousands of observations on height by age from the manifests of US Customs as a byproduct of our work on the internal slave trade. We had been wondering for years what we might do with such data. At the suggestion of Richard Wall of the Cambridge Group, Engerman had written a note for *Local Population Studies* using the cross-sectional data from a subsample of the manifests to represent the growth profiles in the height of male and female slaves. When I showed the profiles to Trussell, he recommended that we show them to James Tanner, who had demonstrated that the mean age of menarche of a population could be estimated by constructing the age-for-height curve from cross-sectional data. He had also shown that the age of menarche followed the peak in the teenage growth spurt by about one year. When we showed Tanner our sample, he suggested that the peak of the teenage growth spurt was probably about age 13 or 14, but warned that a large sample would have to be collected before the issue could be settled.

Thus began our research on the use of anthropometric data to estimate the nutritional status and health of populations between 1720 and 1937. A project on "Secular trends in nutrition, labor welfare, and labor productivity" was established at the National Bureau of Economic Research, and by mid-1984 about 400,000 observations on height by age, covering 16 populations, were in machine-readable form. The data on height by age were integrated with genealogical data to analyze the contribution of secular trends in nutrition to the secular decline in mortality.[10]

Consequently, when the issue arose of creating a life-cycle sample based on the veterans of the Union Army, the task seemed to be a logical extension of the types of synthetic data sets that cliometricians had been working with for some time and would employ research designs and methods that were familiar to them. The main break with the past stemmed from the copious medical histories of both acute and chronic diseases that were available in the military and pension records. Although the medical data required cliometricans to undertake crash courses in epidemiology and medical history, it was apparent that physicians would have to play a central role in the design and execution of the project from the start. Once the appropriate research team was assembled, we were confident that we could manage the challenges of the project. And we were thrilled by the prospect of reconstructing and analyzing the burden of diseases that afflicted the first American cohorts to reach age 65 in the twentieth century.

A principal finding

The main accomplishment to date has been the accurate description of the burden of chronic diseases and disabilities that afflicted males aged 50 and older during the opening decades of the twentieth century and the last decade or two of the nineteenth century.[11] Of course, the array of diseases that afflicted Americans was known to the physicians who treated them, and toward the end of the nineteenth century this knowledge was codified in pathology books that medical students had to read. Not much was known, however, about the frequency of these conditions across the population since nationally representative statistics on civilian health were not collected in the United States until the introduction of the National Health Interview Survey (NHIS) in the 1960s.[12]

Before our project began, quantitative evidence on health came mainly from the information on cause of death in death certificates. However, the diseases that cause most deaths, even when reported accurately, are merely a subset of the disease burden of the living and poorly reflect the chronic conditions and disabilities from which they suffer. Such diseases as arthritis, hernias, and dementia rarely appeared on death certificates, but they sharply reduced the capacity to work and undermined the quality of life for many aging veterans before World War II. Consequently, reliance on death certificates distorted the characterization of the chronic disease burdens of the living and the changes in these burdens during the twentieth century. It was one factor that promoted the view, since shown to be incorrect, that for middle-aged and elderly workers the duration of chronic conditions was shorter in a time when deaths were due primarily to infectious diseases rather than chronic diseases (cf. Harris 1997).

The prevalence and severity of chronic diseases and disabilities

The Union Army data reveal the ubiquity of chronic health conditions during the century before World War II. Not only was the overall prevalence rate of these diseases much higher among the elderly than today, but they afflicted teenagers, young adults, and the middle aged to a much greater extent than today. This fact is demonstrated by Table 1, which shows that more than 80 percent of all males aged 16–19 in 1861 and more than 70 percent of men aged 20–24 were examined for the Union Army. These examinees were overwhelmingly volunteers (less than 4 percent were drafted), who presumably thought they were fit enough to serve. Yet disability rates were higher than today. Even among teenagers more than one out of six

TABLE 1   Share of Northern white males of military age unfit for
military service in 1861

Age	Percent of cohort examined	Percent of examinees rejected
16–19	80.9	16.0
20–24	70.4	24.5
25–29	52.3	35.8
30–34	41.0	42.9
35–39	41.6	52.9

SOURCE: Fogel et al. 1991.

was disabled, and among men aged 35–39 more than half were disabled.
Despite their relatively young ages, cardiovascular diseases (mainly rheumatic) accounted for 11 percent of the rejections; hernias another 12 percent; eye, ear, and nose diseases 7 percent; tuberculosis and other respiratory diseases 7 percent; tooth and gum diseases 8 percent. Most of the other rejections were due to orthopedic conditions and general debility (Lee 2001).

These findings about the early onset of chronic diseases cast new light on the debate about the effect of increased longevity on the prevalence rates of chronic diseases. Those who argued that the effect of increased longevity was to increase the average duration of chronic disease assumed no delay in the average age of onset of these diseases. They were also influenced by cross-sectional evidence that showed some increases in disability rates during the 1970s and 1980s, despite the continuing decline in mortality rates (Riley 1990b, 1991; Wolfe and Haveman 1990). It seemed plausible that various health interventions and environmental changes reduced the severity of diseases and thus delayed death without providing cures, as has been the case with AIDS.

As Table 2 shows, however, there has been a significant delay in the onset of chronic diseases during the twentieth century. Men aged 50–54

TABLE 2   Increase in the proportion of white
males without chronic conditions during the
twentieth century

Age	Proportion without chronic conditions	
	1890–1910	c. 1994
50–54	0.33	0.41
55–59	0.21	0.29
60–64	0.10	0.25
65–69	0.03	0.14

SOURCE: Helmchen 2003.

were 24 percent more likely to be free of all chronic conditions in 1994 than a century earlier. At ages 60–64, white males today are two-and-a-half times more likely to be free of chronic diseases than their counterparts a century ago. Further light is shed on the issue by considering specific diseases (see Table 3). Arthritis began 11 years later among men who turned 65 between 1983 and 1992 than among those who turned 65 between 1895 and 1910. The delay in the onset of a chronic condition was about 9 years for heart diseases, about 11 years for respiratory diseases (despite much higher rates of cigarette smoking), and nearly 8 years for neoplasms.[13]

Union Army veterans who endured poor health did not typically die quickly. Veterans who lived to be at least age 50 and who entered the pension system before age 51 lived an average of 24 years past age 50. Moreover, at their last examination on or before age 51 their average degree of disability was 58 percent, where 100 percent indicates complete incapacity for manual labor. Between ages 50 and 60 disability ratings (controlled for age at death) continued to rise sharply, and then increased at a decreasing rate. Of the veterans who lived to be age 50, about 29 percent lived to age 80 or older. For these "old old," the level of disability for manual labor averaged between 85 and 100 percent for a decade or more. Indeed, some survived with such high levels of disability for as much as a quarter of a century (Helmchen 2003). As Table 4 shows, survivors usually acquired more and more co-morbidities as they aged.[14] Those who lived past age 85 had twice as many co-morbidities as those who died by age 55.

Consideration of the sweep of the twentieth century affords a new perspective on the debate over the relationship between the increase in life expectancy and the change in the burden of chronic disease among the elderly. It now appears that the decline in morbidity rates paralleled the decline in mortality rates. Indeed, the delay in the onset of chronic disabilities between 1900 and the 1990s for those who lived to age 50 was greater than the increase in life expectancy at age 50 over the same period. The average delay in the onset of chronic conditions over the century was more than 10 years (Helmchen 2003),[15] whereas, the average increase in male life expectancy was about 6.6 years (Bell, Wade, and Goss 1992).

TABLE 3 Average age of onset of some chronic conditions among American males near the beginning and near the end of the twentieth century

Condition	Men born 1830–45	Men born 1918–27
Heart disease	55.9	65.4
Arthritis	53.7	64.7
Neoplasm	59.0	66.6
Respiratory disease	53.8	65.0

SOURCE: Helmchen 2003.

TABLE 4   Average number of co-morbidites among veterans who lived to be at least age 50

Average age at death	Percent of veterans who lived to at least age 50 who died in interval	Average number of co-morbidities at last examination before death
50–54	3.9	4
55–59	6.4	5
60–64	9.8	6
65–69	14.0	6
70–74	18.3	7
75–79	19.1	7
80–84	15.5	7
85–89	9.0	8
90–94	3.4	8
95 and older	0.7	7

SOURCE: Helmchen 2003.

Measuring and explaining the decline in the burden of chronic diseases

Several investigators in the *Early Indicators* project have begun the difficult task of constructing a comprehensive index of the change in the burden of chronic diseases at ages 50 and older during the twentieth century. One approach involves the creation of an index based on the number and particular combination of co-morbidities. Initial analysis of the correlation of such an index with the degree of disability that surgeons assigned to pensioners is promising (Canavese and Linares 2003).

Co-morbidities of chronic diseases are also one of the main determinants of the rate of deterioration in health today, predicting the rate of decline in both functional capacity and longevity. According to one scale, an increase in one unit of a co-morbidity index is the equivalent of being a decade older (Landi et al. 1999; Penninx et al. 1999; Stuck et al. 1999; Kazis et al. 1998; Charlson et al. 1994). It thus seems likely that functional forms relating a co-morbidity index to both functional capacity and longevity can be estimated and the way in which these functions have shifted during the twentieth century can be described. These functional forms can also be used to forecast advances in health and longevity during the twenty-first century.

Explaining changes in specific chronic conditions and in functional limitations

One step in formulating a global measure of change in the burden of chronic diseases is to explain the decline in specific conditions. Dora Costa (2000) has estimated the impact of public health and socioeconomic status factors at late developmental and young adult ages on risks of incurring chronic conditions at middle and late ages. Significant predictors included mortality rates in counties of enlistments, infectious diseases experienced during the Civil War, and being a prisoner of war. She focused on a set of chronic conditions for which clinical diagnoses were essentially the same in the early 1900s as today (such as lower back pain, joint problems, decreased breath or adventitious sounds, irregular pulse, and valvular heart disease). This procedure permitted her to estimate how much of the observed decline in the prevalence rates of comparable conditions was due to the reduction in specific risk factors. Prevalence rates for 1971–80 were computed from the National Health and Nutrition Examination Survey (NHANES).

She found that elimination of exposure to specific infectious diseases during developmental and young adult ages explained between 10 and 25 percent of the declines in the specified chronic diseases of middle and late ages between 1900–10 and 1971–80. Occupational shifts were also important, accounting for 15 percent of the decline in joint problems, 75 percent of the decline in back pain, and 25 percent of the decline in respiratory diseases.

Costa (2002) extended this line of analysis by documenting the decline in functional limitations among US men between ages 50 and 74 throughout the twentieth century. A central issue is the factoring of the decline in functional limitations among three processes: the decline in the prevalence rates of specific chronic diseases, the reduction in the debilitating sequelae of these diseases, and the influence of new medical technologies that relieve and control the sequelae. Her analysis turned on five functional limitations: difficulty walking, difficulty bending, paralysis, blindness in at least one eye, and deafness in at least one ear. Prevalence rates of these limitations among men aged 50–74 were computed for the Union Army and for NHANES (1988–94) and NHIS (1988–94).

On average these five functional limitations declined by about 40 percent during the twentieth century. Using probit regressions, Costa attributed 24 percent of the decline to reduction in the debilitating effect of chronic conditions and 37 percent to the reduced rates of chronic conditions.

The significance of changes in body size

The contribution of improvements in body size as measured by stature, body mass index (BMI), and other dimensions has run through the research of the *Early Indicators* project like a red line. The discovery of correlations in time series going back to the colonial period between changes in stature and changes in life expectancy for the United States was reported first in 1986, although it was known as early as 1978.[16] Pursuit of a variety of issues called attention to the significance of changes in body size for the long-term decline in chronic conditions and mortality. For example, Diane Lauderdale and Paul Rathouz (1999) investigated the impact of unhealthy environments on the genetic component of height. They hypothesized that an unhealthy environment might attenuate the effects of genotype. To test their hypothesis, they constructed a sample of brothers who served in the Union Army. Their analysis showed that brothers from unhealthy counties had both higher variances in height and lower covariance in the heights of siblings than was expected from standard equations for measuring genetic influences on the heights of siblings. Study of the likelihood of developing specific diseases while in the army also pointed to the importance of stature. For example, short recruits were more likely to develop tuberculosis while in service than taller ones (Birchenall 2003; cf. Lee 1997).

The Gould sample

In 1995 Dora Costa discovered a sample of 23,000 Civil War recruits who were, for scientific reasons, more intensively examined than the typical recruit (Costa 2004). Benjamin A. Gould, a leading astronomer and one of the founders of the National Academy of Sciences, who was in charge of the project, collected information on waist and hip circumference, lifting strength, vital capacity of lungs, height, weight, shoulder breadth, and chest circumference. The sample included whites, blacks, and Native Americans. Costa linked a subsample of 521 white recruits who survived to 1900 to their pension records. She also compared the Union Army soldiers with soldiers measured in 1946–47, 1950, and 1988.

Over a span of 100 years men in the military became taller and heavier, but their waist-to-hip and chest-to-shoulder ratios were unchanged. Their height increased by 5 cm and the BMIs of men aged 31–35 increased from 23 to 26. Controlling for BMI and age, the waist–hip and chest–shoulder ratios (both measures of abdominal fat) were significantly greater in the Gould sample than in the 1950 and 1988 samples.

Using an independent competing-risk hazard model to estimate the effect of changes in body shape on the risk of death from cerebrovascular and ischemic heart disease at older ages, Costa found that a low waist-to-hip ratio increased mortality by 4.4 times relative to the mean and controlling for BMI, while a high waist–hip ratio increased mortality risk by 2.9 times. Substituting into her regression model the characteristics of soldiers in 1950, who reached age 65 or older during the late 1980s, produced a 15 percent decline in all-cause mortality above age 64, implying that changes in frame size explain about 47 percent of the total decline in all-cause mortality at older ages between the beginning and the end of the twentieth century.

The implication of changes in the body size of women

Changes in the body builds of women have had a far-reaching effect on the reduction of perinatal and infant death rates since 1800.[17] The impact of the improved builds of women is illustrated by Figure 1. The lines on this graph are normal approximations of the frequency distributions of birth weights. Birth weight is represented on the vertical axis, and the horizontal axis represents z-scores (deviations of birth weight from the mean measured in units of the standard deviations). Hence, the cumulative frequency distribution is represented by a straight line. The lowest line represents the distribution of US nonwhites in 1950. They had a mean birth weight of 3,128 grams and, as indicated by Figure 1, about 13 percent of the neonates weighed less than 2,501 grams at birth. The second line is the distribution of birth weights for lower-class women in Bombay (Jayant 1964). The figure indicates the mean birth weight in this population was just 2,525 grams. In this case nearly half (46 percent) of the births were below the critical level, although the women in the sample were not the poorest of the poor.

The third curve is the probable distribution of the birth weights of the children of impoverished English workers around 1800 (Fogel 1986). The distribution of the birth weights in this class around 1800 probably had a mean of 2,276 grams, which is about 249 grams (about half a pound) below the average of the births to lower-class women in Bombay. It follows

FIGURE 1 **Percent of male births with weights below 2,501 grams in two modern populations and among poor English workers in the early nineteenth century**

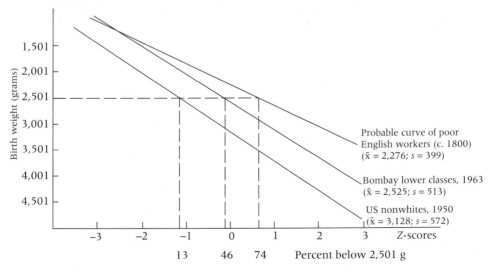

that about 74 percent of the births among impoverished English workers around 1800 were at weights below 2,501 grams.[18]

The implication of this distribution of birth weights is revealed by Table 5. Column 2 represents the actual schedule of neonatal death rates by weight for nonwhite US males in 1950, and column 3 gives the actual distribution of their birth weights.[19] The product of these two columns yields an implied neonatal death rate of 26.8 per thousand, which, of course, was also the actual death rate. If, however, this population had had the distribution of the birth weights of the impoverished English workers of 1800, their neo-natal death rates would have been 173.0 per thousand (see col. 4). The implication of Table 5 is that improvements in nutrition sufficient to shift the mean birth weight from 2,276 grams to 3,128 grams would have re-duced the infant death rate by 83 percent.

Figure 1 reflects an important intergenerational influence on health before the era of cesarean sections and neonatal intensive care units. Mal-nourished mothers were small in stature and had small pelvic cavities, and they produced small children because of deficiencies in their diet and expo-sure to disease during pregnancy. As a result, the birth weight that mini-mized perinatal deaths was about 700 grams below that of the nonwhite US women referred to in Figure 1. In other words, a condition for surviving the birth process was such a low birth weight that the neonate was at very

TABLE 5   Effects of a shift in the distribution of birth weights on the neonatal death rate, holding constant the schedule of death rates (by weight)

Weight (grams) (1)	Neonatal death rate of singleton nonwhite US males in 1950 (per 1,000) (2)	Distribution of birth weights of singleton nonwhite US males in 1950 ($\bar{x}$ = 3,128 g; σ = 572 g) (3)	Distribution of birth weights in a population with $\bar{x}$ = 2,276 g σ = 399 g (4)
1,500 or less	686.7	0.0117	0.1339
1,501–2,000	221.3	0.0136	0.2421
2,001–2,500	62.1	0.0505	0.3653
2,501–3,000	19.7	0.1811	0.2198
3,001–3,500	10.7	0.3510	0.0372
3,501–4,000	12.1	0.2599	0.0017
4,001–4,500	13.0	0.0865	—
4,501 or more	23.2	0.0456	—
Implied neonatal death rate (per 1,000)		26.8	173.0
Possible infant death rate (per 1,000)		48.9	288.3

SOURCE: Cols. 2 and 3: US National Office of Vital Statistics 1954; Col. 4: see Fogel 1986, nn. 21, 23, 24, and 26.

high risk of dying shortly after birth. The escape from that dilemma is now almost universal in rich countries. Poor women accumulated biological capital at an intergenerational rate that was rapid enough to shift the birth weight of their children to a range that is about 1.5 times what it was two centuries ago. This means that fewer than 8 percent of all births in the United States and other rich countries are now below 2,501 grams (Martin et al. 2002; Graafmans et al. 2002; Wilcox et al. 1995).[20]

The theory of technophysio evolution

Recognition of environmentally induced changes in human physiology during the twentieth century that had a profound impact on the process of aging did not become apparent until mid-1993. The key finding was that prevalence rates for the main chronic diseases among Union Army veterans aged 65 and older in 1910 were much higher than among veterans of World War II of the same ages during the mid-to-late 1980s. That finding was first set forth in a 1993 working paper (Fogel, Costa, and Kim 1993) and was elaborated and subsequently characterized as a "theory of technophysio evolution" (Fogel 1994 and 1997; Fogel and Costa 1997; Pope and Wimmer 1998; Fogel 1999, 2000, and 2002). The theory of technophysio evolution arose out of intense discussion among the senior investigators, consultants, and research assistants during 1993–94, with the physicians providing much of the intellectual leadership. This theory points to the synergism between technological and physiological improvements that has produced a form of human evolution that is biological (but not genetic), rapid, culturally transmitted, and not necessarily stable. The process is ongoing in both rich and developing countries.

Interpretation of the theory

Unlike the genetic theory of evolution through natural selection, which applies to the whole history of life on earth, technophysio evolution applies only to the last 300 years of human history, and particularly to the last century.[21] Despite its limited scope, technophysio evolution appears to be relevant to forecasting likely trends over the next century or so in longevity, the age at onset of chronic diseases, body size, and the efficiency and durability of vital organ systems (Fogel and Costa 1997). It also has a bearing on such pressing issues of public policy as the growth in populations, in pension costs, and in health care costs.

The theory rests on the proposition that during the last 300 years human beings have gained an unprecedented degree of control over their environment—a degree of control so great that it sets them apart not only from all other species, but also from all previous generations of *Homo sapi-*

ens. This new degree of control has enabled *Homo sapiens* to increase its average body size by over 50 percent, to increase its average longevity by more
than 100 percent, and to greatly improve the robustness and capacity of
vital organ systems.[22]

Implications of technophysio evolution for analysis and measurement

Technophysio evolution implies that certain theoretical propositions that
underlie some current economic models are misspecified. For example, it is
frequently assumed that individuals are born with a specific amount of health
capital that depreciates over time. It is also assumed that the rate of depreciation depends on gross investments in health and on the level of health
care technology (which is assumed to be both exogenous to the individual
and independent of the date of birth—i.e., neglects cohort effects) (cf.
Grossman 1972; Wagstaff and Dardanoni 1986; Wagstaff 1986). While these
assumptions greatly simplify estimating procedures, they are inconsistent
with accumulating evidence that successive birth cohorts are experiencing
later onset of chronic diseases and disabilities, lower age-specific prevalence
rates, and less severe conditions (Crimmins, Reynolds, and Saito 1999; Larson
1999; Jette et al. 1998; Freedman and Martin 1998).

The theory of technophysio evolution implies that individuals' initial
endowments of health capital increased over the course of the twentieth
century. This implication has been supported by recent research demon-
strating that the curve of age-specific prevalence rates of chronic diseases
has been shifting outward throughout the century at what appears to be an
increasing rate (Manton, Corder, and Stallard 1997; Reynolds, Crimmins,
and Saito 1998; Crimmins, Reynolds, and Saito 1999; Costa 2000 and 2002;
Waidmann and Liu 2000; Manton and Gu 2001; Cutler 2001; Freedman,
Martin, and Schoeni 2002).[23]

If the theory is correct, some of the assumptions currently used by
economists and others to measure and analyze the contribution of health
interventions to improvements in life expectancy are misleading. In the standard models, endowments of individuals at birth are assumed to be the same,
regardless of the year of birth. Without investments in improving health
capital, different birth cohorts are assumed to experience the same average
rates of decline in their original health endowments (i.e., no allowance is
made for the slower average rates of decline in the untreated endowments
of different "vintages" of health capital). Another problem is that a single
health technology is presumed to exist that is exogenous to the individual.

The assumption that the endowment of human physiological capacity
is fixed, so that medical intervention can only slow the rate of deterioration
in the original endowment, means that ways of forecasting future improve-

ment in human physiology are sometimes neglected and possible paths of increase in health endowments play little role in forecasting future health care costs or longevity.[24]

Our theory implies that health endowments in a given population change with the year of birth. It also points to complex interactions between date of birth and the outcome of exposures to given risk factors. Hence, not all improvements in the outcome of exposure to health risks between, say, 1970 and 1990 are due to health interventions during that period. Improvements in life expectancy may depend only partly on the more effective medical technologies of those years. They could also reflect the improved physiologies experienced by later birth cohorts that are due to improved technologies in food production, public health practices, personal hygiene, diets, and medical interventions put into place decades before 1970, and hence that cannot be attributed exclusively, perhaps even primarily, to health inputs between 1970 and 1990.[25]

The same set of considerations applies to efforts to explain the decline in disabilities during the twentieth century. The discovery that the average age of onset of disabilities is more than a decade later today than it was in 1900 focuses attention on factors that might have improved the health endowments of successive cohorts or might have slowed down rates of depreciation before remedial medical interventions became necessary.[26]

The theory of technophysio evolution is also useful in circumstances where the standard models of health capital provide a useful first approximation. Improvements in health capital by date of birth have income effects that would lead individuals to make greater investments in health services. They also have substitution effects because they reduce the relative price of an additional year of life expectancy. Life at late ages becomes relatively more attractive, holding prices constant, because the later onset of chronic disabilities and a slower natural rate of deterioration in health increase the discounted present value of a year of consumption at late ages.

Endogenous treatment technology

The theory of technophysio evolution also suggests the need to reconsider which health variables are endogenous and which are exogenous to individuals and families. For one thing, it implies that health technology is not static but in constant flux. Moreover, there is not just one useful technology available to individuals at any point in time but many coexisting technologies of different vintages, and the rate of production of new technologies is accelerating. Hence, individuals may create their own unique technologies by the way they string together choices from among current and future technologies. For example, a person with a given degree of osteoarthritis may first choose to treat the condition with over-the-counter anti-inflammatory drugs, then shift to oral prescription drugs while waiting for improvements in surgical techniques and new plastics to emerge that reduce costs, increase the degree of success of an operation, and increase the durability of joint replacement. Such a string of choices defines an endogenous technology of treatment. Individuals thus create wide-ranging, person-specific technologies among which they can choose through the numerous permutations of strings of options.

Finally, the effectiveness of the numerous alternative technologies is not independent of the date of birth of a cohort. Studies indicate that the effectiveness of given treatments varies by physiological capacities that vary not only by age for a given cohort, but also across cohorts of different vintages. Race, ethnicity, sex, and nutritional status are significant variables in explaining the outcome of given health risks and the responses to different health interventions (Johnson 2000; Ferraro, Farmer, and Wybraniec 1997; Mendes de Leon et al. 1997; Davis et al. 1992 and 1994; Ostchega et al. 2000; Scrimshaw 1993, 1995, and 1997).

The point is not merely that a more complicated theory is needed, which recognizes the importance and implications of technologically based improvements in human physiology, some of which begin in utero, but that the increasing availability of longitudinal data sets, including the Union Army sample, is making it possible to estimate the critical change in the variables and parameters of dynamic models over time (cf. Parker 2000; Dasgupta 1993 and 1998; Manton and Land 2000a and b).

Postscript

I am keenly aware that I have neglected several important lines of research in the *Early Indicators* project. These include a series of papers by Chulhee Lee on the factors that influenced the health and mortality of soldiers during the Civil War and the effect of wartime stress on subsequent health and labor force participation (Lee 1997, 1998, 1999a and b, 2003a and b, 2005). There has also been a series of studies of specific diseases and disabilities, some of which are still at the working paper stage (Birchenall 2003; Wilson 2003; Wilson, Burton, and Howell 2003). One of the most promising new lines of research focuses on the impact of improved water supplies and other public health policies between 1880 and World War II on health and mortality (Troesken 2002, 2003, 2004; Troesken and Beeson 2003). The way in which politics and ideology affected the formulation of Union Army pension law and the application of pension policy has been examined by Peter Blanck and Chen Song (2001, 2002, 2003; Blanck, Linares, and Song 2002).

Notes

I have benefited from the comments and criticisms on an earlier draft by A. J. Aiseirithe, Dawn Alley, Javier Birchenall, Peter Blanck, Dora Costa, Lance Davis, Bernard Harris, Elaine Heisler, Max Henderson, Kwang-sun Lee, Robert Margo, Robert Mittendorf, Douglass North, Louis Nguyen, Georgeanne Patmios, Robert Pollak, Melissa Ptacek, Nevin Scrimshaw, Kenneth Sokoloff, Chen Song, Dejun Su, Richard Suzman, James Tanner, Werner Troesken, Sven Wilson, and E. A. Wrigley. The *Early Indicators* project is funded by NIA grant P01 AG10120.

1 On such variables as wealth of parental households in 1850 and 1860, number of months unemployed in 1900 and 1910, and persons living in the veterans' households, the census records are superior, since this information is not contained in the pension records. That is why we linked the manuscript schedules of the census to the pension records.

2 Congress established the Union Army pension system in July 1862, providing pensions to soldiers who incurred permanent disabilities while in the service. The amount of the pension depended on the degree of disability. All recruits, regardless of age, who served at least 90 days and were honorably discharged could apply. In June 1890, Congress extended the pension to any veteran who was disabled, even if the disability was unrelated to war service. In 1904, by Executive Order, veterans aged 62 were declared to be 50 percent disabled in their ability to perform manual labor. Thereafter, age alone made veterans eligible for pensions, although the amount of the pension still varied with the degree of disability (Glasson 1918).

3 The behavioral factors do not explain much of the variation in the odds of linking in either the prewar or the postwar censuses. The chi-square and R-square values are especially low in the postwar censuses, with the behavioral factors accounting for less than 3 percent of the variation in the probability of making a link.

4 Deserters were in most cases ineligible for a pension, and many soldiers who died during the war had no eligible dependents. The

foreign dummy is also significant in part because many of the foreigners who died during the early postwar years had no eligible dependents or served behind the front and so were less likely to incur war-related disabilities. However, those who survived to become eligible under the pension law of 1890 were as likely as natives to be linked to pension records.

5 These enterprises were highly successful, providing insights into processes that had heretofore been obscure and promoting many new studies that exploited these sources and analytical techniques. They also promoted new skills in sampling design, in analyzing sample selection biases, and in methods of correcting these and other biases by reweighting and by use of simulation models to estimate probable ranges of error and their impact on particular analytical issues.

6 The genealogies of Mormons, called "family histories," consist of three generations, but they can be linked together to construct large genealogies.

7 For example, persons outside the family line cannot be brought into the sample until marriage, because they are not at risk of dying before marriage. When such caveats are heeded, it is possible to draw cross-sections of persons alive in 1860 or 1870 from a sample of genealogies and compare these distributions of selected characteristics with the distributions of the same characteristics in the censuses. Such comparisons revealed that the genealogies produced representative cross-sections when tested against such variables as wealth, household size, and age distributions.

8 This experience with genealogies provides the inspiration for future projects we are planning, and it influenced the conception of a new project on "The effect of family on adult health and welfare," led by Clayne Pope. A project using the genealogies has been in the planning for more than a decade. Much expertise has been accumulated in the use of this source of evidence. (See Wimmer and Pope 1975; Pope 1986, 1992; cf. Wimmer 2003; Wilson and Pope 2003; Costa 2003.)

9 In fact, the figure of 17 years for Norwegian girls was revised in subsequent publi-

cations, when better data had become available, to about 15.5 years; see Tanner 1981.

10 I have omitted a number of important developments in quantitative history between 1955 and 1985. More complete surveys are presented in Fogel and Elton 1983; Fogel 1992; Bogue 1983; and Jensen 1984, among other places.

11 We are exploring the possibility of drawing a representative sample of hospital records to measure the burden of chronic diseases among women at the beginning of the twentieth century.

12 Of course, the Public Health Service had long collected information on notifiable (contagious) diseases.

13 Since current diagnostic techniques make it possible to diagnose heart disease and neoplasms sooner in the development of these diseases than was the case around 1910, the figures given in the text should be considered lower bounds on the delay in the onset of these conditions.

14 Co-morbidity: the coexistence of two or more disease processes.

15 The delay in the average age at onset of chronic diseases can be decomposed into two parts: (1) the shift in the age-specific disease schedule; (2) the change in the distribution of ages due to the increase in life expectancy and the decline in the fertility rate. Although we have not yet completed this decomposition, preliminary estimates indicate that the contribution of the change in the age distribution was small.

16 For reviews of earlier work dealing with the use of height, BMI, and other anthropometric measures as indexes of changes in health and the standard of living over time, see Steckel 1995; Komlos and Cuff 1998.

17 For information on what is known about change in body size, and in rates of development of women over time and differences over space in recent decades, see Tanner 1981; Eveleth and Tanner 1976 and 1990; Friedman 1982; and John 1988 and 1992.

18 Tanner (1982) estimated that the Marine Society boys were 62 inches at maturity. Compared with the British military recruits of the same birth cohorts, the mature graduates

of the Marine Society were about 5 inches shorter (Floud, Wachter, and Gregory 1990: Table 4.1), suggesting that they belonged to the shortest 10 percent of the British laboring classes. It is likely that the women of this class were shorter than 59 inches. In populations stunted to this extent, the differential in mean heights between men and women is in the range of 3 to 5 inches (cf. Friedman 1982; Eveleth and Tanner 1976: Tables 77, 78, 44, 45).

19 The distribution of birth weights is not strictly normal because it is a convolution of two distributions: a main distribution of full-term babies and a smaller distribution of preterm babies. Hence in fitting normal approximations of birth weights, it is common to discard the small distribution of preterm babies (Wilcox and Russell 1983; Wilcox et al. 1995; Graafmans et al. 2002). The weight distribution displayed in column 3 of Table 5 is estimated from the fitted normal curve, and it differs slightly from the original data as follows:

Birth weight (g)	Fitted distribution	Original distribution
1,500 or less	0.012	0.012
1,501–2,000	0.014	0.015
2,001–2,500	0.051	0.055
2,501–3,000	0.181	0.188
3,001–3,500	0.351	0.356
3,501–4,000	0.260	0.253
4,001–4,500	0.087	0.082
4,501 or more	0.046	0.040

I am grateful to Kwang-sun Lee for providing the comparison. As he pointed out in his letter of 7 July 2003, the difference in the two distributions is so small that it does not affect the thrust of my discussion of Table 5.

20 However, obstructed labor is still a serious problem for small women in poor countries, where it kills many mothers and children (Rush 2000).

21 Costa and I limit technophysio evolution to the last 300 years for two reasons. It was not until about 1700 that changes in technology permitted population growth far in excess of previous rates. Moreover, after 1700 body weight and stature increase to unprecedented levels. See Figure 1 in Fogel and Costa 1997.

22 Although considerable empirical evidence indicates that a "good" environment both speeds up biological development at young ages and delays the onset of chronic conditions at middle and late ages, there is as yet no agreed-upon theory about the cellular and molecular processes that explain these observations.

23 Costa has noted that the annual rate of decline in functional limitations between 1900 and 1980 was substantially below the rate of decline since 1980. That point is important because it bears on forecasts of the likely improvements in functional limitations during the twenty-first century.

Another question arises: How much of the total decline in the burden of disease and functional limitation that occurred in the United States during the twentieth century took place before 1980 and how much since then? A reliable answer requires new data sets that will provide a more detailed picture of the temporal pattern of changes in the burden of chronic disabilities for cohorts who turned age 65 between 1915 and 1980. An illustration of what that division might be is suggested by Costa's estimate that functional limitation declined at 0.6 percent per annum between 1900 and 1980, and Manton and Gu's estimate that during the 1980s and 1990s the average rate of decline in disability was 1.7 percent per annum. Together these estimates suggest a total decrease of 56 percent in the burden of disability after age 65. About two-thirds of the decline took place before 1980 and one-third after 1980.

This computation illustrates some of the problems that need to be overcome in measuring and explaining the decline in disabilities during the twentieth century. The measure of functional limitations needs to be consistent over the century (Costa and Manton and Gu used different measures of disability). There is also the question of how to define the severity of different sets of conditions in different social and economic contexts. It is likely that several alternative indexes will have to be constructed, involving issues similar to those encountered in constructing indexes of prices over long periods.

24 Among the exceptions are Rosenzweig and Schultz 1988 and Dasgupta 1993.

25 Much recent research indicates that waiting time to the onset of chronic diseases is a function of exposure to insults in utero and in infancy. See Barker 1998; Scrimshaw 1997.

26 Although I have focused on new technology for treatment, much has been done to prevent early onset of chronic diseases by promoting better nutritional habits and lifestyles.

References

Alter, George and James C. Riley. 1989. "Frailty, sickness, and death: Models of morbidity and mortality in modern populations," *Population Studies* 43(1): 25–45.

Barker, D. J. P. 1998. *Mothers, Babies, and Health in Later Life*. 2d ed. Edinburgh: Churchill Livingstone.

Bell, Felicitie C., Alice H. Wade, and Stephen C. Goss. 1992. *Life Tables for the United States Social Security Area 1900–2080*. Actuarial Study No. 107. Baltimore: U.S. Department of Health and Human Services, Social Security Administration, Office of the Actuary.

Birchenall, Javier A. 2003. "Airborne diseases: Tuberculosis in the Union Army," paper presented at the Joint Meeting of the *Early Indicators of Later Work Levels, Disease, & Death* Program Project and Cohort Studies groups, National Bureau of Economics, 25–26 April 2003, Cambridge, MA.

Blanck, Peter D., Claudia Linares, and Chen Song. 2002. "Evolution of disability in late 19th century America: Civil War pensions for Union Army veterans with musculoskeletal conditions," *Behavioral Sciences and the Law* 20(6): 681–697.

Blanck, Peter D. and Chen Song. 2001. "'With malice toward none; with charity toward all': Civil War pensions for native and foreign-born Union Army veterans," *Transnational Law and Contemporary Problems* 11(1): 1–75.

———. 2002. "Civil War pension attorneys and disability politics," *University of Michigan Journal of Law Reform* 35(1&2): 137–217.

———. 2003. "'Never forget what they did here': Civil War pensions for Gettysburg Union Army veterans and disability in nineteenth century America," *William and Mary Law Review* 44(3): 1109–1171.

Bogue, Allan G. 1983. *Clio and the Bitch Goddess: Quanitification in American Political History.* Beverly Hills: Sage Publications.

Canavese, Paula and Claudia Linares. 2003. "Alternative measures to the total disability rates, surgeon's certificates data," CPE Working Paper Series #2003-2.

Ceruzzi, Paul E. 2003. *A History of Modern Computing,* 2nd ed. Cambridge, MA: MIT Press.

Charlson, M., T. P. Szatrowski, J. Peterson, and J. Gold. 1994. "Validation of a combined comorbidity index," *Journal of Clinical Epidemiology* 47(11): 1245–1251.

Costa, Dora L. 2000. "Understanding the twentieth-century decline in chronic conditions among older men," *Demography* 37(1): 53–72.

———. 2002. "Changing chronic disease rates and long-term declines in functional limitation among older men," *Demography* 39(1): 119–137.

——— (ed.). 2003. *Health and Labor Force Participation over the Life Cycle.* Chicago: University of Chicago Press for NBER.

———. 2004. "The measure of man and older age mortality: Evidence from the Gould Sample," *Journal of Economic History* 64(1): 1–23.

Crimmins, Eileen M., Sandra L. Reynolds, and Yasuhiko Saito. 1999. "Trends in health and ability to work among the older working-age population," *Journals of Gerontology* 54B(1): S31–S40.

Cutler, David M. 2001. "The reduction in disability among the elderly," *Proceedings of the National Academy of Sciences, USA* 98(12): 6546–6547.

Dasgupta, Partha. 1993. *An Inquiry into Well-Being and Destitution.* Oxford: Clarendon.

———. 1998. "The economics of poverty in poor countries," Working paper, STICERD, London School of Economics Discussion Papers Series.

Davis, Maradee A., John M. Neuhaus, Deborah J. Moritz, and Mark R. Segal. 1992. "Living arrangements and survival among middle-aged and older adults in the NHANES I Epidemiologic Follow-Up Study," *American Journal of Public Health* 82(3): 401–406.

Davis, Maradee A. et al. 1994. "Health behaviors and survival among middle-aged and older men and women in the NHANES I Epidemiological Follow-Up Study," *Preventive Medicine* 23(3): 369–376.

Eveleth, Phyllis B. and J. M. Tanner. 1976. *Worldwide Variation in Human Growth.* Cambridge: Cambridge University Press.

———. 1990. *Worldwide Variation in Human Growth,* 2d ed. Cambridge: Cambridge University Press.

Ferraro, Kenneth F., Melissa M. Farmer, and John A. Wybraniec. 1997. "Health trajectories: Long-term dynamics among black and white adults," *Journal of Health and Social Behavior* 38(1): 38–54.

Floud, Roderick, Kenneth Wachter, and Annabel Gregory. 1990. *Height, health and history: Nutritional status in the United Kingdom, 1750–1980.* Cambridge: Cambridge University Press.

Fogel, Robert William. 1986. "Nutrition and the decline in mortality since 1700: Some preliminary findings," in Stanley L. Engerman and Robert E. Gallman (eds.), *Long-Term Factors in American Economic Growth.* Chicago: University of Chicago Press, pp. 439–555.

———. 1992. "Introduction: Notes on the art of empirical research in the social sciences during an age of plunging costs in data processing," in *Without Consent or Contract,* vol. 2, *Evidence and Methods,* eds. Robert William Fogel, Ralph A. Galantine, and Richard L. Manning. New York: W. W. Norton, pp. 1–41.

———. 1993. "New sources and new techniques for the study of secular trends in nutritional status, health, mortality, and the process of aging," *Historical Methods* 26(1): 5–43.

———. 1994. "Economic growth, population theory, and physiology: The bearing of long-term processes on the making of economic policy," *American Economic Review* 84(3): 369–395.

———. 1997. "Economic and social structure for an ageing population," *Philosophical Transactions of the Royal Society of London* 353B(1356): 1905–1917.

———. 1999. "Catching up with the economy," *American Economic Review* 89(1): 1–21.

———. 2000. *The Fourth Great Awakening and the Future of Egalitarianism.* Chicago: University of Chicago Press.

———. 2002. "Auxology and economics," in G. Gilli, L. M. Schell, and L. Benso (eds.), *Human Growth from Conception to Maturity.* London: Smith-Gordon, pp. 1–11.

Fogel, Robert William and Dora L. Costa. 1997. "A theory of technophysio evolution, with some implications for forecasting population, health care costs, and pension costs," *Demography* 34(1): 49–66.

Fogel, Robert William, Dora L. Costa, and John M. Kim. 1993. "Secular trends in the distribution of chronic conditions and disabilities at young adult and late ages, 1860–1988: Some preliminary findings." Paper presented at the National Bureau of Economic Research (NBER) Summer Institute, Economics of Aging Program, 26–28 July, Cambridge, MA.

Fogel, Robert William and Geoffrey R. Elton. 1983. *Which Road to the Past? Two Views of History.* New Haven: Yale University Press.

Fogel, Robert William and Stanley L. Engerman. 1974. *Time on the Cross: The Economics of American Negro Slavery.* 2 vols. Boston: Little, Brown.

Fogel, Robert William, Stanley L. Engerman, James Trussell, Roderick Floud, Clayne L. Pope, and Larry T. Wimmer. 1978. "The economics of mortality in North America, 1650–1910: A description of a research project," *Historical Methods* 11(2): 75–108.

Fogel, Robert William, Michael Haines, Clayne L. Pope, Irwin H. Rosenberg, Nevin S. Scrimshaw, James Trussell, and Larry T. Wimmer. 1991. "Aging of Union Army men: A longitudinal study, 1830–1940." Program Project proposal submitted to the National Institute on Aging. Typescript, University of Chicago.

Foust, James D. 1968. *The Yeoman Farmer and Westward Expansion of U.S. Cotton Production.* Ann Arbor, MI: University Microfilms.

Freedman, Vicki A. and Linda G. Martin. 1998. "Understanding trends in functional limitations among older Americans," *American Journal of Public Health* 88(10): 1457–1462.

Freedman, Vicki A., Linda G. Martin, and Robert F. Schoeni. 2002. "Recent trends in disability and functioning among older adults in the United States," *Journal of the American Medical Association* 288(24): 3137–3146.

Friedman, Gerald C. 1982. "The heights of slaves in Trinidad," *Social Science History* 6(4): 482–515.

Glasson, William Henry. 1918. *Federal Military Pensions in the United States.* New York: Oxford University Press.

Graafmans, Wilco C., Jan Hendrik Richardus, Gerard J. J. M. Borsboom, Leiv Bakketeig, Jens Langhoff-Roos, Pers Bergsjø, Alison Macfarlane, S. Pauline Verloove-Vanhorick, Johan P. Mackenbach, and the EuroNatal working group. 2002. "Birth weight and perinatal mortality: A comparison of 'optimal' birth weight in seven Western European countries," *Epidemiology* 13(5): 569–574.

Grossman, Michael. 1972. "On the concept of health capital and the demand for health," *Journal of Political Economy* 80(2): 223–255.

Harris, Bernard. 1997. "Growing taller, living longer? Anthropometric history and the future of old age," *Ageing and Society* 17(5): 491–512.

Helmchen, Lorens A. 2003. "Changes in the age at onset of chronic disease among elderly Americans, 1870–2000," typescript, Center for Population Economics, University of Chicago.

Jayant, K. 1964. "Birth weight and some other factors in relation to infant survival: A study on an Indian sample," *Annals of Human Genetics* 27(3): 261–267.

Jensen, Richard J. 1984. "Historiography of American political history," in *Encyclopedia of American Political History: Studies of the Principal Movements and Ideas*, vol. 1, ed. J. P. Greene. New York: Scribner's.

Jette, Alan M., Susan F. Assmann, Dan Rooks, Bette Ann Harris, and Sybil Crawford. 1998. "Interrelationships among disablement concepts," *Journals of Gerontology* 53A(5): M395–M404.

John, A. Meredith. 1988. *The Plantation Slaves of Trinidad, 1783–1816: A Mathematical and Demographic Inquiry*. Cambridge: Cambridge University Press.

———. 1992. "Logistic models of slave child mortality in Trinidad," in Robert William Fogel and Stanley L. Engerman (eds.), *Without Consent or Contract*, Technical Papers, vol. 2, *Conditions of Slave Life and the Transition to Freedom*. New York: W. W. Norton, pp. 413–434.

Johnson, Nan E. 2000. "The racial crossover in comorbidity, disability, and mortality," *Demography* 37(3): 267–283.

Kazis, L. E., D. R. Miller, J. Clark, K. Skinner, A. Lee, W. Rogers, A. Spiro III, S. Payne, G. Fincke, A. Selim, and M. Linzer. 1998. "Health-related quality of life in patients served by the Department of Veterans Affairs: Results from the Veterans Health Study," *Archives of Internal Medicine* 158(6): 629–632.

Komlos, John and Timothy Cuff (eds.). 1998. *Classics in Anthropometric History*. St. Katharinen, Germany: Scripta Mercaturae Verlag.

Landi, F., G. Zaccala, G. Gambassi, R. A. Incalzi, L. Manigrasso, F. Pagano, P. Carbonin, and R. Bernabei. 1999. "Body mass index and mortality among older people living in the community," *Journal of the American Geriatrics Society* 47(9): 1072–1076.

Larson, James S. 1999. "The conceptualization of health," *Medical Care Research and Review* 56(2): 123–136.

Lauderdale, Diane S. and Paul J. Rathouz. 1999. "Evidence of environmental suppression of familial resemblance: Height among U.S. Civil War brothers," *Annals of Human Biology* 26(5): 413–426.

Lee, Chulhee. 1997. "Socioeconomic background, disease, and mortality among Union Army recruits: Implications for economic and demographic history," *Explorations in Economic History* 34(1): 27–55.

———. 1998. "Long-term unemployment and retirement in early-twentieth-century America," *Journal of Economic History* 58(3): 844–856.

———. 1999a. "Farm value and retirement of farm owners in early-twentieth-century America," *Explorations in Economic History* 36(4): 387–408.

———. 1999b. "Selective assignment of military positions in the Union Army: Implications for the impact of the Civil War," *Social Science History* 23(1): 67–97.

———. 2001. "Exposure to disease during growing ages and service," in *Early Indicators of Later Work Levels, Disease, & Death*, program project proposal submitted to the N. I. A. Typescript, Center for Population Economics, University of Chicago.

———. 2003a. "Health and economic mobility of Union Army recruits, 1860–1870," paper presented at the NBER *Early Indicators of Later Work Levels, Disease, and Death* and Cohort Studies Groups Joint Meeting, Boston, 25–26 April.

———. 2003b. "Prior exposure to disease and later health and mortality: Evidence from Union Army medical records," in Dora L. Costa (ed.), *Health and Labor Force Participation over the Life Cycle: Evidence from the Past*. Chicago: University of Chicago Press for NBER, pp. 51–87.

———. 2005. "Labor market status of older males in the United States, 1880–1940," *Social Science History* (forthcoming).

Manton, Kenneth G., Larry Corder, and Eric Stallard. 1997. "Chronic disability trends in elderly United States populations: 1982–1994," *Proceedings of the National Academy of Sciences, USA* 94(6): 2593–2598.

Manton, Kenneth G. and XiLiang Gu. 2001. "Changes in the prevalence of chronic disability in the United States black and nonblack population above age 65 from 1982 to 1999," *Proceedings of the National Academy of Sciences, USA* 98(11): 6354–6359.

Manton, Kenneth G. and Kenneth C. Land. 2000a. "Active life expectancy estimates for the U.S. elderly population: A multidimensional continuous-mixture model of functional change applied to completed cohorts, 1982–1996," *Demography* 37(3): 253–265.

———. 2000b. "Multidimensional disability/mortality trajectories at ages 65 and over: The impact of state dependence," *Social Indicators Research* 51(2): 193–221.

Martin, J. A., B. E. Hamilton, S. J. Ventura, F. Menacker, M. M. Park, and P. D. Sutton. 2002. "Births: Final data for 2001," *National Vital Statistics Reports* 51(2): 1–102.

Mendes de Leon, Carlos F., Laurel A. Beckett, Gerda G. Fillenbaum, Dwight B. Brock, Laurence G. Branch, Denis A. Evans, and Lisa F. Berkman. 1997. "Black-white differences in risk of becoming disabled and recovering from disability in old age: A longitudinal analysis of two EPESE populations," *American Journal of Epidemiology* 145(6): 488–497.

Menn, Joseph Karl. 1964a. *The Large Slaveholders of Louisiana, 1860*. New Orleans, LA: Pelican.

———. 1964b. "The large slaveholders of the deep South, 1860," Ph.D. dissertation, University of Texas.

Murray, Christopher J. L. and Lincoln C. Chen. 1992. "Understanding morbidity change," *Population and Development Review* 18(3): 481–503.

———. 1993a. "In search of a contemporary theory of understanding mortality change," *Social Science and Medicine* 36(2): 143–155.

———. 1993b. "Understanding morbidity change: Reply to Riley," *Population and Development Review* 19(4): 812–815.

Omran, Abdel R. 1971. "The epidemiological transition: A theory of the epidemiology of population change," *Milbank Memorial Fund Quarterly* 49(4): 509–538.

Ostchega, Yechiam, Tamara B. Harris, Rosemarie Hirsch, Van L. Parsons, and Raynard Kington. 2000. "The prevalence of functional limitations and disability in older persons in the US: Data from the National Health and Nutrition Examination Survey III," *Journal of the American Geriatrics Society* 48(9): 1132–1135.

Parker, Philip M. 2000. *Physioeconomics: The basis for long-run economic growth*. Cambridge, MA: MIT Press.

Penninx, B. W., S. Leveille, L. Ferrucci, J. T. van Eijk, and J. M. Guralnik. 1999. "Exploring the effect of depression on physical disability: Longitudinal evidence from the established populations for epidemiologic studies of the elderly," *American Journal of Public Health* 89(9): 1346–1352.

Pope, Clayne L. 1986. "Native adult mortality in the U.S.: 1770–1870," in Robert William Fogel (ed.), *Long-Term Changes in Nutrition and the Standard of Living*. Bern: International Economic History Association, pp. 76–85.

———. 1992. "Adult mortality in America before 1900: A view from family histories," in Claudia Goldin and Hugh Rockoff (eds.), *Strategic Factors in Nineteenth Century American Economic History*. Chicago: University of Chicago Press for NBER, pp. 267–296.

Pope, Clayne L. and Larry T. Wimmer. 1998. "Ageing in the early twentieth century," *American Economic Review* 88(2): 217–221.

Preston, Samuel H. and Michael Haines. 1991. *Fatal Years: Child Mortality in Late Nineteenth-Century America*. Princeton, NJ: Princeton University Press.

Preston, Samuel H., Nathan Keyfitz, and Robert Schoen. 1972. *Causes of Death: Life Tables for National Populations*. New York: Seminar Press.

Reynolds, Sandra L., Eileen M. Crimmins, and Yasuhiko Saito. 1998. "Cohort differences in disability and disease presence," *Gerontologist* 38(5): 578–590.

Riley, James C. 1989. *Sickness, Recovery and Death: A History and Forecast of Ill Health*. Iowa City, IA: University of Iowa Press.

———. 1990a. "Long-term morbidity and mortality trends: Inverse health transitions," in *What We Know about Health Transition: The Cultural, Social and Behavioural Determinants of Health, The Proceedings of an International Workshop, Canberra, May 1989*. Canberra: Health Transition Centre, Australian National University.

———. 1990b. "The risk of being sick: Morbidity trends in four countries," *Population and Development Review* 16(3): 403–432.

———. 1991. "The prevalence of chronic diseases during mortality increase: Hungary in the 1980s," *Population Studies* 45(3): 489–496.

———. 1997. *Sick, Not Dead: The Health of British Workingmen during the Mortality Decline*. Baltimore: Johns Hopkins University Press.

Riley, James C. and George Alter. 1996. "The sick and the well: Adult health in Britain during the health transition," *Health Transition Review* 6(suppl.): 19–44.

Rosenzweig, Mark R. and T. Paul Schultz. 1988. "The stability of household production technology: A replication," *Journal of Human Resources* 23(4): 535–549.

Rush, David. 2000. "Nutrition and maternal mortality in the developing world," *American Journal of Clinical Nutrition* 72(1 Suppl.): 212S–240S.

Scrimshaw, Nevin S. 1993. "Malnutrition, brain development, learning and behavior." The Twentieth Kamla Puri Sabharwal Memorial Lecture presented at Lady Irwin College, New Delhi, India, 23 November 1993.

——— (ed.). 1995. *Community-Based Longitudinal Nutrition and Health Studies: Classical Examples from Guatemala, Haiti and Mexico*. Boston: International Nutrition Foundation for Developing Countries (INFDC).

———. 1997. "More evidence that foetal nutrition contributes to chronic disease in later life," *British Medical Journal* 315(7112): 825–826.

Soltow, Lee. 1975. *Men and Wealth in the United States 1850–1870*. New Haven: Yale University Press.

Steckel, Richard H. 1995. "Stature and the standard of living," *Journal of Economic Literature* 33(4): 1904–1940.

Stuck, A. E., J. M. Walthert, T. Nikolaus, C. J. Bula, C. Hohmann, and J. C. Beck. 1999. "Risk factors for functional status decline in community-living elderly people: A systematic literature review," *Social Science & Medicine* 48(4): 445–469.

Tanner, J. M. 1981. *A History of the Study of Human Growth*. Cambridge: Cambridge University Press.

———. 1982. "The potential of auxological data for monitoring economic and social well-being," *Social Science History* 6(4): 571–581.

Troesken, Werner. 2002. "The limits of Jim Crow: Race and the provision of the water and sewerage services in American cities, 1880–1925," *Journal of Economic History* 62(3): 734–72.

———. 2003. "Lead water pipes and infant mortality in turn-of-the-century Massachusetts," NBER Working Paper No. 9549.

———. 2004. *Water, Race, and Disease*. Cambridge: MIT Press.

Troesken, Werner and Patricia E. Beeson. 2003. "The significance of lead water mains in American cities: Some historical evidence," in Dora L. Costa (ed.), *Health and Labor Force Participation over the Life Cycle*. Chicago: University of Chicago Press for NBER, pp. 181–201.

Trussell, James and Richard Steckel. 1978. "The age of slaves at menarche and their first birth," *Journal of Interdisciplinary History* 8(3): 477–505.

U.S. National Office of Vital Statistics. 1954. "Weight at birth and its effect on survival of the newborn in the United States, early 1950," *Vital Statistics Special Report* 39(1).

Verbrugge, Lois M. 1984. "Longer life but worsening health? Trends in health and mortality of middle-aged and older persons," *Milbank Memorial Fund Quarterly Health and Society* 62(3): 475–519.

———. 1989. "Recent, present, and future health of American adults," *Annual Review of Public Health* 10: 333–361.

Verbrugge, Lois M. and Alan M. Jette. 1994. "The disablement process," *Social Science & Medicine* 38(1): 1–14.

Wagstaff, Adam. 1986. "The demand for health: Theory and applications," *Journal of Epidemiology and Community Health* 40(1): 1–11.

Wagstaff, Adam and Valentino Dardanoni. 1986. "The demand for health: A simplified Grossman model/A note on a simple model of health investment," *Bulletin of Economic Research* 38(1): 93–100.

Waidmann, Timothy, John Bound, and Michael Schoenbaum. 1995. "The illusion of failure: Trends in self-reported health of the U.S. elderly," *Milbank Memorial Fund Quarterly* 73(2): 253–287.

Waidmann, Timothy A. and Korbin Liu. 2000. "Disability trends among elderly persons and implications for the future," *Journals of Gerontology* 55B(5): S298–S307.

Wilcox, A., R. Skjaerven, P. Buekens, and J. Kiely. 1995. "Birth weight and perinatal mortality: A comparison of the United States and Norway," *Journal of the American Medical Association* 273(9): 709–711.

Wilcox, A. J. and I. T. Russell. 1983. "Birthweight and perinatal mortality: II. On weight-specific mortality," *International Journal of Epidemiology* 12(3): 319–325.

Wilcox, Nathaniel T. 1992. "The overseer problem: A new data set and method," in Robert William Fogel, Ralph A. Galantine, and Richard L. Manning (eds.), *Without Consent or Contract*, vol. 2, *Evidence and Methods*. New York: W. W. Norton, pp. 84–108.

Wilson, Sven E. 2003. "The prevalence of chronic respiratory disease in the industrial era: The United States, 1895–1910," in Dora L Costa (ed.), *Health and Labor Force Participation over the Life Cycle: Evidence from the Past*. Chicago: University of Chicago Press for NBER, pp. 147–180.

Wilson, Sven E., Joseph Burton, and Benjamin Howell. 2003. "Work disability among non-elderly adult males: The United States, 1893–2001," typescript, Brigham Young University.

Wilson, Sven E. and Clayne L. Pope. 2003. "The height of Union Army recruits: Family and community influences," in Dora L. Costa (ed.), *Health and Labor Force Participation over the Life Cycle*. Chicago: University of Chicago Press for NBER, pp. 113–145.

Wimmer, Larry T. 2003. "Reflections on the Early Indicators project: A partial history," in Dora L. Costa (ed.), *Health and Labor Force Participation over the Life Cycle: Evidence from the Past*. Chicago: University of Chicago Press for NBER.

Wimmer, Larry T. and Clayne L. Pope. 1975. "The Genealogical Society Library of Salt Lake City: A source of data for economic and genealogical historians," *Historical Methods Newsletter* 8(2): 51–58.

Wolfe, Barbara L. and Robert Haveman. 1990. "Trends in the prevalence of work disability from 1962 to 1984, and their correlates," *Milbank Memorial Fund Quarterly* 68(1): 53–80.

The Biodemography
of Aging

James W. Vaupel

Is there a looming limit to human life expectancy? Will the life expectancy of any sizable population ever exceed 85 years? These were the research questions that seized my attention in 1986. I would like to start with them by way of offering an account of the course of my life as a researcher interested in the biodemography of aging.

The question of limits to life expectancy was a hot topic in 1986, and the subject remains of considerable interest today. In 1980 James Fries wrote a widely cited article in the *New England Journal of Medicine* in which he quantified some notions that gerontologists had been talking about for a long time. Fries made the following assertions. There are two kinds of death: premature and senescent. Premature death results from accidents and various illnesses that cut life short. Senescent death strikes as an individual approaches his or her maximum potential life span. Every human is born with a maximum potential life span. This maximum differs from person to person and is normally distributed with a mean of 85 years and a standard deviation of 7 years. Nothing can be done to alter a person's maximum potential life span: it is innate, fixed, and beyond the influence of any currently conceivable environmental, behavioral, or medical intervention. When a person's age nears his or her maximum potential life span, then the person becomes increasingly susceptible to many proximate causes of death. If a person does not die of cancer today, then he or she will die of a heart attack or influenza or a serious fall or something else tomorrow. Because the maximum potential life span of individuals has a mean of 85 years, it follows that under no foreseeable conditions can a population's life expectancy exceed 85 years.

The kernel of Fries's theory can be traced back to Aristotle. Aristotle also asserted that there were two kinds of death, premature and senescent. He compared premature death to a fire extinquished by throwing water on it, and he compared senescent death to a fire burning itself out. Each individual, Aristotle wrote, was born with a fixed amount of "fuel," analogous to the wood in a fire. No new fuel could be added. Hence, each individual has a maximum potential life span. For 24 centuries this Aristotelian view has been widely accepted and is still viewed by many experts as well as laypeople as undeniably correct. The value of Fries's contribution was to clearly specify the elements of the theory and to quantify particular values for the mean and standard deviation of the distribution of maximum potential life spans.

Evolutionary biologists, starting with Medawar, Williams, and Hamilton in the 1950s and 1960s, developed a theory of aging that is consistent with the Aristotelean notion of limited life spans. Their basic reasoning can be simply summarized. Evolution is driven by the survival of the fittest. By definition, individuals who are more fit have more descendants than those who are less fit. That is, fit individuals are more likely to survive to reproductive age and to give birth to numerous offspring who survive to reproduce as well. Hence the genes of the individuals in a population tend to be the genes of fit individuals.

But how does age affect this process? Older individuals have few if any additional progeny. Over the long course of human evolution, the elderly contributed to the survival and reproductive success of their children and grandchildren by providing them with food and other resources. Such contributions tend to diminish with age. Moreover, only a small proportion of individuals, before the twentieth century, survived to age 70 or older. Hence, individuals with mutations that increased the chances of death at older ages—but not at younger ages—were almost as fit as individuals without such mutations. As such mutations gradually occurred and were passed on from generation to generation, their frequency tended to increase. This process was accelerated for mutations that are deleterious at older ages but that reduce mortality or increase fertility at younger ages. In any case, however, harmful mutations that affect only older individuals accumulate over many generations, and this results in an increase in death rates with age. In particular, death rates reach very high levels at ages when individuals make little contribution to the survival or fertility of their descendants. This high level of mortality imposes an effective limit to any individual's life span. Because the burden of late-acting mutations affects various individuals differently, maximum potential life span also varies across individuals. For humans, it does not seem unreasonable that the mean of this distribution might be 85 years or so, perhaps with a standard deviation of roughly 7 years, because the fitness contribution of older individuals is certainly modest by age 85, very small by age 92, minuscule by age 99, and not large at age 78 or even 71.

Because Fries's arguments seemed reasonable to many people, because he expressed his views clearly, cogently, and with admirable specificity, because he presented some indirectly relevant evidence to support his position, and because his theory is consistent with the evolutionary theory of aging, the "Fries theory" was widely accepted in the 1980s. Some scholars, however, had doubts, especially about whether 85 years was the true limit to human life expectancy but also about the general notion of limited life spans. Kenneth Wachter and Sheila Ryan Johansson at the University of California at Berkeley made a crucial contribution by organizing a stimulating research workshop in 1988 to discuss the evidence for the theory and the doubts about it.

Immediately after participating in this workshop, James Carey, Shripad Tuljapurkar, and I discussed possible analyses that might be done to test the Fries theory. At the University of Minnesota I had organized a series of weekly meetings at which scholars interested in demography could discuss their research. Following the Berkeley workshop, the Minnesota meetings increasingly focused on Fries's theory and how to test it. Working together with Carey, at the University of California at Davis, we developed a program of research. We were encouraged by various people, most importantly by Richard Suzman at the US National Institute on Aging, and also by Michael Teitelbaum at the Sloan Foundation and by Tuljapurkar, Robert Fogel, Nathan Keyfitz, Peter Laslett, and Samuel Preston, among others. Before I describe our program of research, let me briefly recount how I arrived at the University of Minnesota and how my research career there got started.

My early research career

After studying international business at Harvard Business School, getting a Master's degree in public policy, and starting Ph.D. research at the Kennedy School of Government at Harvard, I joined the public policy faculty at Duke University. At Harvard I began three Ph.D. dissertations. The first focused on mathematical methods for deciding when it is time to cease analyzing a decision dilemma. The second concerned public regulation of multinational corporations. And the third, which I finished after I started working at Duke, evaluated public policies to reduce "early death" before age 65. My interest in mortality led me to start reading and thinking about demography. This resulted in my first research article in *Demography*, a piece by Vaupel, Manton, and Stallard (1979) on the impact of heterogeneity in frailty on the dynamics of mortality. For three years, spread out over the first half of the 1980s, I was employed by the International Institute for Applied Systems Analysis (IIASA), near Vienna, Austria, where I deepened my understanding of demography by working with such outstanding researchers as Brian Arthur, Nathan Keyfitz, Andrei Rogers, Michael Stoto, and Anatoli Yashin.

At the end of my stay at IIASA, I moved to Minneapolis and began working in 1986 as a full professor at the Humphrey Institute for Public Affairs and Planning at the University of Minnesota. It was immediately made clear to me that I would have to learn how to raise grant funding. In part because of the pressure to do so and in part because of my by-now deep interest in demography, I decided to find colleagues at Minnesota who were also interested in demography. So I used the Science and Social Science Citation Indexes to find the names of everyone in Minnesota who had written a cited article with the word "demography" or "population" in the title, abstract, or key words. I found almost 200 names. Some had left Minnesota, some lived in Minnesota but a long way from Minneapolis, and some clearly had interests that were distant from demographic research. Many, however, seemed relevant and others, such as the author of "The population of timber wolves on Isle Royale," seemed at least to be worth meeting. So I started telephoning people and asking whether they would like to have lunch with me. Very few people turned me down. Altogether I had lunch with about 100 new people over the course of my first year at Minnesota.

As it turned out, many of these people were interested in survival and longevity, in some cases for humans and in other cases for various nonhuman species. A group of about 30 of these researchers decided to meet for an hour once a week to discuss research on the demography of aging. These participants included about a dozen scholars with backgrounds in social and behavioral sciences, about half a dozen with degrees in medicine and public health, another half dozen from various branches of biology, and a final half dozen from statistics, biostatistics, and actuarial mathematics. Robert Kane, who then was Dean of the School of Public Health, offered us use of a seminar room and provided some financial support. Other financial support came from the Humphrey Institute, from the central administration of the University, and from a program directed by Michael Teitelbaum at the Sloan Foundation. We used this money to start some pilot research projects.

None of the participants was able to attend every meeting, but typically between 12 and 20 researchers came—and almost all the meetings, which started in 1987 and ended in 1991, were lively and stimulating. Numerous research projects were developed or furthered by the meetings, including David Snowdon's study of elderly Catholic nuns, the work by Steven Ruggles and Robert McCaa on census data, Richard Paine's compilation of lifetables for prehistoric European populations, Stanley Hill's evaluation of the impact of longer lives on life insurance companies, and Peter Abrams's research on evolutionary forces that shape the age trajectory of mortality for any species.

Throughout the four years of the weekly series and especially after the aforementioned Berkeley workshop, the main interest focused on Fries's theory and how to test it. As a result of our discussions, we were able to develop a multi-university program of research that we submitted to the US National Institute on Aging. Richard Suzman encouraged and facilitated this application. We started the research on 1 January 1990. Funding for the research we began then has been renewed three times, and we are currently in the fifteenth year of work. Of course we are now studying new topics, and there has been considerable change in personnel as well as a shift in the location of the coordinating center of the grant from the University of Minnesota to Duke University. For a decade and a half, however, we have focused on the general topic of life span limits versus life span plasticity.

Research strategy: The Scientific Method

Let me now turn to the strategy we decided to pursue to investigate the Fries theory in general and, more specifically, whether there is a looming limit to human life expectancy at age 85. Our key decision was to adopt the so-called Scientific Method. Let me emphasize that most demographic research, including most research of the highest standards and greatest interest, is based on other strategies. Let me also admit that most of my own research is based on other approaches to knowledge, although it seems to me that my involvement in the application of the Scientific Method to the Fries theory is perhaps my biggest contribution to knowledge and, in light of this, I plan to base much of my future research on that method. Various population scientists—James Smith of the RAND Corporation comes immediately to mind—have demonstrated how powerful the Scientific Method can be in research on the demography (and economics) of aging, and I believe that demographers should emphasize this strategy more than most of us do.

The Scientific Method involves three main elements. First, a theory must be explicitly and precisely specified. Fries's contribution was to add such flesh and bones to misty gerontological speculation. Second, falsifiable predictions of the theory have to be deduced. Much of our thinking at Minnesota was devoted to formulating such testable propositions. Third, highly reliable data have to be gathered to determine whether the predictions hold true. If they do, this adds to the credibility of the theory; if not, the theory has been shown to be wrong. All theories are eventually proven wrong, but some theories are useful, at least in some contexts. Newton's theory of gravity is an example. So the crucial task in testing a theory is to develop predictions that are not only falsifiable but that are also important in terms of the purposes of the theory.

With substantial help from James Carey and from others not at the University of Minnesota, we developed four falsifiable predictions of the Fries theory. Then instead of using convenient datasets already at hand—a tempting approach to research—we thought long and hard about how to assemble the most compelling datasets to test the four predictions. We gathered the data, tested the propositions, and published refereed articles in *Science* and other outstanding journals. Various objections were raised, and we systematically pursued research to respond to each serious concern.

The first of the predictions we tested can be adumbrated as follows. According to the Fries theory, nearly all mortality at advanced ages is due to senescent death, and nothing can be done to reduce senescent death. Specifically, the prediction is that death rates after age 85 years, and especially after age 92 or 99, should be about the same today as they always have been. Fries explicitly makes this claim in his seminal article. So we decided to compile reliable statistics on the age-specific probabilities of death after age 85 over an extended period of time. The most reliable long-term data on death rates pertain to Sweden: outstanding data have been collected since 1861 and serviceable data since 1750. Although appropriate data had been collected, however, statistics on Swedish death rates after age 85 had not been systematically compiled, checked, and published. So we asked Hans Lundstrom of Statistics Sweden to undertake this task. Subsequently, the work of Roger Thatcher permitted study of long-term trends in mortality at the oldest ages in England and Wales, and the monumental efforts of Väinö Kannisto extended this work to more than a dozen additional countries. Hence we were able to test our first falsifiable prediction of Fries's theory. Have death rates above age 85, and particularly above age 100, remained more or less constant over time? In particular, have death rates at these advanced ages remained unchanged in Sweden since 1861 (and in various other countries over extended periods)?

Our second testable hypothesis ran as follows. If everyone is born with a maximum potential life span, then two identical twins should be born with the same maximum. The world's best twin registry, at least for our purposes, was in Denmark. Two professors of medicine, Mogens Hauge and Bent Harvald, set up the Danish Twin Registry, the world's first such national registry, half a century ago. They and their colleagues were able to follow nearly all Danish twins born since 1870. By 1990 the Registry had 120 years of twin data, and the dataset included many elderly twin pairs. In early 1988 I contacted Niels Holm, who was then head of the Danish Twin Registry, and invited him to visit us in Minneapolis. That summer I went to Denmark and we started to do some collaborative research on the Registry. The collaboration flourished to such an extent that I was offered a professorship at Odense University Medical School in Denmark. In June 1991 I moved to Denmark and started work as professor of epidemiology and demography, with responsibility to advance research using the Twin Registry and, more generally, to develop research on the epidemiology and demography of aging. One of my colleagues was Kaare Christensen, then a young epidemiologist and now one of the world's leading twin researchers and a well-known epidemiologist of aging.

When I started to collaborate on research using the Danish Twin Registry, the data were not computerized: the information for each person was on an index card. The first thing we did, with funding from the

US National Institute on Aging, was to computerize the data. Then we were able to undertake sophisticated analyses. In particular, we fit various survival-analysis models to the data we had on the life spans of twins. Some models included a term that captured the maximum potential life span that two identical twins were hypothesized to share. And we fit simpler models, so-called nested models, that did not have this term. The key question was whether the life span term improved the fit of the models to the data.

Our third testable prediction concerned the shape of the age trajectory of mortality. Both the Fries theory and the evolutionary theory of aging assert that mortality should increase rapidly—exponentially or even faster—at advanced ages. So we decided to use Swedish data to determine the veracity of this prediction.

Furthermore, we tested this prediction using data from some nonhuman species. The evolutionary theory of aging applies not only to humans: it is supposed to apply to all species of animals. Nor is the central notion of Fries's theory—that each individual is born with a maximum potential life span—limited to humans. We decided to try to find another species for which large numbers of individuals had been followed from birth to death. James Carey and I took the lead on this project. The largest study we were able to find was done by Raymond Pearl in the 1920s. Pearl, one of the founders of the Population Association of America, conducted demographic research on various animals as well as on humans. In one experiment he compiled life span data on a few thousand fruit flies (*Drosophila*) held in his laboratory. Until our research in the 1990s, that experiment was apparently the largest ever done to determine the distribution of life spans for any nonhuman species. Thus, little was known about the trajectory of mortality at older ages for any species except humans—and even for humans the data available on mortality at advanced ages were limited and of questionable reliability.

Carey decided which nonhuman species to investigate first and where to carry out the study. The best option was to compile data on one million Medflies in a laboratory in Tapachula, Mexico. Subsequently, large populations of several other species were also studied in this laboratory. The laboratory is housed in a factory, just over the border from Guatemala, that rears billions of Medflies that are sterilized and then released along the border. When Guatemalan Medflies attempt to invade Mexico, they mate with the sterile Mexican flies and do not have any offspring: this is a way of controlling the invasion from Guatemala. Our project staff were given use of a small corner of the factory, and local technicians were hired to follow one million Medflies from birth to death.

In our first experiment, Medflies were put, one by one, into small containers with food and water. The technicians were supposed to look at each container daily and determine whether the Medfly was alive or dead. After they had followed about 10,000 flies, they refused to continue the work—it was too tedious. So Carey designed a second experiment with smaller containers that were assembled in blocks of several containers. Work with these devices also proved too tedious. Finally, Carey designed an experiment with sizable cages, each holding about 5,000 flies. When a fly died it fell to the floor of the cage. A technician could "aspirate" (i.e., carefully suck up through a small hose) dead flies and array them on white paper. Then the males could be separated from the females and the dead counted. When the last fly died, the cumulative count of the number of dead flies provided an accurate estimate of the initial population of flies, permitting the calculation of death rates. (That is, we used the "extinct generation" method.) This laboratory procedure held the interest of the technicians. They successfully completed the study of just over one million Medflies. Then they went on to further studies of Medflies and other insects, aspirating close to 10 million flies by now.

Let me now turn to the fourth falsifiable prediction we deduced from Fries's theory. A drawback of studies based on human twins is that there are only two members of a twin pair. Determining whether they share a common maximum potential life span therefore requires application of sophisticated statistical models. The analysis would be much more straightforward if there were thousands of individuals who were identical "twins," that is, who were genetically identical with each other. Indeed, if a population of several thousand genetically identical individuals could be followed from birth to death, then a simple test of the Fries theory would be feasible. The survival curve for such a population would gradually decline from 100 percent toward zero as premature death took its toll. When the common maximum potential life span of the genotype was approached, the survival curve should then plunge to zero, with no individual living past the maximum. Such a test of the theory is possible with inbred lines of animals. In particular, it is not difficult to rear thousands of genetically identical *Drosophila* fruitflies. James Curtsinger of the University of Minnesota undertook this experiment with several different populations of fruitflies.

Findings

We started work in 1990 on the four falsifiable predictions of the Fries theory. Within two years we had publishable results, but we continued to refine and extend our tests for several more years. Our findings can be summarized as follows.

The first falsifiable prediction we deduced from the theory was that Swedish death rates at advanced ages should have remained unchanged over time. This is not true. Even at age 100, Swedish death rates fell sub-stantially, being less than half as high in 1990 as they were a century ear-lier. Subsequent analysis of data from various other countries with long life expectancies confirmed this finding. Mortality after age 85 is not fixed: it is highly plastic and has been dramatically reduced, especially since 1950.

Fries's theory also failed our second test. Simpler statistical models of the survival of Danish identical twins fit the data as well as more complicated models that included a term that captured the effect of a shared maximum potential life span. We know that identical twins die at more similar ages than do fraternal twins. And fraternal twins die at more similar ages than do unrelated individuals. We used this information to estimate that about a quar-ter of the variation in adult longevity could be attributed to genetic variation among individuals (McGue et al. 1993; Herskind et al. 1996). Genes, then, do have an impact on the length of life, but we could find no evidence that they determined a maximum potential life span.

Fries's third prediction was that death rates should rise rapidly at ad-vanced ages. Our studies revealed, however, that Swedish death rates—and death rates for other countries with reliable data at oldest-old ages—increase more and more slowly after age 85. Furthermore, the age trajectory of mor-tality for Medflies reached a maximum and then declined. Subsequent re-search that our team and others have done on large populations of various species, including nematode worms and different kinds of insects, has shown that such mortality deceleration is the rule rather than the exception. This unexpected result has led to a stream of biodemographic research aimed either at trying to rescue the current evolutionary theory of aging or at find-ing a more valid evolutionary theory of aging. In any case, the prediction of the Fries theory is wrong.

Finally, our fourth test of the theory was whether survival curves for thousands of genetically identical *Drosophila* are characterized by a cliff of plunging survival followed by no survival when the maximum potential life span for the genotype is reached. In James Curtsinger's experiments there was no evidence of such a cliff: the survival curves gradually fell off and petered out. Thomas Johnson subsequently replicated this negative re-sult in large populations of genetically identical nematode worms.

In sum, our research team demonstrated that all four central predic-tions of Fries's theory are false.

On the other hand, I admit that our findings, especially our early find-ings, were not beyond reasonable criticism. Various scholars advanced le-gitimate caveats and objections concerning our results. After the first burst of research results in the early 1990s, marked by two major articles in *Sci-ence* (Carey et al. 1992 and Curtsinger et al. 1992), we devoted considerable effort during the rest of the decade to refining and extending our findings. As I noted above, Väinö Kannisto and Roger Thatcher compiled data on oldest-old mortality in many countries besides Sweden and this resulted in an influential article (Kannisto et al. 1994). We replicated our studies in various species in addition to humans, Medflies, and *Drosphila*. An important concern about our insect experiments was that the density of individuals in a Medfly cage or a *Drosophila* vial declined as survival declined. Consequently, James Curtsinger's group and, to a somewhat lesser extent James Carey's group, undertook laborious experiments to hold density constant—and to hold all other conditions as constant as feasible. Another effort of ours was to replicate the Danish twin results in other populations of twins and to develop more powerful methods to analyze the data; among other investigators, Anatoli Yashin worked on this. A research report in *Science* with many coauthors summarized our main results as of the mid-1990s (Vaupel et al. 1998).

We gradually convinced ourselves—and most of our colleagues who were willing to change their minds when presented with compelling evidence—that individuals are not born with limited life spans. A key milestone was reached recently: female life expectancy in Japan in 2002 rose above 85—to 85.23 years. The diehards who believe in a looming limit to human life expectancy have retreated to higher ages—88 for instance. Jim Oeppen and I reviewed the sorry saga of broken limits to life expectancy in an article in *Science* (Oeppen and Vaupel 2002). We showed that best-practice life expectancy—that is, life expectancy in the national (female) population that holds the record—has increased linearly by three months per year since 1840, with no sign of any slowdown. If this trend continues, then the new alleged maximum of 88 years will be broached in less than a dozen years.

The future of human life expectancy is uncertain. Deadly epidemics, environmental collapse, economic depression, global war, terrorism, and various other calamities could make life once again nasty, brutal, and short. Furthermore, it is possible there will turn out to be a limit to human life expectancy at some age that few if any individuals currently reach and for some reason we do not yet understand. On the other hand, biomedical and other research may permit the acceleration of progress in reducing mortality, as well as morbidity and disability. And new kinds of health interventions, based for instance on new knowledge about genetics or about ways of regenerating or even rejuvenating organs, may lead to life expectancies far exceeding 100 years.

In this regard it seems to me that a key issue is whether to focus research on limits to longevity or on the plasticity of longevity. As James Carey, Kaare Christensen, and I recently argued (Vaupel, Carey, and Christensen 2003), data on humans and on various nonhuman species suggest that mortality is remarkably malleable, even at advanced ages and even for cohorts of individuals who have suffered poor conditions earlier in life. To what extent and how quickly human death rates can be reduced and to what extent longevity can be extended in laboratory populations of nonhuman species are open questions that may remain of great interest for decades as the frontiers of survival are further advanced. Nematode worms typically live a week or two under favorable laboratory conditions. Genetic and environmental manipulations have led to life spans exceeding half a year. Will we soon be reading about nematode worms that live more than a year? The key question does not seem to be the one that used to be popular, namely, Why and how do evolutionary forces impose species-specific limits on longevity? Rather, the key question based on our current knowledge is, Why and how do evolutionary forces license the remarkable plasticity of death rates and longevity?

Consequently, the researchers supported by our ongoing grant from the US National Institute on Aging—and various other researchers as well—have shifted their focus away from limits and toward explaining the genetic and nongenetic factors that influence why some individuals in various species live much longer than others, why humans are living longer and longer, and, more broadly, why longevity is so plastic. This is the thrust of much of the best recent research on aging in general and on the biodemography of aging in particular.

Broadening of research

An idiosyncratic essay on my voyage of discovery in the field of the biodemography of aging is not the place to review either the history or the current status of biodemography. (See Carey and Vaupel (2004) for a recent attempt at this.) Let me mention, however, four research areas within the broad field that my colleagues and I have worked on over the past decade or so.

The first area might be called the biomedical demography of aging. With support from the US National Institute on Aging and from elsewhere, I have been principal investigator on various initiatives to survey and examine elderly people in Denmark, China, Sardinia, and Russia, and I am currently the deputy director of a very large survey, funded by the European Union, of elderly sibling pairs in Europe. My contribution to this research was only a small part of the total work; many other people deserve as much or more credit than I, including Kaare Christensen and Bernard Jeune in Denmark; Zeng Yi in China; Luca Deiana, Giovanella Baggio, and Graziela Caselli in Italy; Maria Shkolnikova in Russia; and Claudio Franceschi and others for the nascent European project.

In these surveys, older individuals were (and are being) asked to answer various questions about themselves, to perform various tests of physical and cognitive functioning, and to give blood samples for genetic and biochemical analysis. Some of the surveys, including one in Denmark and ongoing surveys in China and Sardinia, included many centenarians. My original hope was to find a few key "secrets to longevity," among them perhaps a few genetic variants and some crucial behavioral or environmental factors. To date, however, our findings and those of other groups suggest that there are many ways of living a long, healthy life; that hundreds and perhaps thousands of genetic variants play a significant but modest role; and that beyond the advice we get from our mothers—to eat sensibly, to exercise appropriately, not to smoke, not to drink excessively, to smile and keep a good sense of humor—there is little that any of us can do to change our behavior or environment in order to live substantially longer. Life expectancy today is decades longer than it was a century or two ago, and life expectancy in the future may be decades longer than it is today—but we do not know today how to take the actions necessary to live substantially beyond current life expectancy. Careful people who follow sound advice might, on average, live five or ten years beyond the life expectancy of their national population, but not two or three decades beyond.

This does not mean I think that the findings from biomedical and demographic research are uninteresting or unimportant. On the contrary, these findings will help people live longer, healthier lives. My point is different: the findings suggest that there are not a handful of secrets of longevity, but rather that a great many genetic and nongenetic factors contribute to determining a person's life span. This multiplicity of causal mechanisms is consistent with the finding that aging is remarkably plastic. The complexity may also help explain why so many people for so many years have erroneously concluded that we are close to the ultimate limit of human life expectancy.

A second branch of the biodemography of aging that has captured much of my attention over the past decade might be called the biological demography of aging (in contrast to the biomedical demography of aging described above). As a demographer I have been able to contribute to research on longevity in various species, including several kinds of insects, nematode worms, and yeast. An important thrust of this research has been to investigate the deep relationship between mortality and fertility.

Third, I have been intrigued by paleodemography in general and by the problem of estimating age from skeletal remains in particular. At the University of Minnesota, I was given a secondary appointment as professor of ancient studies and did some teaching and research on paleodemography. Since becoming Founding Director of the Max Planck Institute for Demographic Research in Rostock, Germany, in 1996, I have organized four research workshops on methods of paleodemography, helped edit a book (Hoppa and Vaupel 2001), and set up a paleodemographic laboratory in Rostock.

Finally, two years ago my interest was seized by another branch of biodemography, namely evolutionary demography or "evodemo." In the first part of the twentieth century Alfred Lotka made seminal contributions to this line of research. In the 1960s William Hamilton, a biologist who studied demography at the London School of Economics, made further advances. For more than a decade, Shripad Tuljapurkar has been productively tilling this field and recently Ronald Lee, Kenneth Wachter, and various others have begun to focus their attention on it. It is sometimes claimed that nothing in biology can be understood except in the light of evolution. What I have learned—and many biologists would agree with me—is that nothing in evolution can be understood except in the light of demography. As just noted, demographers have made some contributions to understanding the processes of evolution, but demographers could surely make many more.

My interest in evodemo was stimulated by research by Deborah Roach, a professor at the University of Virginia whose studies are supported in part by our grant from the National Institute on Aging. She uses *Plantago lancealota* —a common plant, indeed a weed, known as plantain—as her experimental model. As this plant gets older, it tends to get bigger, and as it gets bigger its fecundity tends to increase and its chances of morbidity and mortality tend to decrease. It seemed to me that this could be called "negative senescence" and that to understand aging it would be useful to compare species characterized by negative senescence with species, such as humans, that get weaker and less fertile with age.

William Hamilton, in 1968, published a highly influential article in which he claimed to prove that negative senescence is evolutionarily impossible. So when, a couple of years ago, I uttered the phrase "negative senescence" at a research workshop on the biology of aging, I was assaulted with hisses. This stimulated me all the more. A talented doctoral student, Annette Baudisch, with some help and encouragement from me, showed that Hamilton's "proof" is no such thing. A research team at the Max Planck Institute for Demographic Research is now developing evodemo models of positive versus negative senescence, and we have published an initial article (Vaupel et al. 2004).

The nature of demography

Let me conclude with some remarks about how the course of my research career has shaped the way I have come to see the field of demography more generally. The deepest attraction of demography for me is that it is fundamentally a mathematical discipline. We demographers can prove theorems that hold forever. For the last three winter semesters in Rostock I have taught a course on "The theory of pure demography." In each of the 28 classes in the semester, I prove at least one demographic theorem. This to my mind is the essence of demography, the core that makes demography a discipline.

It seems to me that demography is where the social sciences meet the biological sciences. Some demographers may object that their field is much closer to sociology, economics, and history than it is to biological disciplines such as epidemiology, ecology, population genetics, evolutionary theory, or physical anthropology. This may be true according to the current affiliations of most demographers, but in terms of the scope of demography as a field of study, I would argue that our domain includes large biological as well as social science territories. Death, after all, has biological aspects, as do morbidity, disability, and aging more generally. Fertility also has biological underpinnings.

At Odense University Medical School, I was professor of epidemiology and demography—and I can testify that the two disciplines have many points of contact. The flourishing of biomedical demography has brought epidemiologists and demographers even closer together. Research on the biological demography of aging is creating ties with biologists who study non-human species. Demographers have much to contribute to research in the areas of population genetics, evolutionary theory, ecology, life-history biology, and various other branches of the life sciences. My hunch is that much of the future growth of the field of demography will be in the direction of our legitimate but underexplored territory in the biological sciences.

References

Abrams, P. 1991. "The fitness costs of senescence: The evolutionary importance of events in early adult life," *Evolutionary Ecology* 5: 343–360.

Carey, J. R., P. Liedo, D. Orozco, and J. W. Vaupel. 1992. "Slowing of mortality rates at older ages in large medfly cohorts," *Science* 258(5081): 457–461.

Carey, J. R. and J. W. Vaupel. 2004. "Biodemography," in D. L. Poston (ed.), *The Handbook of Population*. Dordrecht: Kluwer.

Curtsinger, J. W., H. H. Fukui, D. R. Townsend, and J. W. Vaupel. 1992. "Demography of genotypes: Failure of the limited life-span paradigm in *Drosophila melanogaster*," *Science* 258(5081): 461–463.

Fries, J. F. 1980. "Aging, natural death, and the compression of morbidity," *New England Journal of Medicine* 202(3): 130–135.

Hamilton, W. D. 1966. "The moulding of senescence by natural selection," *Journal of Theoretical Biology* 12(1): 12–45.

Herskind, A. M., M. McGue, N. V. Holm, T. I. A. Soerensen, B. Harvald, and J. W. Vaupel. 1996. "The heritability of human longevity: A population-based study of 2872 Danish twin pairs born 1870–1900," *Human Genetics* 97: 319–323.

Hoppa, R. D. and J. W. Vaupel. 2002. "The Rostock Manifesto for paleodemography: The way from stage to age," in: R. D. Hoppa and J. W. Vaupel (eds.), *Paleodemography: Age Distributions from Skeletal Samples*. Cambridge: Cambridge University Press, pp. 1–8 (Cambridge studies in biological and evolutionary anthropology; 31).

Kannisto, V. 1994. *Development of Oldest-old Mortality, 1950–1990*. Odense: Odense University Press.

———. 1996. *The Advancing Frontier of Survival: Life Tables of Old Age*. Odense: Odense University Press.

Kannisto, V., J. Lauritsen, A. R. Thatcher, and J. W. Vaupel. 1994. "Reductions in mortality at advanced ages: Several decades of evidence from 27 countries," *Population and Development Review* 20(4): 793–810, 921–924.

Lee, R. D. 2003. "Rethinking the evolutionary theory of aging: Transfers, not births, shape senescence in social species," *Proceedings of the National Academy of Sciences of the United States* 100(16): 9637–9642.

Lotka, A. J. 1998. *Analytical Theory of Biological Populations* [Théorie analytique des associations biologiques, 1934] . New York: Plenum Press.

McGue, M., J. W. Vaupel, N. Holm, and B. Harvald. 1993. "Longevity is moderately heritable in a sample of Danish twins born 1870–1880," *Journal of Gerontology* 48(6): B237–244.

Medawar, P. B. 1952. *An Unsolved Problem of Biology.* London: H. K. Lewis & Co.

———. 1957. *The Uniqueness of the Individual.* London: Methuen.

Oeppen, J. and J. W. Vaupel. 2002. "Broken limits to life expectancy," *Science* 296(5570): 1029–1031.

Pearl, R. 1925. *The Biology of Population Growth.* New York: Alfred A. Knopf.

Ruggles, S. 1995. "The Minnesota Historical Census Projects—introduction," *Historical Methods* 28(1): 6–10.

Ruggles, S., M. L. King, D. Levison, R. McCaa, and M. Sobek. 2003. "IPUMS-international," *Historical Methods* 36(2): 60–65.

Snowdon, D. 2001. *Aging with Grace: What the Nun Study Teaches Us About Leading Longer, Healthier, and More Meaningful Lives.* New York: Bantam.

Steinsaltz, D., S. N. Evans, and K. W. Wachter. Forthcoming. "A generalized model of mutation-selection balance with applications to aging," *Front for the Mathematics ArXiv.*

Thatcher, A. R. 1993. "Trends in numbers and mortality at high ages in England and Wales," *Population Studies* 46: 411–426.

Vaupel, J. W., A. Baudisch, A. M. Dölling, D. A. Roach, and J. Gampe. 2004. "The case for negative senescence," *Theoretical Population Biology* 65(4): 339–351.

Vaupel, J. W., J. R. Carey, and K. Christensen. 2003. "It's never too late," *Science* 301(5640): 1679–1681.

Vaupel, J. W., J. R. Carey, K. Christensen, T. E. Johnson, A. I. Yashin, N. V. Holm, I. A. Iachine, A. A. Khazaeli, P. Liedo, V. D. Longo, Zeng Yi, K. G. Manton, and J. W. Curtsinger. 1998. "Biodemographic trajectories of longevity," *Science* 280(5365): 855–860.

Vaupel, J. W., T. E. Johnson, and G. J. Lithgow. 1994. "Rates of mortality in populations of *Caenorhabiditis elegans,*" [Comment] *Science* 266(5186): 826.

Vaupel, J. W., K. G. Manton, and E. Stallard. 1979. "The impact of heterogeneity in individual frailty on the dynamics of mortality," *Demography* 163: 439–454.

Williams, G. C. 1957. "Pleiotropy, natural selection, and the evolution of senescence," *Evolution* 11(4): 398–411.

From Alzheimer's Disease to a Demography of Chronic Disease: The Development of Demographic Synthesis for Fitting Multistate Models

Douglas Ewbank

This is the story of a process of discovery that led from a study of Alzheimer's disease to demographic models that incorporate genetics. This in turn led to a generalized demographic approach to estimating multistate models. This evolution is documented in four papers (Ewbank 1999, 2002a, 2002b, 2004). The first uses a basic demographic model to examine the claim that Alzheimer's disease is the fourth leading cause of death in the United States. The second expands this model by incorporating differences in the incidence of Alzheimer's disease by genotype. The next paper applies the demographic model incorporating genotype to all-cause mortality. And the fourth applies the results on mortality by genotype to examine the effects of one gene on the variation in mortality within and among populations.

The discussion of each paper, presented below, is prefaced by a description of how the research question originated and of previous research on the topic. This is followed by a brief description of the logic underlying the demographic model and the data used to answer the question. This description highlights a few elements of the models; they are described in full in the published papers. The main findings that relate to the development of the models are summarized and new insights are described. I make no claim for the originality of any of these ideas. They were merely ideas that were new to me or captured my attention and contributed to the research at hand.

Deaths attributable to Alzheimer's disease in the United States

In early 1992, Alzheimer's disease was labeled the fourth leading cause of death in the United States. This claim originated in an editorial in the *New*

63

England Journal of Medicine by Robert Katzman (1986). The method used to derive the conclusion was not described in detail; however, it was basically a back-of-the-envelope calculation of attributable risk. Although this claim was accepted by many Alzheimer's disease researchers, demographers were generally skeptical.

Alzheimer's disease is the most common cause of severe memory loss in the elderly. It is a chronic disease that causes a decline over a period of years in short-term memory, language, ability to recognize friends and family members, and other basic cognitive abilities. In 1991 Alzheimer's disease was reported as the underlying cause of death for 14,112 deaths in the United States, 13,768 of which involved people over age 65 years (Hoyert 1996). According to these data, Alzheimer's disease would rank as the eleventh most common cause of death among those over age 65—not the fourth leading cause at all ages. Including all deaths for which Alzheimer's disease was mentioned as a contributing cause more than doubles the reported number. Between 1979 and 1991, the reported age-adjusted death rate for Alzheimer's disease increased twelve-fold. Most of this increase was due to increased awareness of Alzheimer's disease and decreasing use of less specific diagnoses for dementia.

Numerous studies have documented excess mortality rates among patients with Alzheimer's disease (Barclay et al. 1985; Evans et al. 1991; Kukull et al. 1994; Larson et al. 2004). It is not clear, however, why this should be the case, at least until the last stages of the disease. It is clear from several studies that Alzheimer's disease is underreported on death certificates in the United States (Macera et al. 1992; Raiford et al. 1994). For example, a study in Rochester, Minnesota, of Alzheimer's disease cases diagnosed between 1960 and 1984 reported that only 11 percent of death certificates mentioned dementia (Beard et al. 1996).

Methods[1]

To estimate deaths from Alzheimer's disease I followed Katzman's use of an attributed risk model. I produced two independent estimates by examining two sets of data using a different method for each set. The first estimate was based on published data from the East Boston Study, which was a large population-based study of the incidence and prevalence of Alzheimer's disease and the excess mortality associated with it (Evans et al. 1989; Evans et al. 1991). The second applied a demographic model and data from several different kinds of studies. It is this second approach that has led to much further research.

The demographic model underlying the second estimate is a relatively simple multistate model. It looks like a life table with additional columns to keep track of individuals by their disease status. Individuals at each age are divided into those who do not have Alzheimer's disease, $S_N(x)$, and those who do $S_A(x,d)$. The second index variable for Alzheimer's disease cases, d, tracks duration of disease. The incidence of disease is modeled using a Weibull distribution with unobserved heterogeneity (Manton, Stallard, and Vaupel 1986). This formulation allows the incidence rate to increase rapidly with age, but can allow the rates to level off (or even decline) at the oldest ages. It summarizes the age-specific incidence rates with three parameters, which are estimated using maximum likelihood as described below. Mortality rates for the model are based on a life table for the United States in 1990 and several published clinical studies of the relative risk of death for Alzheimer's disease cases by duration of disease.

Findings

Although the two estimates were based on different models and different data, the results were surprisingly similar. The East Boston data led to an estimate of 173,000 deaths attributable to Alzheimer's disease in 1995. The simulation led to an estimate of 163,000. These estimates are about four times greater than the number of death certificates that mentioned Alzheimer's disease in 1991 (Hoyert 1996). It now appears that Alzheimer's disease was responsible for about 7 percent of all deaths in 1995. Figure 1 compares the number of Alzheimer's disease deaths with the other major causes of death in the United States in 1995. These estimates place Alzheimer's disease on a

FIGURE 1   Estimated number of deaths from Alzheimer's disease and reported numbers of deaths from heart disease, cancer, cerebrovascular disease, and chronic obstructive pulmonary disease, United States, 1995

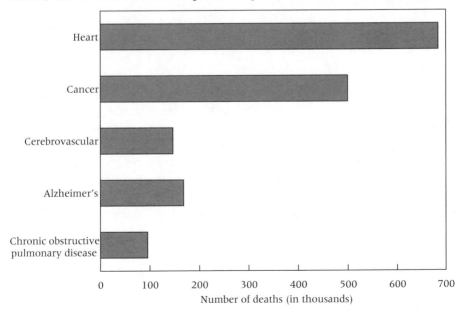

SOURCES: Ewbank 1999; Rosenberg et al. 1996.

par with cerebrovascular diseases as the third leading cause of death in the United States.

Insights

The approach to estimating the parameters of the Weibull function for the incidence of Alzheimer's disease became the foundation for subsequent research described in this chapter using maximum likelihood to estimate the parameters of the multistate model from a variety of types of data.

The details of the Weibull function with heterogeneity are not important. The only important fact is that there are three parameters: the mean of the gamma distribution of risk, α (the level parameter); the parameter that determines the rate at which the risk increases with age, m; and the coefficient of variation in the risk, which slows the rate of increase at the oldest ages, v. The task is to estimate the values of these three parameters for the incidence of Alzheimer's disease.

The maximum likelihood approach to estimation involves finding the values of the model parameters that maximize the probability of observing the recorded data. I started with published incidence rates from a longitudinal study of Alzheimer's disease. Incidence studies involve a baseline survey that tests everyone for Alzheimer's disease. A follow-up survey several years later picks up new cases of the disease among the survivors. The probability of observing $C(x)$ cases at age x among $N(x)$ individuals at risk is binomial with a rate of $\lambda(x|\alpha, m, v)$. The likelihood of observing the data from a single study for a given age-sex group is the probability of observing $C(x)$ and $N(x)$ given values of α, m, and v:

$$L\left(C_x, N_x \middle| \alpha, m, v\right) = \lambda\left(x \middle| \alpha, m, v\right)^{C_x} \left[1 - \lambda\left(x \middle| \alpha, m, v\right)\right]^{\left(N_x - C_x\right)}.$$

Thinking of the model as a multistate life table, we can express $\lambda(x)$ in terms of the number of Alzheimer's disease cases at the appropriate age and various durations, $S_A(x,d)$, and the number who do not have Alzheimer's, $S_N(x)$. In a multiround survey, new cases recorded at the second round are used to estimate "incidence rates." However, these rates do not include new cases among individuals who died between survey rounds. Although this introduces little error, it is possible to match these data with model estimates. For example, if a follow-up survey at three years provided data by single years of age, the estimated rate at age x from the model is:

$$\lambda(x) = \frac{S_A(x,0) + S_A(x,1) + S_A(x,2)}{S_A(x,0) + S_A(x,1) + S_A(x,2) + S_N(x)}.$$

In other words, the observed rate is the number of survivors with new cases within the last three years (i.e., those at duration 0, 1, or 2 years), divided by the number of individuals at risk (i.e., the new cases plus those remaining without Alzheimer's disease). Of course $S_N(x)$ and $S_A(x,d)$ are functions of the values assumed for the three parameters.[2]

The likelihood of observing all of the data is the product of the binomial probabilities for individual age groups from various studies:

$$L = L_{x,i} L_{y,i} \ldots L_{z,j} \ldots$$

where $L_{x,i}$ is the likelihood of observing the incidence rate reported at age x in study i. Then a simple search routine (available in spreadsheet programs) can find the values of the three parameters of the Weibull that maximize the total likelihood, L.

At the time I was doing this research there were very few data on the incidence of Alzheimer's disease, although I found far more data on the prevalence of disease. The model also produces estimates of prevalence since it combines incidence rates with estimates of excess mortality among cases. Therefore, an alternative approach is to use prevalence data. This is possible because the incidence of Alzheimer's disease has probably been relatively constant in the recent past.

The prevalence rate is also binomial where the model estimate of the probability is the ratio of the number of cases between ages x and $x+n$ to the total population at those ages:

$$\frac{\int_x^{x+n} S_A(z)dz}{\int_x^{x+n} S(z)dz}.$$

The binomial probabilities for each age-specific rate in each of several studies would then be multiplied together to get the overall likelihood.

At some point it occurred to me that I did not need to limit the estimation to either incidence rates or prevalence rates. By simply multiplying together the likelihood values from the incidence and prevalence data, it is possible to use data from both types of studies. Therefore, I estimated the Weibull parameters from five prevalence studies and one incidence study.[3]

This approach to estimating the parameters formed the basis for what I later termed "demographic synthesis." It is defined as the use of a multistate model to combine different types of functionally related data to produce estimates of quantities not adequately measured in any single study.

The model serves as a meta-analytic tool which is not limited to combining studies that all have the same research design and produce the same indexes. This is a significant improvement over standard meta-analytic methods that can only use a single type of data (e.g., incidence rates or prevalence rates). For example, Jorm and Jolley (1998) studied the incidence of dementia by combining data from numerous longitudinal studies, but they did not make use of the prevalence estimates that come from the baseline surveys.

This approach can be generalized to combine a wider variety of data. In the next paper I combined rates from longitudinal studies (incidence rates or mortality rates) with cross-sectional data (prevalence rates or genotype frequencies) and odds ratios from case–control studies.

A multistate model of the genetic risk of Alzheimer's disease

The attributable risk approach might overstate mortality from Alzheimer's disease if patients are much more likely than those without Alzheimer's disease to have another major risk factor for mortality. The next research question was whether the deaths attributed to Alzheimer's disease are really a result of another risk factor that is more common in Alzheimer's disease patients.

There are few well-established risk factors for Alzheimer's disease. One that seemed promising in this regard is the alleles of the gene for apolipoprotein-E (APOE). APOE is involved in the transport of fats (lipids) in the blood stream. Three variants of APOE have been shown to be associated with different serum levels of lipids. The most common variant is labeled e3. The second most common is e4, which is a risk factor for both Alzheimer's disease (Farrer et al. 1997) and ischemic heart disease (Eichner et al. 1993; Wilson et al. 1996). The e2 variant is protective against Alzheimer's disease and may protect against heart disease. The three variants (alleles) of the gene that gives the code for APOE are termed $\varepsilon2$, $\varepsilon3$, and $\varepsilon4$.[4] These alleles differ by single nucleic acids at positions 112 and 158: APOE $\varepsilon4$ has arginine at both sites, $\varepsilon3$ has cysteine at 112, and $\varepsilon2$ has cysteine at both sites. An individual's genotype is determined by the copies of the APOE alleles inherited from his or her parents. The most common genotype is e3/3. The initial research question was whether many of the deaths attributed to Alzheimer's disease are really deaths from ischemic heart disease associated with the e4 allele.

Methods[5]

Answering this question required several elaborations of the simple model of mortality and Alzheimer's disease. First, I had to expand to three causes of death: Alzheimer's disease, ischemic heart disease, and all others. Then I divided the population into groups by genotype. Each genotype would have different risks of Alzheimer's disease and ischemic heart disease. I built this model and tested it. However, I dropped this approach for two reasons. First, the model suggested that the APOE–heart disease link was not responsible for many of the excess deaths among individuals with Alzheimer's disease. Second, there were scant data on APOE and ischemic heart disease mortality, although there are plentiful data on APOE and heart disease *morbidity*. Therefore, I dropped back to a simpler model with only two causes of death (Alzheimer's disease and all others) to study differences in the risk of Alzheimer's disease by APOE genotype. After presenting the model, I applied this approach (2002a) to published data on males in populations of European origin.

Although the association of the APOE alleles with the risk of Alzheimer's disease was widely accepted, the estimates of the risks associated with each genotype varied widely from study to study, largely because of sampling variability. In addition, no single study was large enough to produce useful estimates of the risks associated with the rarest genotypes: e2/2 and e2/4. Farrer et al. (1997) published an analysis of data on APOE and Alzheimer's disease from 40 research teams. The sample size of 5,930 patients and 8,607 controls was large enough to examine the risks for e2/2 and e2/4 in addition to examining how the risks changed with age. The analysis relied on a logistic regression that included age and age-squared terms that differed by APOE genotype. Thus the odds ratios for the risk of Alzheimer's disease by genotype were allowed to change with age. The problem with this approach is that it requires any changes with age in the odds ratio to be symmetrical. The mechanisms that might lead to changes with age, however, are very different at the youngest and oldest ages (Ewbank 1998).

I used an approach that models the changes in the odds ratios at the youngest and oldest ages separately. The basic model follows the model used to estimate the deaths attributable to Alzheimer's disease. It assumes that the risk of Alzheimer's disease for each genotype follows a Weibull distribution with the same values of m (the exponent on age) and v (the amount of heterogeneity) for each genotype. The differences in risk among genotypes are modeled by different values for α. After combining the rare e2/2 genotype with the e2/3 and the e2/4 with the e3/3, there are six main parameters to be estimated: the level of Alzheimer's disease risk among the e3/3 at age 80 (which sets α for this reference group), the relative risks for the e2/3, e3/4, and e4/4 (which define the differences in α by genotype), and the values of m and v shared by all four genotypes.

This basic model was modified to allow the odds ratios at the youngest ages to reflect changes in the relative importance of rare genetic forms of Alzheimer's disease (Levy-Lahad and Bird 1996). Several genotypes have been associated with Alzheimer's disease at ages as young as 35. There is some evidence that the risks associated with these rare genotypes are not modified by APOE genotype. Therefore, at the youngest ages APOE genotype has little or no effect on the risk of Alzheimer's disease. As the importance of these rare genotypes declines with age, the effect of APOE becomes apparent.

Extending the model to include genotype was not difficult. Estimating the parameters presented a challenge, however. There are almost no data on the incidence of Alzheimer's disease by genotype and few data on prevalence by genotype. The problem is especially serious for the rarer genotypes. Therefore, we have little or no data from population-based surveys with which to estimate the relative risks.

The solution is to use clinical case–control data on the relative differences in risk among genotypes. The odds ratios from these studies are closely related to the relative risk parameters we need to estimate. Comparable odds ratios can easily be calculated from the demographic model. For example, the odds ratio for e3/4 relative to e3/3 is given by the standard equation for an odds ratio:

$$OR_{3/4} = \frac{P_{3/4}(x) \Big/ \left[1 - P_{3/4}(x)\right]}{P_{3/3}(x) \Big/ \left[1 - P_{3/3}(x)\right]}$$

where $p_{3/4}(x)$ is the proportion with Alzheimer's disease among the observed e3/4:

$$P_{3/4}(x) = \frac{S_A^{3/4}(x)}{S_A^{3/4}(x) + S_N^{3/4}(x)}.$$

Similar odds ratios can be calculated using incidence rates to match clinical studies of the onset of Alzheimer's disease.

The model was fitted to published data on the incidence and prevalence of Alzheimer's disease and relative risks of Alzheimer's disease by APOE genotype.

Findings

The first finding was that the APOE connection with ischemic heart disease does not explain much of the excess risk previously attributed to Alzheimer's disease. Because I dropped ischemic heart disease mortality from the model, my published findings relate to the age pattern of incidence of Alzheimer's disease and differences in incidence among APOE genotypes.

Among men aged 80, the relative risks of Alzheimer's disease relative to e3/3 are: $R_{3/4}$: 3.4 (95 percent CI: 2.5–4.4), $R_{4/4}$: 9.4 (3.8–26.6), and $R_{2/3}$: 0.43 (0.24–0.72). The differences between genotypes are slightly larger at age 65, change rapidly after age 85, and essentially disappear by age 100. The heterogeneity model assumes that this declining importance of APOE holds only for the average survivor. For example, if you could change a centenarian's genotype from e3/4 to e3/3, you would reduce his risk of Alzheimer's disease by a factor of about 3.4. However, centenarians with the e3/4 genotype who have not developed Alzheimer's disease probably have numerous unknown characteristics that protect them against the disease. It is only because of these other protective characteristics that centenarians with the e3/4 genotype do not on average have higher risks than those with the e3/3 genotype.

These effects of heterogeneity are probably responsible for much of the leveling off of the incidence levels at the oldest ages. Some of this is caused by the fact that the riskier genotypes (e3/4 and e4/4) form a smaller proportion of the population at risk at the older ages. Similarly, unobserved heterogeneity (the v parameter) causes the incidence rate among the riskier genotypes to level off. This is most evident in the incidence rates for the e4/4 genotype (see below). The model also estimated that about 0.20 percent of the population have rare genotypes that are associated with a risk of Alzheimer's disease of about 4 percent per year.

Insights

The first insight is that we can combine estimates of the odds ratios from case–control studies with incidence and prevalence rates from population-based surveys to estimate incidence rates by age, sex, and genotype. It is not feasible to estimate these relative risks from a single large longitudinal study.

The second insight relates to the estimate of v, the coefficient of variation of unobserved heterogeneity. Unobserved heterogeneity arises because we cannot control for every factor affecting the risk of Alzheimer's disease. The effects of unobserved heterogeneity are generally described in terms of the age pattern of mortality. The solid line in Figure 2 shows the estimated incidence of Alzheimer's disease at each age among males with APOE e3/3. The gray line shows what the rates would be for this group with the same level of risk in the Weibull distribution (α) and the same rate of increase in the absence of heterogeneity (m) but without any heterogeneity (v set to 0).

Figure 2 also shows the estimated incidence rates for the e4/4 genotype. Heterogeneity affects the e3/3 and the e4/4 genotypes differently even though they are based on the same amount of heterogeneity (i.e., the same value of v). The reason is that heterogeneity selects out the most frail faster when the incidence rates are high; the combination of the high risks from e4/4 and other unobserved risk factors is quite powerful. The incidence rates for the e4/4 level off by about age 90, but the rates for the e3/3 are still climbing. Therefore, the relative risks (the ratio of the values of the two curves at the same age) decline at the oldest ages (Figure 3).

This leads to the second insight: changes in the relative risks with age provide information about the amount of heterogeneity. This is very important because the confidence intervals for the reported incidence rates

FIGURE 2   Estimated incidence rates for Alzheimer's disease, APOE genotypes e3/3 and e4/4 and the curve for e3/3 without unobserved heterogeneity

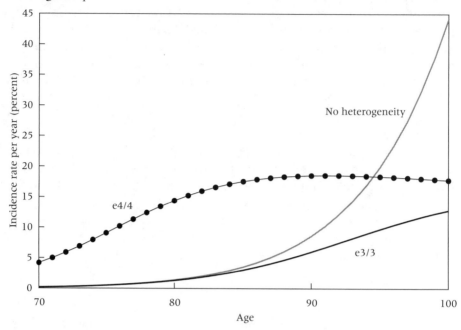

SOURCE: Ewbank 2002a.

FIGURE 3   Estimated risk of Alzheimer's disease, APOE e4/4 genotype relative to the e3/3 genotype

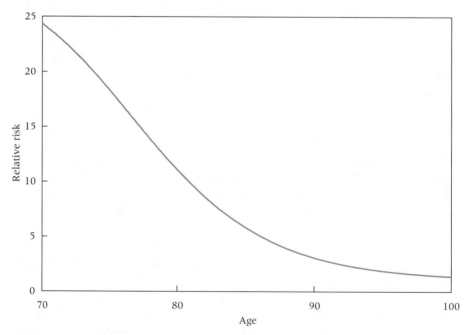

SOURCE: Based on parameter estimates in Ewbank 2002a.

become very large at the oldest ages and do not provide much information about heterogeneity. The confidence intervals on the relative risks at the oldest ages are also large. However, the combination of numerous studies of each kind can lead to more precise estimates of heterogeneity.

Mortality differentials by APOE genotype

There are good reasons to believe that the risk of overall mortality differs substantially by APOE genotype since it affects the risks of two major causes of death: ischemic heart disease (IHD) and Alzheimer's disease. The previous paper modeled the differentials in mortality associated with Alzheimer's disease, but there were not enough data relating APOE and IHD mortality. Therefore, the mortality differences by genotype were understated. Thus, my next paper (2002b) addressed two questions: 1) how much do all-cause mortality rates differ by APOE genotype, and 2) do the effects of APOE genotype on mortality differ by sex or area of residence?

A number of longitudinal studies have examined mortality rates by APOE genotype. Contrary to expectations, not all of them have found significant differences. For example, three of four prospective studies did not find a significant difference in mortality by APOE genotype (Tilvis et al. 1998; Vogt et al. 1997; Skoog et al. 1998; Juva et al. 2000). All four failed to find (or did not test for) differences associated with the e2 alleles. Traditional meta-analytic methods are not well suited to this issue. A logistic regression with proper controls for differences in sample size and length of observation could address this issue with appropriate controls for an interaction between the gene effect and age. It is not clear, however, what form that interaction should take.[6] In addition, there are no standard age groups used in published studies, which makes it difficult to properly control for age differences using logistic regression.

Cross-sectional studies of genotype frequencies by age provide additional information on mortality by genotype. A lower frequency of a genotype at the oldest ages suggests that individuals with that genotype died out at a faster rate. Traditional meta-analytic approaches are not capable of combining cross-sectional and longitudinal data. Genotype frequencies by age have been used by Yashin et al. (2000) and Toupance et al. (1998) to estimate excess mortality from cross-sectional surveys, but they did not include data from longitudinal studies. I used demographic synthesis to combine these two types of data from five European countries and American whites.

Methods[7]

The estimation included longitudinal data from six studies that followed almost 6,000 individuals for an average of 5.6 years of observation.[8] The genotype frequencies come from 12 cross-sectional studies of APOE genotype frequencies by age. These studies include data from young or middle-aged adults and nonagenarians or centenarians. The total sample size for cross-sectional data is 7,264 (including the baseline surveys from the longitudinal studies).

The model used to estimate mortality by APOE genotype is a simplified version of the model of Alzheimer's disease incidence and prevalence. It does not specify causes of death and there is no onset of disease.

An important new element in this study was the use of cohort life tables. The estimation used 56 cohort life tables for different countries by sex and year of birth. The model forced the mortality rates by genotype to add up to the rates in the life table for an appropriate cohort. This was done using the equation:

$$\mu(x) = \frac{R_{2/3}(x)\mu_{3/3}(x)S_{2/3}(x) + \mu_{3/3}(x)S_{3/3}(x) + R_{3/4}(x)\mu_{3/3}(x)S_{3/4}(x) + \ldots}{S_{2/3}(x) + S_{3/3}(x) + S_{3/4}(x) + \ldots}$$

which merely states that $\mu(x)$, the reported mortality rate for the cohort at age x, is equal to the weighted average of the mortality rates for each genotype. The weights are the proportion of each genotype that survived to age x, for example $S_{2/3}(x)$. It is easy to solve this equation to derive $\mu_{3/3}(x)$ given values of $S(x)$ and the $R(x)$.

$R(x)$ can be derived from equations like the following:

$$R_{3/4}(x) = R_{3/4}(0)\left(\frac{S_{3/4}(x)}{S_{3/3}(x)}\right)^{v^2}$$

which relates the relative risk at every age to the rate at birth if the variation in risk follows a Gamma distribution. This can be rewritten to use any age as the reference rate in place of age 0. I used age 60 in order to get confidence intervals at a useful age. By using a cohort life table and parameterizing the $R(x)$, we do not have to impose a functional form (for example, a Gompertz curve) on the age-specific mortality rates. This removes one assumption and two parameters that are usually necessary for this type of analysis.

The use of a life table and the assumption about the relative risks are similar to some of the methods proposed by Yashin et al. (1999) for the analysis of cross-sectional data on genotype frequencies. There are a few differences. First, the life tables used here are cohort life tables. Second, instead of assuming that the relative risk is the same at all ages, I assume that they change with age in a way that is consistent with a Gamma distribution of frailty. In addition, multiple types of data are used to estimate the model.

Findings

The differences in mortality by genotype are all significant. The relative risks at death for the main APOE genotypes relative to e3/3 at age 60 are 1.4 for e3/4 and 0.81 for e2/3. The relative risk for e4/4 is not significantly different from the square of the risk for e3/4, 1.96, which means the effects of the e4 allele follow a dose–response pattern. There were no significant differences in the relative risks of death between men and women. In addition, there were no significant differences between northern and southern Europe. This is an interesting finding. Since APOE plays an important role in managing the transport of fats in the blood stream, we might expect the effect of the e4 allele on IHD mortality to be greater in populations whose diet is higher in cholesterol and fats. This effect is not discernible in the available data.

The differences by genotype become small after age 100 (the three relative risks approach 1.0) because of the effects of unobserved heterogeneity. The changes in the relative risks with age differ substantially from cohort to cohort because of large differences in mortality. For example, Figure 4 shows the relative risks by age for the e3/4 and e4/4 genotypes for males in Finland born in 1886–90 and for Swedish females born in 1905–09. Only 7.5 percent of the men in the Finnish cohort survived from age 60 to age 90, whereas

FIGURE 4   Risk of death, APOE genotypes e3/4 and e4/4 relative to e3/3, Swedish females born 1905–09 and Finnish males born 1886–90

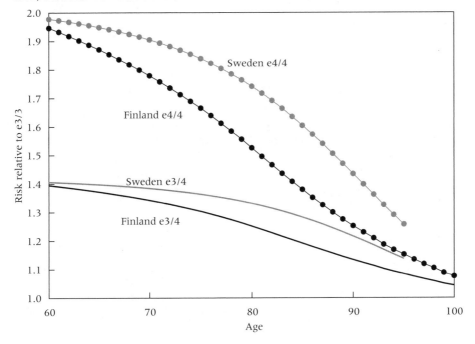

25.1 percent of the women in the Swedish cohort survived to that age. With the higher mortality rates among the Finnish males, those with numerous risk factors die out very quickly and those e4 carriers who survive to the oldest ages probably carry numerous unobserved protective factors.

Insights

The most important methodological finding is that it is possible to introduce heterogeneity into the model without imposing a Weibull or a Gompertz curve on the mortality rates. Instead, we can use an existing life table to define overall mortality rates and simply assume a distribution of frailty that determines changes in the relative risks by age.

Second, the use of cohort life tables does make a difference in the estimates because the relative risks approach 1.0 faster with higher mortality. However, it is differences in mortality at the older ages that are important. Therefore, it is not necessary to have very precise mortality rates for the earliest cohorts at young ages.

The APOE gene and differences in life expectancy in Europe

My fourth paper (Ewbank 2004) addresses two questions of great interest to demographers and others concerned with population-level effects: what are the implications of differences by APOE genotype for mortality differences within and among European countries? Since the three APOE alleles are relatively common and are associated with different risks of mortality, it is likely that APOE genotype frequencies may play an important role. Therefore, we can ask how much of the difference in life span (age at death) among individuals in a population is explained by APOE genotype. In addition, the frequencies of the APOE alleles differ among European countries: for example, the e4 allele frequency varies from 9.4 percent in Italy to 21.6 percent in Sweden. In general, the e4 allele is much more common in northern Europe (here represented by Denmark, Finland, and Sweden) than in southern Europe (Italy and France). This north–south gradient has been noted by several authors (Lucotte, Loirat, and Hazout 1997; Panza et al. 1999). The e2 frequencies vary from 3.9 percent in Finland to 9.5 percent in Sweden and do not follow any simple geographic pattern in Europe.

Some evidence on this comes from a study by Stengärd, Weiss, and Sing (1998). They examined data on middle-aged males from nine European populations to study the relationship between APOE and coronary heart disease (CHD). They found that differences in the frequency of the e4 allele explained 75 percent of the variance in CHD mortality. Although this is an impressive result, the ecological fallacy states that associations found at the population level do not necessarily reflect differences at the individual level.

An alternative approach is to cumulate data at the individual level (e.g., longitudinal studies on APOE and mortality) to estimate differences at the population level.

Methods[9]

The methods used here are simple analysis of variance and standardization. To study the effects of APOE on the life span of individuals in a cohort, I examine the sum of squared deviations in age at death around the mean age at death, e(x). These calculations are based on the $_1d_x$ column of the life table (in survival analysis terms: $D(x) = S[x]-S[x+1]$). To calculate the proportion of the variation in life span that is attributable to differences by genotype, we compare the sum of squares around e(x) with the sum of squares around the genotype-specific mean ages at death, e.g., $e^{3/4}(x)$ for genotype e3/4.

The effect of differences in genotype frequencies on mortality differences among countries is also based on an analysis of variance. The variance among countries in a mortality measure (for example, e(0) or a mortality rate) is compared to the variance among values standardized to a common set of genotype frequencies. For example, to examine the effect on life expectancy at birth, e(0), I standardize life expectancy using a standard set of gene frequencies at birth. The life expectancy at birth in Denmark standardized to the gene frequencies in Italy is:

$$e_D^I(0) = f_{2/3}^I e_{2/3}^D(0) + f_{3/3}^I e_{3/3}^D(0) + \ldots + f_{4/4}^I e_{4/4}^D(0)$$

where $f_{2/3}^I$ is the proportion with genotype e2/3 at birth in Italy and $e_{2/3}^D(0)$ is the life expectancy at birth for the e2/3 genotype in Denmark. Similarly, for e(65) I weight the genotype-specific life expectancies at age 65 in Denmark by the genotype frequencies at age 65 in Italy.

Findings

The differences in age at death among genotypes are quite large. For example, in the cohort born in Denmark 1895–99 the estimates of e(15) for both sexes combined for the relatively common e2/3 and e3/4 genotypes differ by 3.1 years. Although this is a substantial difference, it is relatively small compared to the standard deviation in life span after age 15, 17.6 years. Calculating the sum of squared differences around the genotype-specific e(15), I find that the differences by APOE genotype explain 0.9 percent of the variation in life span over age 15 in Denmark. For survivors to age 65, the proportion of the variance in remaining life span explained by APOE genotype is 1.8 percent.

No single factor explains a large proportion of the variation in age at death. We can put these percentages into perspective by comparing them to the proportions explained by sex and an estimate of the proportion explained by all gene effects. Differences in adult mortality by sex are substantial. For example, for the cohort born in Denmark in 1895–99 the female life expectancy at age 15 exceeds the male value by 3.3 years. These differences by sex explain the same proportion of the variation in life span as APOE genotype: 0.9 percent. At age 65, sex explains about twice as much as APOE genotype: 3.5 percent compared to 1.8 percent.

The proportion of the variance in age at death attributable to APOE depends on the gene frequencies. For example, the frequencies of the e2 and e4 alleles in France are smaller than in Denmark. Therefore, for the same birth cohort in France APOE explains less of the variation in life span after age 65 than in Denmark: 1.2 percent compared to 1.8 percent. In addition, the differences in e(65) by sex are much larger in France than in Denmark. Sex explains 5.5 percent of the variance after age 65 compared to only 3.5 percent in Denmark. In general, in Western Europe the effect of APOE on life span after age 65 is comparable to, but generally less than, the effect of sex.

The proportion of the variation in life span estimated for the Danish cohort can also be compared to an estimate of the proportion of the variance explained by all genetic effects. Herskind et al. (1996) used data on Danish twins born in 1870–1900 to estimate the proportion of life span after age 15 that is explained by genetic differences. They estimated that about 25 percent of the variation in adult life span is attributable to genetics. Therefore, in this Danish cohort, differences in mortality by APOE genotype explain about 3.5 percent (i.e., 0.009/0.25) of the contribution of genetics.

The differences in APOE genotype frequencies explain a large share of the differences among European countries. Table 1 provides the data re-

TABLE 1   Estimated life expectancy at age 65 for males by APOE genotype for Denmark in the mid-1990s and APOE genotype frequencies at age 65 in Denmark and Italy

	e2/2 and e2/3	e3/3 and e2/4	e3/4	e 4/4
Life expectancy at age 65, Denmark (years)	15.9	14.6	12.7	10.9
APOE genotype frequencies at age 65 (%)				
Denmark	14.1	59.1	24.3	2.5
Italy	13.3	71.4	14.5	0.7

SOURCE: Based on Ewbank 2004.

quired to adjust the e(65) for males in Denmark to the APOE genotype frequencies in Italy. In the mid-1990s, Italian males had an e(65) of 15.5 years compared to 14.3 for Danish males. The e3/4 and e4/4 genotypes— which have the lowest values of e(65)—are much less common in Italy than in Denmark (Table 1). Combining the e(65) values from Denmark with the genotype frequencies in Italy leads to a standardized e(65) of 14.5, 0.25 years higher than the actual value in Denmark. Therefore, differences in APOE genotype frequencies explain 20 percent of the observed difference between these two countries in e(65) in males. Standardizing the values of e(65) for Denmark, Finland, France, the Netherlands, and Sweden to the genotype frequencies in Italy, I find that differences in APOE genotype frequencies explain 16 percent of the differences in e(65) for males and 17 percent of the differences for females. Therefore, APOE explains a substantial share of the differences in mortality after age 65 among these countries.

Insights

These results demonstrate one of the advantages of demographic synthesis over other meta-analytic techniques. By estimating a multistate life table, demographic synthesis produces estimates of quantities that cannot be measured reliably from longitudinal studies with feasible sample sizes. In this case, the model provides estimates of e(x) by genotype that are not available from any of the published studies. These estimates can be used for comparisons within and among populations. They can also be used to simulate the effects of reducing or eliminating the differences by genotype. For example, we could estimate what would happen if we had a therapy that reduced the excess mortality associated with the e4/4 genotype. This approach can be used to study the effects of any fixed factors on differences in life span.

A demographic approach to synthesizing data on risk factors for chronic disease

This approach to modeling chronic disease relies on one of the fundamental concepts in epidemiology: the relationship between prevalence and cumulated incidence rates is determined by the duration of disease and differences in survival rates by disease status. In the case of chronic diseases, the duration is the time to death. Epidemiologists have generally not exploited this relationship in the study of chronic diseases. Instead this link between incidence and prevalence is central to demographic thinking. For example, the prevalence of people at each age (i.e., the age distribution) is determined by the history of birth, death, and migration incidence rates. This difference between epidemiology and demography reflects a fundamental difference between the two disciplines.

Most epidemiologists are primarily interested in determining factors associated with the onset of disease. Research on the progression of disease is usually left to clinical researchers, biostatisticians, and clinical epidemiologists. Prevalence studies are generally used to demonstrate the population burden of a disease or they are used as proxies for incidence rates in association studies. In general, epidemiologists model the relationship between incidence and prevalence for infectious diseases only where the prevalence of infectious cases in the population drives the incidence of new cases (e.g., HIV/AIDS, malaria, and measles). However, it is rarely necessary for epidemiologists to pay much attention to the linkage between incidence and prevalence.

Demographers, on the other hand, start with an interest in both prevalence and entrances to and exits from the population (births, deaths, and migrations). The study of the incidence or onset of various states (for example, marriage rates) is often driven by an interest in the prevalence of the state (for example, family structure or the prevalence of unmarried young adults). Therefore, demographers start with an interest in how dynamic processes determine the distribution of the population (the prevalence) by various characteristics. This perspective is the foundation for the way in which demographic synthesis estimates multistate models.

Multistate models have been used by demographers to study disease processes (e.g., Crimmins, Saito, and Ingegneri 1997; Al Mamun 2003) and social processes (e.g., Hayward and Grady 1990; Schoen and Standish 2001). The applications have often been based on transition rates (denoted as $_nm_x$ or $\mu(u)$) or on transition probabilities ($_nq_x$ or $S(x+1)/S(x)$) from multiround surveys or vital statistics (Keyfitz 1985). In the absence of data on transitions, researchers have used current status data (i.e., prevalence rates) to estimate measures such as years of life free of chronic disease or disability (Crimmins, Saito, and Ingegneri 1989). However, demographic synthesis can combine a wide range of inputs including incidence, prevalence and odds ratios. In this way, the models that I have used to study Alzheimer's disease and the risks associated with APOE genotypes emphasize the fundamentally demographic nature of multistate models.[10]

By combining data from numerous studies, demographic synthesis performs a meta-analytic function. Unlike typical meta-analytic methods, however, this approach can integrate information from a wide range of study designs. It also produces estimates of quantities that cannot be, or have not been, adequately measured directly (e.g., life expectancy). The process is one of combining disparate pieces of a whole (synthesis) rather than the more typical social science activity of identifying the components or causes of a socially defined entity (analysis).

Demographic synthesis is ideally suited to the study of Alzheimer's disease and the effects of APOE genotypes. Alzheimer's is a chronic disease for which there is no cure. The treatments that are available only slow the process for a short time. This makes it much easier to model than infectious or acute conditions that would require modeling of recovery and, possibly, re-infection. In addition, there is no evidence that the risk of Alzheimer's disease has changed in recent decades (although there is some evidence of a decline in dementia and impaired cognitive functioning). These characteristics of Alzheimer's disease simplify both the modeling and the data requirements. However, it is possible to use this approach for infectious diseases and in situations in which the incidence rates have been changing. For example, some of the basic concepts underlying demographic synthesis have been used by Heuveline for the study of HIV/AIDS, the prevalence of which has increased rapidly in the past two decades (Heuveline 2003).

The ability to generalize these models to other chronic diseases was demonstrated in a paper I wrote with Robbins (Robbins and Ewbank 2001). We used demographic synthesis to study the onset of Parkinson's disease and dementia among cases of Parkinson's. We combined data on the incidence and prevalence of Parkinson's with data on the onset of dementia by duration of Parkinson's and estimates of the relative risk of mortality among Parkinson's cases and cases of Parkinson's with dementia. This approach provides estimates of numerous useful summary statistics such as dementia-free life expectancy of patients with Parkinson's disease.

APOE is also well suited to demographic synthesis. First, it meets the three criteria for what I have termed a "demogene"—a gene that has noticeable effects at the population level (Ewbank 2000). Demogenes must have variants that are associated with sizable differences in the risk of common conditions, and these variants must be common in the population (e.g., carried by more than 5 percent of the population). The importance of a demogene is enhanced if the frequency of the variants differs substantially across populations. To date, the gene for APOE is the only gene proven to meet all three of these criteria. Demographic synthesis can be applied to genes that do not meet some or all of these characteristics if there is sufficient population-level data. However, the full benefits of demographic synthesis for population genetics are realized for demogenes.

The applicability of demographic synthesis to the study of other fixed traits has been demonstrated by Stone (2004). She has used this approach to study the mortality of individuals who have a sibling who survived to age 110. The advantage of this approach is that it is semi-parametric—it models the changes in the relative risks without imposing a parametric form for the full life table. In that regard it improves on the nonparametric Kaplan–Meier approach without imposing a Gompertz or Weibull distribution on the age pattern of risk.

The value of this approach is not limited to applications to chronic disease and mortality. It can be applied to estimate any multistate model. The modeling is easier if the risks (or the relative risks) have stayed constant. Even this assumption is not necessary, however.

Postscript

This chapter has described the evolution of demographic synthesis from a specific application (the study of Alzheimer's disease as a cause of death) to a generalized approach to studying chronic disease and the population-level effects of genetic variability. Demographic synthesis also offers an alternative way to fit multistate models. I illustrated the development of this approach through references to four previously published papers. However, this discussion makes the process of discovery look far more orderly than it was. When describing an intellectual process, the chronological approach can be at odds with the logical. The situation that led to a discovery is rarely the best example for explaining it. Over time, what began as a solution to a small problem at hand slowly becomes an approach with more general applications. Therefore, this retrospective look obscures what was really a process of rediscovery, refinement, and restatement.

This voyage of discovery is not complete. Currently, I am expanding the model of the risk of Alzheimer's disease by APOE genotype and applying it to the raw data from a large number of case–control studies. I am beginning a study of the effects of several fixed characteristics on mortality at the oldest ages. I also plan to modify the models of genetic effects to address questions that involve latent classes and to develop applications to the study of centenarians. Variants of these models can find wide applicability in both demography and epidemiology.

Notes

This research was supported by National Institute on Aging (NIA) grant R01-AG16683.

1 This section and the subsequent section, "Findings," are based on "Deaths attributable to Alzheimer's disease in the U.S." (Ewbank 1999).

2 The published data are actually for much larger age groups. Therefore, we need to weight the $\lambda(x)$ using an appropriate age distribution by single years of age.

3 The model also relied on estimates of excess mortality among Alzheimer's disease cases by duration of disease. These were estimated by averaging data from several clinic-based studies.

4 In many articles and in discourse, the distinction between the gene forms ($\varepsilon2$, $\varepsilon3$, and $\varepsilon4$) and the resulting gene products (e2, e3, and e4) is often ignored.

5 This section and the subsequent section, "Findings," are based on "A multistate model of the genetic risk of Alzheimer's disease" (Ewbank 2002a).

6 For a brief discussion of some of these issues, see Ewbank 1998.

7 This section and the subsequent section, "Findings," are based on "Mortality differences by APOE genotype estimated from demographic synthesis" (Ewbank 2002b).

8 Since the time this paper was published in *Genetic Epidemiology*, I have updated the estimates using two new data sets from the Netherlands and two from the United States. Therefore, the sample sizes and the results given here are slightly different from those given in the paper. These more recent estimates are described briefly in the fourth paper discussed below.

9 This section and the subsequent section, "Findings," are based on "The APOE gene and differences in life expectancy in Europe" (Ewbank 2004).

10 One of the risks in using current status (prevalence) data is that they may be affected by past trends in incidence rates or relative risks. The applications described here are all based on the assumption that the Alzheimer's disease incidence rates and all relative risks at young ages have remained constant. These assumptions can easily be relaxed if sufficient data are available.

References

Al Mamun, Abdullah. 2003. *Life History of Cardiovascular Disease and Its Risk Factors: Multistate Life Table Approach and Application to the Framingham Heart Study*. Amsterdam, Netherlands: Rozenberg Publishers.

Barclay, Laurie L., Alexander Zemcov, John P. Blass, and Joseph Sansone. 1985. "Survival in Alzheimer's disease and vascular dementias," *Neurology* 35: 834–840.

Beard, C. Mary, Emre Kokmen, Cathy Sigler, Glenn E. Smith, Tanya Petterson, and Peter C. O'Brien. 1996. "Cause of death in Alzheimer's disease," *Ann Epidemiology* 6(3): 195–200.

Crimmins, Eileen M., Yasuhiko Saito, and Dominique Ingegneri. 1989. "Changes in life expectancy and disability-free life expectancy in the United States," *Population and Development Review* 15(2): 235–267.

———. 1997. "Trends in disability-free life expectancy in the United States, 1970–90," *Population and Development Review* 23(3): 555–572.

Eichner, June E. et al. 1993. "Relation of apolipoprotein E phenotype to myocardial infarction and mortality from coronary artery disease," *Am J Cardiol* 71: 160–165.

Evans, Denis A. et al. 1989. "Prevalence of Alzheimer's disease in a community population of older persons," *Journal of the American Medical Association* 262: 2551–2556.

Evans, Denis A., Laurel A. Smith, Paul A. Scherr , Marilyn S. Albert, H. Harris Funkenstein, and Liese E. Hebert. 1991. "Risk of death from Alzheimer's disease in a community population of older persons," *Am J Epidemiol* 134(4): 403–412.

Ewbank, Douglas C. 1998. "Effects of age and ethnicity on the link between APOE ε4 and Alzheimer's disease," *Journal of the American Medical Association* 279(8): 580–581.

———. 1999. "Deaths attributable to Alzheimer's disease in the U.S.," *Am J Public Health* 89(1): 90–92.

———. 2000. "Demography in the age of genomics: A first look at the prospects," in Caleb E. Finch, James W. Vaupel, and Kevin Kinsella (eds.), *Cells and Surveys: Should Biological Measures Be Included in Social Science Research?* Washington, DC: National Academy Press.

———. 2002a. "A multistate model of the genetic risk of Alzheimer's disease," *Exp Aging Res* 28(4): 477–499.

———. 2002b. "Mortality differences by APOE genotype estimated from demographic synthesis," *Genet Epidemiol* 22(2): 146–155.

———. 2004. "The APOE gene and differences in life expectancy in Europe," *J Gerontol A Biol Sci Med Sci* 59A(1): 8–12.

Farrer, Lindsay A. et al. 1997. "Effects of age, sex, and ethnicity on the association between apolipoprotein E genotype and Alzheimer disease," *Journal of the American Medical Association* 278: 1349–1356.

Hayward, Mark D. and William R. Grady. 1990. "Work and retirement among a cohort of older men in the United States, 1966–1983," *Demography* 27(3): 337–356.

Herskind, Anne Marie, Matthew McGue, Niels V. Holm, Thorkild I. A. Sörensen, Bent Harvald, and James W. Vaupel. 1996. "The heritability of human longevity: A population-based study of 2872 Danish twin pairs born 1870–1900," *Hum Genet* 97(3): 319–323.

Heuveline, Patrick. 2003. "HIV and population dynamics: A general model and maximum-likelihood standards for East Africa," *Demography* 40(2): 217–245.

Hoyert, Donna L. 1996. "Mortality trends for Alzheimer's disease, 1979–1991," *Vital Health Stat 20*(28).

Jorm, A. F. and D. Jolley. 1998. "The incidence of dementia: A meta-analysis," *Neurology* 51(3): 728–733.

Juva, K., A. Verkkoniemi, P. Viramo, T. Polvikoski, K. Kainulainen, K. Kontula, and R. Sulkava. 2000. "APOE epsilon4 does not predict mortality, cognitive decline, or dementia in the oldest old," *Neurology* 54(2): 412–415.

Katzman, R. 1986. "Alzheimer's disease," *New England Journal of Medicine* 314: 964–973.

Keyfitz, Nathan. 1985. *Applied Mathematical Demography*. New York : Springer-Verlag.

Kukull, W. A., D. E. Brenner, C. E. Speck, D. Nochlin, J. Bowen, W. McCormick, L. Teri, M. L. Pfanschmidt, and E. B. Larson. 1994. "Causes of death associated with Alzheimer disease variation by level of cognitive impairment before death," *J Am Geriatr Soc* 42(7): 723–726.

Larson, Eric B., Marie-Florence Shadlen, Li Wang, Wayne C. McCormick, James D. Bowen, Linda Teri, and Walter A. Kukull. 2004. "Survival after initial diagnosis of Alzheimer disease," *Ann Intern Med* 140(7): 501–509.

Levy-Lahad, Ephrat and Thomas D. Bird. 1996. "Genetic factors in Alzheimer's disease: A review of recent advances," *Ann Neurol* 40(6): 829–840.

Lucotte, G., F. Loirat, and S. Hazout. 1997. "Pattern of gradient of apolipoprotein E allele ε4 frequencies in Western Europe," *Hum Biol* 69 (2): 253–262.

Macera, Caroline A., R. K. Sun, Kimberly K. Yeager, and Debra A. Brandes. 1992. "Sensitivity and specificity of death certificate diagnoses for dementing illnesses, 1988–1990," *J Am Geriatr Soc* 40(5): 479–481.

Manton, Kenneth G., Eric Stallard, and James W. Vaupel. 1986. "Alternative models for the heterogeneity of mortality risks among the aged," *JASA* 81(395): 635–644.

Panza, Francesco et al. 1999. "Decreased frequency of apolipoprotein E ε4 allele from Northern to Southern Europe in Alzheimer's disease patients and centenarians," *Neurosci Lett* 277: 53–56.

Raiford, K., S. Anton-Johnson, Z. Haycox, K. Nolan, A. Schaffer, C. Caimano, G. Fillenbaum, and A. Heyman. 1994. "CERAD Part VII: Accuracy of reporting dementia on death certificates of patients with Alzheimer's disease," *Neurology* 44(11): 2208–2209.

Robbins, Jessica M. and Douglas C. Ewbank. 2001. "Dementia in Parkinson's disease: Demographic models and estimates," paper presented at the Annual Meeting of the Population Association of America, Washington, DC, 29–31 March.

Rosenberg H. et al. 1996. "Births and deaths: United States, 1995," *Monthly Vital Statistics Report* 45(3) suppl 2.

Schoen, R. and N. Standish. 2001. "The retrenchment of marriage: Results from marital status life tables for the United States, 1995," *Population and Development Review* 27(3): 553–563.

Skoog, I., C. Hesse, O. Aevarsson, S. Landahl, J. Wahlstrom, P. Fredman, and K. Blennow. 1998. "A population study of ApoE genotype at the age of 85: Relation to dementia, cerebrovascular disease, and mortality," *J Neurol Neurosurg Psychiatry* 64(1): 37–43.

Stengård, Jari H., Kenneth M. Weiss, and Charles F. Sing. 1998. "An ecological study of association between coronary heart disease mortality rates in men and the relative frequencies of common allelic variations in the gene coding for apolipoprotein E," *Hum Genet* 103(2): 234–241.

Stone, Leslie. 2004. "Studies in the demography of supercentenarians in the United States." Unpublished doctoral dissertation, University of Pennsylvania.

Tilvis, R. S., T. E. Strandberg, and K. Juva. 1998. "Apolipoprotein E phenotypes, dementia and mortality in a prospective population sample," *J Am Geriatr Soc* 46(6): 712–715.

Toupance, Bruno, Bernard Godelle, Pierre-Henri Gouyon, and François Schächter. 1998.

"A model for antagonistic pleiotropic gene action for mortality and advanced age," *Am J Hum Genet* 62: 1525–1534.

Wilson, Peter W. F., Ernst J. Schaefer, Martin G. Larson, and Jose M. Ordovas. 1996. "Apolipoprotein E alleles and risk of coronary disease: A meta-analysis," *Arterioscler Thromb Vasc Biol* 16: 1250–1255.

Vogt, M. T., J. A. Cauley, and L. H. Kuller. 1997. "Apolipoprotein E phenotype, arterial disease, and mortality among older women: The study of osteoporotic fractures," *Genet Epidemiol* 14(2): 147–156.

Yashin, A. I., G. De Benedictis, J. W. Vaupel, Q. Tan, K. F. Andreev, I. A. Iachine, M. Bonafe, M. DeLuca, S. Valensin, L. Carotenuto, and C. Franceschi. 1999. "Genes, demography and life span: The contribution of demographic data in genetic studies of aging and longevity," *Am J Hum Genet* 6511: 78–93.

Yashin, A. et al. 2000. "Genes and longevity: Lessons from studies of centenarians," *J Gerontol* 55A(7): B319–B328.

II. HEALTH AND SOCIOECONOMIC STATUS

Integrating Biology into the Study of Health Disparities

EILEEN M. CRIMMINS
TERESA E. SEEMAN

Socioeconomic status, ethnicity, and other salient social and demographic characteristics contribute to differences in health outcomes with age through multiple biological pathways. Investigators at the USC/UCLA Center on Biodemography and Population Health seek to clarify the multiple proximate biological mechanisms through which health differentials arise in mortality, cardiovascular disease, cancer, and physical and cognitive functioning. Founded in 1999, the center has developed multidisciplinary research teams and projects, incorporating biological, epidemiologic, and medical researchers along with more traditional demographic, behavioral, and psychosocial researchers to promote integrative research. Clarification of the effect of various biological risk factors on health outcomes as well as better understanding of their relationships to demographic, behavioral, psychological, and medical factors will provide more complete explanations of the sources of differentials in the health of populations and may improve our ability to develop effective interventions to reduce these differentials.

Population health disparities

A vast body of evidence documents that people who are poorer and who have less education are more likely to suffer from diseases, to experience loss of physical functioning, to be cognitively and physically impaired, and to experience high mortality rates (Adler et al. 1993; Hayward et al. 2000; Smith 1999; Williams 1990). Lower educational attainment has been linked to higher mortality from most causes (Rogers, Hummer, and Nam 2000; Steenland, Henley, and Thun 2002). Some chronic causes of mortality and morbidity are particularly associated with low education level; these include diabetes, hypertension, and heart disease. Disability, loss of functioning, and cognitive impairment are also higher among those with lower levels of socioeconomic status (Crimmins, Hayward, and Seeman 2004; Jones and Gallo 2002; Seeman et al. 1994b; Albert et al. 1995).

The large health differentials by race and ethnicity in the United States are at least partially the result of differences in socioeconomic status. Blacks have significantly higher prevalence and incidence of many of the major chronic diseases, including hypertension, diabetes, and stroke, as well as greater levels of loss of functioning and disability (Hayward et al. 2000; Smith and Kington 1997). Hispanics are less clearly disadvantaged; most estimates of Hispanic life expectancy indicate that it is either similar to or longer than that of non-Hispanic whites and higher than that of black Americans (Hayward and Heron 1999; Rogers et al. 1996). Hispanics also appear to have lower mortality from cancer, cardiovascular disease, and chronic lung conditions (Markides et al. 1997; Sorlie et al. 1993). There are, however, some conditions from which Hispanics are more likely to die; the statistically most important is diabetes (Sorlie et al. 1993). Because the Hispanic population comprises a high proportion of immigrants, selectivity complicates the interpretation of these differentials (Crimmins et al. 2004; Palloni and Morenoff 2001).

Understanding health differentials

During the past four years, the Center on Biodemography and Population Health has contributed to clarifying the relative burden of mortality, disease, and disability among population groups, using demographic approaches to summarizing the life cycle effects of health differences. Center researchers have used the concepts of "years of life lost" and "healthy life expectancy" to clarify the relative life cycle effects of population health differentials. "Years of life lost" indicates how many years are not lived relative to the longest-lived group; "healthy life expectancy" divides years of life lived into healthy and unhealthy. Such methods can be linked to population composition to summarize effects of health differentials in actual populations; or they can eliminate population composition effects through the use of life table populations to compare the forces of mortality and morbidity across population subgroups (Robine et al. 2003; Crimmins and Cambois 2003). Multistate approaches to active life expectancy can be used to clarify the implications of changes in mortality and morbidity for population health (Crimmins, Hayward, and Saito 1994).

Crimmins and colleagues have estimated differences in healthy life expectancy for blacks and whites (Crimmins and Saito 2001; Crimmins, Hayward, and Saito 1996; Molla et al. 2003). Black Americans can expect to live more years than whites with a disabling health problem that has begun at an earlier age, and the differentials in healthy life are greater than differentials in total life. Within both racial groups, differences in healthy life expectancy by education are large, and over time individuals with the highest levels of education among both blacks and whites have experienced the greatest increase in healthy life (Crimmins and Saito 2001). Coupling the years-of-life-lost approach with the years-of-healthy-life approach, we have documented that the most marked differentials manifest themselves in the far lower likelihood that black men with low education will reach old age (Crimmins and Saito 2001).

Using years of life lost, Wong and colleagues (2002) measured the impact of specific causes of death on differences in mortality by socioeconomic status and race. Before age 75, relatively few diseases account for most of the mortality disparities: cardiovascular disease accounts for about a third of both the educational and the black/white differences; lung cancer is another important contributor to the disparities by education.

We have also used the healthy-life-expectancy approach to estimate the length of time men and women spend living with specific diseases and impairments (Crimmins, Kim, and Hagedorn 2002). For instance, an average woman lives more years with heart disease than an average man even though men have higher incidence of and mortality from heart disease (Crimmins et al. submitted). This approach has also shown that on average women live longer with cognitive impairment than men because of lower female mortality (Suthers, Kim, and Crimmins 2003).

Much of the evidence that we have used in evaluating health differences points to an earlier onset of health problems among individuals with lower socioeconomic status and among blacks. This is analogous to an earlier "aging" of disadvantaged people. In an attempt to clarify this facet of population health differences, we have used data from the Health and Retirement Survey to estimate "equivalent ages," or ages at which education subgroups of the population experience the same rates of prevalence or incidence of age-related health problems (Crimmins, Hayward, and Seeman 2004). Logistic and hazard equations relating age and education to prevalence and onset are the basis for estimates of age-specific rates of disease prevalence and onset for those with 8, 12, and 16 years of education (Figure 1). The base rate is that of the lowest education group at age 51 years, and equivalent ages are those at which individuals with 12 and 16 years of education experience the same rates. For those with 16 years of education, equivalent ages for onset and prevalence of disease are reached 5 to 15 years later than among those with less education.

Our use of demographic approaches to health differentials has clarified the importance of integrating life cycle effects into the study of health differences. While we focus on socioeconomic and race/ethnic differences, it is clear that age is an additional consideration in examining disparities across groups. Differentials tend to be greater before old age, and some dif-

FIGURE 1 Estimated equivalent ages of disease prevalence and onset for three educational groups: Health and Retirement Survey, persons aged 51 to 61 years at baseline

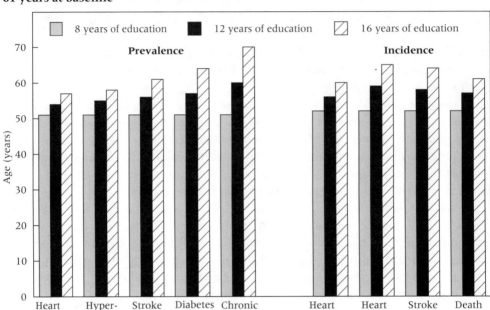

SOURCE: Crimmins, Hayward, and Seeman 2004.

ferentials disappear (Crimmins, Hayward, and Seeman 2004). And while socioeconomic status and race are related to most health outcomes, differentials are larger for some outcomes than others. At older ages differentials in disability and loss of functioning are greater than differentials in the presence of major mortal diseases. All of these results point to a complex interaction of age-specific mortality and morbidity rates in producing health differentials in populations.

Seeman has pioneered research on the social and psychological pathways that are hypothesized to act as partial mediators of socioeconomic effects on health and mortality. She has documented the links between social and psychological factors and cardiovascular disease (Seeman and Syme 1987; Seeman 1991), as well as the links between such factors and patterns of cognitive and physical decline (Seeman et al. 1993, 1995, 1996, 1999, 2001; Unger et al. 1999) and mortality (Seeman et al. 1987, 1993). Most recently, she has elucidated the biological pathways through which social and psychological factors affect health and longevity, documenting links between social integration, support, and social conflict, and biological parameters known to affect health, including neuroendocrine function (Seeman et al. 1994a) and major cardiovascular and metabolic factors (Seeman and McEwen 1996).

Moving to a more integrative model

Integrative, multidimensional models linking social status and race/ethnicity to health outcomes through social, psychological, behavioral, and biological causal mechanisms have increasingly become a focus of research among demographers and health researchers. Center researchers have been in the forefront of efforts to integrate demographic and health approaches (Crimmins and Seeman 2001; Seeman and Crimmins 2001). Figure 2 provides a heuristic model of the multiple (and possibly interacting) pathways that are a focus of research sponsored by the USC/UCLA center. While the model appears static, this research recognizes that levels of biological risk and chronic health conditions grow out of social, psychological, economic, and medical conditions over the entire life cycle and are at the root of differences in healthy life and years of life lost (Link and Phelan 1995; Adler et al. 1993; Garber 1989).

While these mechanisms combine over the life cycle and contribute to differences in health in myriad ways, all the mechanisms must eventually work through biological factors to affect the "premature aging" or earlier

FIGURE 2 Heuristic biopsychosocial model of health outcomes

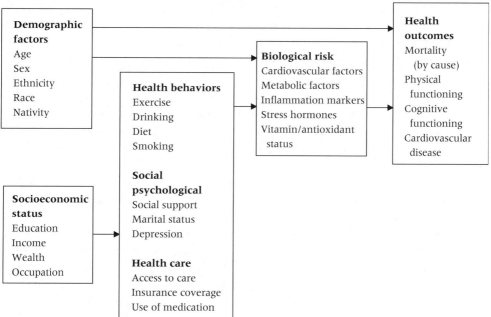

onset of disease and disability among disadvantaged people. Indeed, many of these biological risk factors are at play decades before disease is clinically evident, and their early identification and treatment would be a promising approach to reducing mortality and morbidity at older ages. The cumulative lifetime levels of adversity and disadvantage experienced by persons of lower status are likely to result in higher levels of physiological deterioration at younger ages (Finch and Seeman 1999).

Understanding biological pathways

The USC/UCLA Biodemography Center has undertaken a number of projects to enhance our understanding of the biological processes through which population health differentials are generated. A particular approach has been to demonstrate the biological pathways through which traditional demographic variables (e.g., socioeconomic status, race/ethnicity, age, sex) affect health outcomes such as disease, disability, and mortality. The pathways we have considered include those that progress through multiple physiological systems including the cardiovascular, metabolic, endocrine, immune and inflammation, and sympathetic nervous systems. Genetic factors have also been a more recent focus of research.

Evidence links individual biological risk factors to education, other measures of socioeconomic status, race and ethnicity, and health outcomes. Biological variables frequently found in models explaining education/socioeconomic status, and race/ethnic differences in health in the United States include indicators of cardiovascular and metabolic processes such as blood pressure, lipid profiles, and relative weight (Winkleby at al. 1998, 1999; Kaplan and Keil 1993). More recently, markers of inflammation and coagulation processes have been recognized as potentially important predictors of vascular conditions (Finch et al. 2001; Wilson, Finch, and Cohen 2002). Inflammatory markers have been related to cardiovascular diseases and also have been shown to be distributed negatively by socioeconomic status, with lower educational status being associated with higher levels of such markers of inflammation (Danesh et al. 1998, 1999, 2000; Ishizaki et al. 2000; Wamala et al. 1999).

One focus of center researchers has been on the question of whether biological factors previously shown to be associated with health risks in general populations remain significant risk factors among older adults and how the importance of risk factors changes with age. Findings indicate that while some biological factors continue to be associated with increased health risks in older adults, others do not. For example, higher burdens of inflammation continue to be associated with increased risks for cognitive declines (Weaver et al. 2002) as well as with mortality in older adults (Hu et al. 2004). Higher homocysteine levels (generally the result of low dietary folate intake) are associated with significantly increased risks for both physical and cognitive decline (Kado et al. 2002; Kado et al., in press). Elevations in other "stress" hormones (e.g., cortisol, epinephrine) are associated with increased risks for cognitive decline (Seeman et al. 1997a; Karlamangla et al., in press a) as well as risks for onset of new depression among older persons (Karlamangla, Chodosh, Seeman, in preparation). A recently completed project has provided intriguing evidence that lower reported happiness may be linked to increased risk for fracture in older adults through an association with higher cortisol exposures (Karlmangla, Singer, Greendale, Seeman, in preparation).

While the foregoing research has largely provided evidence of the continued impact of biological factors on risks for mortality and functional decline at older ages, center researchers have also recently documented potentially important age-related declines in the salience of several risk factors. Analyses have shown that, at older ages, not only is higher cholesterol not a risk factor for mortality but higher cholesterol levels are associated with less risk of mortality and lower risk for cognitive decline (Karlamangla et al. 2004). While surprising in light of the considerable evidence linking higher total cholesterol to increased risks for cardiovascular disease, these findings are consistent with a growing body of evidence indicating that total cholesterol is not associated with increased mortality among older adults (Anderson, Catelli, and Levy 1987; Corti et al. 1997; Volpato et al. 2001).

Center research has also examined the changing relationship with age between behavioral risk factors and mortality. The link between smoking and mortality is reduced in old age (Crimmins 2001), and the lack of a relationship between obesity and mortality in old age has been demonstrated in both the United States and Japan (Crimmins 2001). Research on variability of risk with age is providing a basis for developing life cycle models of health outcomes for which age-specific risk relationships are a crucial input. One aim of the research is to understand how risk varies over the life cycle and results in changes with age in the distribution of risk or heterogeneity of the population.

Cumulative biological risk

Center faculty have pioneered efforts to develop more comprehensive, cumulative models of biological risk and its impact on health and functioning over the life course. The search for summary scores that incorporate multiple biological risk factors is motivated by the observation that many individuals are exposed to several risk factors and small increases in multiple risk factors can lead to a substantial increase in overall risk, even if no single factor exceeds its clinically accepted threshold. Research on the metabolic syndrome (also known as Syndrome X, Insulin resistance syndrome, and cardiovascular risk factor cluster), for example, has demonstrated the significantly increased risks for cardiovascular disease and mortality associated with the presence of a constellation of risk factors, including hyperinsulinemia, trunkal obesity, dyslipidemia, and hypertension (Trevisan et al. 1998; Lindblad et al. 2001; Lakka et al. 2002). Similarly, research from the Framingham Study has shown that a composite score created from multiple cardiovascular risk factors strongly predicts risk of coronary heart disease in the Framingham cohort as well as other population-based cohorts (Wilson et al. 1998; ATP III 2001).

The concept of allostatic load has been proposed as a more comprehensive, multisystem view of the cumulative physiological toll that may be exacted on the body through attempts to adapt to life's demands (McEwen and Stellar 1993; McEwen 1998). Allostatic load is a measure of the cumulative impact of adaptive physiological responses that chronically exceed optimal operating ranges, resulting in wear and tear on the body's regulatory systems. Such a multisystem approach may be useful in conceptualizing biological mediation of the effects of education/socioeconomic status and race/ethnicity on health and longevity.

The idea that allostatic load is a cumulative phenomenon derives from evidence in both animal and human studies that profiles of physiological dysregulation are frequently cumulative, with evidence of a narrowing of systems' ranges of response and an overall reduction in the capacity to adapt with increasing age (Seeman and Robbins 1994; Young et al. 1980; Rowe and Troen 1980; Shock 1977; Lipsitz and Goldberger 1992). The cumulative burden of physiological wear and tear is, at least partially, a product of the individual's interaction with the environment throughout life, with older individuals having more cumulative dysregulation but with substantial variability within any one age group.

A multisystem approach to biological risk similar to "allostatic load" provides a more comprehensive framework for conceptualizing the concurrent biological pathways through which education, other indicators of socioeconomic status, stressors, health behaviors, and other factors may affect health outcomes over the life course. Biological risk measurements also have the potential to provide some of the earliest evidence of pathophysiological processes that ultimately progress to clinical disease. A multisystem view of biological foundations of health risks seems well suited to investigating influences of broad sets of factors that are associated with differences in socioeconomic status. These biological systems are the pathways through which the individual's interaction with his/her environment is translated into physiologically adaptive (or nonadaptive) responses.

The multisystem approach attempts to incorporate information about the multiplicity of potentially additive and/or synergistic biological processes that operate continually as we interact with our environment. A multisystem approach to investigation of biological "health risk" profiles seeks to move us beyond traditional approaches that have identified individual "risk factors." The approach explicitly considers the simultaneous and potentially cumulative impacts of physiological effects from multiple regulatory systems—consistent with growing evidence of counter-regulatory links between various major physiological systems, with changes in one leading to alterations in the patterns of activity in others.

Initial efforts to test empirically the concept of allostatic load were undertaken by an interdisciplinary team, including Teresa Seeman, Bruce McEwen, Burton Singer, Ralph Horwitz, and Jack Rowe (Seeman et al. 1997a). The initial conceptualization of allostatic load was based on available data from the MacArthur Study of Successful Aging and included ten biological parameters: systolic blood pressure, diastolic blood pressure, waist-to-hip ratio, ratio of total/HDL cholesterol, HDL cholesterol, glycosylated hemoglobin, cortisol, norepinephrine, epinephrine, and DHEA-S. These represent physiological activity across the cardiovascular system, the metabolic system, the hypothalmic–pituitary axis, and the sympathetic nervous system. In subsequent analyses, additional indicators have included renal functioning, lung capacity, markers of inflammation and coagulation, and these have added to the explanatory power of the measure (Seeman et al. 2004).

The initial conceptualization of allostatic load in the MacArthur Study was based on a simple count of the number of markers (from a set of ten) for which the subject scored in the upper 25 percent of the distribution, a summary measure that has been shown to predict mortality as well as risk for decline in physical and cognitive functioning among a sample of initially healthy older persons (Seeman et al. 1997b; Seeman et al. 2001). Subsequent analyses have explored several alternative techniques whereby individual indicators can contribute differentially and through their entire range of values to risks for outcomes of interest (e.g., through use of factor analyses, cannonical correlation, and recursive partitioning techniques; Seeman et al. 2004; Karlamangla et al. 2002; Singer, Ryff, and Seeman 2004). Use of these more refined approaches has clarified that the optimal weighting of the individual components of biological risk differs depending on the outcome of interest and suggests that levels of risk follow a continuous pattern (e.g., risks accrue not only from clear deviations from "normal/optimal" levels of functioning, but from more modest deviations as well)—providing support for the use of the full continuum of values for the various biological indicators. Despite the apparent gains in predictive ability with more complex operational definitions of biological risk, comparisons of the simple count index with the more refined measures do not indicate major differences in their ability to predict health outcomes, and the simple summed measure has the advantage of being easily defined and interpreted across populations.

While current conceptualizations of allostatic load include most of the components of the Framingham risk score and the metabolic syndrome (i.e., traditional cardiovascular risk factors such as blood pressure, cholesterol, relative weight, and glucose dysregulation), analyses of the relative contributions to health risks of these traditional risk factors for cardiovascular disease versus the additional factors (e.g., stress hormones) have indicated that both sets of factors make significant independent contributions, so that the more inclusive allostatic load measure is a better predictor of health outcomes (Seeman et al. 2001; Seeman et al. 2004; Karlamangla et al. 2002).

Most recently, center researchers in collaboration with others have begun to examine differences in allostatic load by socioeconomic status. Analyses based on the MacArthur Successful Aging Study have demonstrated that a summary index of cumulative allostatic load is related to education, with lower education being associated with greater allostatic load (Seeman et al. 2004). These analyses also demonstrate that differential allostatic load mediates approximately 35 percent of the education-related differences in mortality among the study group of persons 70 to 79 years of age at the beginning of observation. Levels of social integration (known to be negatively related to mortality; Seeman 1996) are significantly and negatively associated with allostatic load in older men, with parallel though nonsignificant patterns seen among older women (Seeman et al. 2002). Similar findings have been reported for middle-aged adults (Singer and Ryff 1999).

Biological risk pathways at younger ages are being investigated, with particular attention to the trajectories of biological risk development at younger ages. Analyses of trajectories of developing cardiovascular risk based on data from the Coronary Artery Risk Development in Young Adults Study (CARDIA) have shown that socioeconomic status differences in risk profiles are evident in young adulthood (e.g., beginning when subjects were aged 18–30) and that these socioeconomic status–associated differences tend to become more accentuated over time. Those at highest risk initially show the steepest trajectories of increasing risk over the next ten years (Karlamangla et al., in press b). These associations hold true for childhood socioeconomic status as measured by parental educational attainment and participant's own educational attainment. In each case, socioeconomic status was found to be negatively associated with a summary index of cardiovascular risk in whites. Although the trends were similar for blacks, the "gains" from college education in terms of lower cardiovascular disease risk scores were smaller and did not achieve statistical significance in men (Karlamangla et al., in press b).

Additional work based on the National Health and Nutrition Examination Survey (NHANES) is investigating socioeconomic status and ethnic differences in age-related patterns of cumulative biological dysregulation in a nationally representative sample of persons aged 20 years and older. Our initial analysis indicates that differences in biological risk by race/ethnicity and socioeconomic status will provide significant explanations for the mechanisms producing observed health differences. Defining biological risk using clinical guidelines where available and definition of risk as used in the MacArthur data where not available, we examined the average number of risk indicators out of 13 markers by education and race/ethnicity for persons from ages 20 to 90 years (Wong and Crimmins 2002). Average age-specific numbers of biological risk markers by education level are shown in Figure 3a. Similar to results reported above for the CARDIA sample, educational differentials in biological risk appear as early as age 20 years; however, they are particularly marked in the age range 35 to 65 years. Those with more than 12 years of education have markedly lower biological risk up until the older ages; at ages over 70, biological risk appears to level off, perhaps because death removes those with high levels of biological risk from the population (Crimmins et al. 2003).

The National Health and Examination Study III data collected by the US National Center for Health Statistics also provides the opportunity to examine differences in biological risk among large samples of blacks and Hispanics (primarily of Mexican origin) (Wong and Crimmins 2002). While blacks and Hispanics have similar levels of biological risk, they have higher average age-specific levels of biological risk than non-Hispanic whites up until the older ages (Figure 3b). Evidence of the earlier aging of these minority groups is demonstrated: levels of biological risk for Hispanics and blacks at age 45 are characteristic of whites at age 55. Race/ethnic differentials are also greatest in the 35 to 65 age range. At the older ages, the three groups have similar levels of biological risk, again perhaps linked to the selection by mortality for low biological risk at older ages.

Genetic markers

Center research has begun to include genetic factors along with other biological risk markers. In the MacArthur sample, the presence of APOE4 alleles has been linked to cognitive decline (Bretsky et al. 2003; Ewbank, this volume). Most recently, research has examined possible gene–environment interactions. To date, this research has focused on possible interactions between the APOE genotype and potentially "protective" factors such as education or serum antioxidant levels in relation to risks for cognitive decline. Our general hypothesis has been that such protective factors might be more important in protecting against risks for decline among those with the e4 allele (i.e., the group at higher risk based on genotype). For education, we found no evidence for an interaction with APOE genotype (i.e., those with and without the e4 allele show parallel education differences in risks for cognitive decline) (Seeman et al., in press). By contrast, antioxidant levels appear to contribute significantly to reduction of risk for cognitive decline for those with

FIGURE 3   Mean number of biological risk factors by education and ethnicity

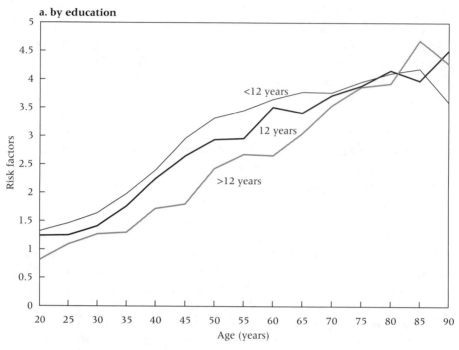

a. by education

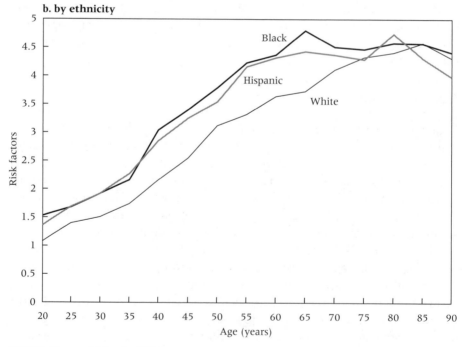

b. by ethnicity

SOURCE: Wong and Crimmins 2002.

the e4 allele, while differences in antioxidant levels do not affect risks for those without the e4 allele (Hu et al., submitted). Additional analyses are examining possible synergistic relationships between presence of the e4 allele and comorbidities associated with increased risk for cognitive decline (e.g., diabetes, hypertension, cardiovascular disease).

The center has also recently funded an innovative project to examine possible relationships between socioeconomic status and other indexes of psychosocial disadvantage and evidence of DNA damage (e.g., shorter telomere length, greater mitochondrial damage). Future work will include additional genetic markers and their relationships to more traditional biological risk factors as well as demographic and social characteristics.

Summary and future directions

During its first four years of funding, the USC/UCLA Center on Biodemography and Population Health has integrated biological and medical results with demographic measures of population health. Evidence has been amassed linking factors central to demographic models of population health (e.g., socioeconomic status, ethnicity, sex) to various health outcomes; specific attention has been given to evidence for mediating pathways through biological, behavioral, and psychosocial factors (Crimmins, Hayward, and Seeman 2004; Crimmins and Seeman 2001; Seeman and Crimmins 2001). Empirical work has examined the effect of socioeconomic status and race/ethnic differentials on years of healthy life and years of life lost to various major causes of death (Wong et al. 2002; Crimmins and Saito 2001). A series of papers have identified biological processes likely to mediate socioeconomic status differences in a variety of health outcomes (e.g., Seeman et al. 2004; Hu et al. 2004; Karlamangla et al., in press b). Multiple interactive processes account for observed variation in health, including processes relating to socioeconomic status and genotype, as well as biological systems. Integrative research, incorporating attention to biological, epidemiologic, and medical data, along with more traditional demographic, behavioral, and psychosocial factors, is necessary to understanding and projecting demographic trends and to designing interventions to reduce undesirable differences in population health.

Plans for coming years at the center focus on three major areas of interest: 1) better and more comprehensive assessment of biological factors as well as development of better operational measures of cumulative biological risks; 2) additional attention to the role of genetic factors, and in particular to possible gene–environment interactions in relation to health risks; and 3) expansion of modeling approaches that reflect lifecourse influences affecting population health as well as continued attention to the overarching (and possibly interactive) effects of socioeconomic status and race/ethnicity.

References

Adler, Nancy E., Thomas W. Boyce, Margaret A. Chesney, Sheldon Cohen, Susan Folkman, and Leonard S. Syme. 1993. "Socioeconomic inequalities in health: No easy solution," *Journal of the American Medical Association* 269: 3140–3145.

Adult Treatment Panel III. 2001. "Executive summary of the third report of the national cholesterol education program (NCEP) expert panel on detection, evaluation, and treatment of high blood cholesterol in adults," *The Journal of the American Medical Association* 285: 2486–2497.

Albert, Marilyn S., Kenneth Jones, Cary R. Savage, Lisa Berkman, Teresa Seeman, Dan Blazer, and John W. Rowe. 1995. "Predictors of cognitive change in older persons: MacArthur Studies of Successful Aging," *Psychology and Aging* 10: 578–589.

Anderson, K. M., W. P. Catelli, and D. Levy. 1987. "Cholesterol and mortality: 30 years of follow-up from the Framingham Study," *Journal of the American Medical Association* 257: 2176–2180.

Bretsky, Phillip, Jack Guralnik, Lenore Launer, Marilyn Albert, and Teresa E. Seeman. 2003. "The role of APOE-e4 in longitudinal cognitive decline in an elderly cohort: MacArthur Studies of Successful Aging," *Neurology* 60: 1077–1081.

Corti, Maria-Chiara, Jack M. Guralnik, Marcel E. Salive, Tamara Harris, Luigi Ferrucci, Robert J. Glynn, and Richard J. Havlik. 1997. "Clarifying the direct relation between total cholesterol levels and death from coronary heart disease in older persons," *Annals of Internal Medicine* 126: 753–760.

Crimmins, Eileen. 2001. "Mortality and health in human life spans," *Experimental Gerontology* 36: 885–897.

Crimmins, Eileen M. and Emmanuelle Cambois. 2003. "Social inequalities in health expectancy," in J. M. Robine, C. Jagger, C. D. Mathers, E. M. Crimmins, and R. M. Suzman (eds.), *Determining Health Expectancies*. West Sussex, England: John Wiley & Sons, pp. 111–125.

Crimmins, Eileen M., Mark D. Hayward, and Yasuhiko Saito. 1994. "Changing mortality and morbidity rates and the health status and life expectancy of the older U.S. population," *Demography* 31 (Feb.): 159–175.

———. 1996. "Differentials in active life expectancy in the older population of the United States," *Journal of Gerontology* 51B(3): S111–S120.

Crimmins, Eileen M., Mark D. Hayward, Hiroshi Ueda, and Yasuhiko Saito. "Life with and without heart disease among men and women over 50" (submitted).

Crimmins, Eileen M., Mark D. Hayward, and Teresa Seeman. 2004. "Race/ethnicity, socioeconomic status, and health," in N. Anderson, R. Bulatao, and B. Cohen (eds.), *Critical Perspectives on Race and Ethnic Differences in Health in Later Life*. Washington, DC: The National Academies Press, pp. 310–352.

Crimmins, Eileen M., Melanie Johnston, Mark Hayward, and Teresa Seeman. 2003. "Age differences in allostatic load: An index of physiological dysregulation," *Experimental Gerontology* 38: 731–734.

Crimmins, Eileen, Jung-Ki Kim, and Aaron Hagedorn. 2002. "Life with and without disease: Women experience more of both," *Journal of Women and Aging* 14: 47–59.

Crimmins, Eileen and Yasuhiko Saito. 2001. "Trends in disability free life expectancy in the United States, 1970–1990: Gender, racial, and educational differences," *Social Science and Medicine* 52: 1629–1641.

Crimmins, Eileen M. and Teresa E. Seeman 2001. "Integrating biology into demographic research on health and aging (with a focus on the MacArthur Study of Successful Aging)," in C. E. Finch and J. W. Vaupel (eds.), *Cells and Surveys: Should Biological Measures Be Included in Social Science Research*. Washington, DC: National Academy Press, pp. 9–41.

Danesh, John, Rory Collins, Paul Appleby, and Richard Peto. 1998. "Association of fibrinogen, C-reactive protein, albumin, or leukocyte count with coronary heart disease: Meta-analyses of prospective studies," *Journal of the American Medical Association* 270(18): 1477–1482.

Danesh, John, Y.-K. Muir, M. Wong, J. R. Ward, Ruth J. Gallimore, and Mark B. Pepys. 1999. "Risk factors for coronary heart disease and acute-phase proteins: A population based study," *European Heart Journal* 20: 954–959.

Danesh, John, Peter Whincup, Mary Walker, Lucy Lennon, Andrew Thomson, Paul Appleby, Ruth J. Gallimore, and Mark B. Peyps. 2000. "Low grade inflammation and coronary heart disease: Prospective study and updated meta-analysis," *British Medical Journal* 321: 199–204.

Finch, Caleb E., Valter Longo, A. Miyao, et al. 2001. "Amyloids, inflammatory mechanisms in Alzheimer disease and aging," in M. F. Chesselet (ed.), *Molecular Mechanism in Neurodegenerative Diseases*. Towota, NJ: Humana Press, pp. 87–110.

Finch, Caleb E. and Teresa E. Seeman. 1999. "Stress theories of aging," in Vern L. Bengston and K. Warner Schaie (eds.), *Handbook of the Theories of Aging*. New York: Springer Publishing.

Garber, Alan M. 1989. "Pursuing the links between socioeconomic factors and health: Critique, policy implications, and directions for future research," in J. P. Bunker, D. S. Gomby, and B. H. Kehrer (eds.), *Pathway to Health: The Role of Social Factors*. Menlo Park, CA: Henry J. Kaiser Family Foundation, pp. 271–313.

Hayward, Mark D., Eileen M. Crimmins, T. Miles, and Y. Yang. 2000. "The significance of socio-economic status is explaining the race gap in chronic health conditions," *American Sociological Review* 65: 910–930.

Hayward, Mark D. and Melonie Heron. 1999. "Racial inequality in active life among adult Americans," *Demography* 36: 77–91.

Hu, Peifeng, P. Bretsky, Eileen M. Crimmins, Jack M. Guralnik, David B. Reuben, and Teresa Seeman. "The effects of serum beta-carotene levels on decline of cognitive function in high-functioning older persons with or without Apolipoprotein E 4 alleles: MacArthur Studies of Successful Aging" (submitted).

Hu, Peifeng, David B. Reuben, Eileen M. Crimmins, Tamara B. Harris, Mei H. Huang, and Teresa E. Seeman. 2004. "The effects of serum beta-carotene level and burden of inflammation on all-cause mortality in high-functioning older persons: MacArthur Studies of Successful Aging," *Journal of Gerontology: Medical Sciences* 59: 849–854.

Ishizaki, Masao, Pekka Martikainen, Hideaki Nakagawa, and Michael Marmot. 2000. "The relationship between employment grade and plasma fibrinogen level of Japanese male employees," *Atherosclerosis* 151(2): 415–421.

Jones, Richard N. and Joseph J. Gallo. 2002. "Education and sex differences in the minimental state examination: Effects of differential item functioning," *Journal of Gerontology: Psychological Science* 57B: P548–P558.

Kado, Deborah M., Alexander S. Bucur, Jacob Selhub, John W. Rowe, and Teresa E. Seeman. 2002. "Homocysteine and decline in physical function: MacArthur Studies of Successful Aging," *American Journal of Medicine* 113: 537–542.

Kado, Deborah M., Arun Karlamangla, Mei Hua Huang, A. Troen, John W. Rowe, Jacob Selhub, and Teresa E. Seeman. "Homocysteine versus the vitamins folate, B_6 and B_{12} as predictors of cognitive function and decline in older high functioning adults: MacArthur Studies of Successful Aging," *American Journal of Medicine* (in press).

Kaplan, George A. and Julian E. Keil. 1993. "Socioeconomic factors and cardiovascular disease: A review of the literature," *Circulation* 88: 1973–1998.

Karlamangla, Arun, Joshua Chodosh, and Teresa Seeman. "Stress hormones and risk of incident depression: MacArthur Studies of Successful Aging" (manuscript in preparation).

Karlamangla, Arun S., Burton Singer, Gail Greendale, and Teresa E. Seeman. "Increase in epinephrine excretion is associated with cognitive decline in elderly men: MacArthur Studies of Successful Aging," *Psychoneuroendocrinology* (in press a).

———. "Happiness, cortisol and risk of fractures: MacArthur Studies of Successful Aging" (manuscript in preparation).

Karlamangla, Arun S., Burton H. Singer, Bruce S. McEwen, John W. Rowe, and Teresa E. Seeman. 2002. "Allostatic load as a predictor of functional decline: MacArthur Studies of Successful Aging," *Journal of Clinical Epidemiology* 55(7): 696–710.

Karlamangla, Arun, Burton Singer, David Reuben, and Teresa E. Seeman. 2004. "Increase in serum non–high-density lipoprotein cholesterol may be beneficial in some high-functioning older adults: MacArthur Studies of Successful Aging," *Journal of the American Geriatrics Society* 52: 487–494.

Karlamangla, Arun, Burton S. Singer, David R. Williams, Joseph Schwartz, Karen Matthews, Catarina I. Kiefe, and Teresa E. Seeman. "Impact of socio-economic status on longitudinal accumulation of cardiovascular risk in young adults: The CARDIA Study," *Social Science and Medicine* (in press b).

Lakka, Hanna M., David E. Laaksonen, Timo A. Lakka, Leo K. Niskanen, Esko Kumpusalo, Jaakko Tuomilehto, and Jukka T. Salonen. 2002. "The metabolic syndrome and total and cardiovascular disease mortality in middle-aged men," *Journal of the American Medical Association* 288(21): 2709–2716

Lindblad, Ulf, Robert D. Langer, Deborah L. Wingard, Ronald G. Thomas, and Elizabeth L. Barrett-Connor. 2001. "Metabolic syndrome and ischemic heart disease in elderly men and women," *American Journal of Epidemiology* 153(5): 481–489.

Link, Bruce G. and Jo Phelan. 1995. "Social conditions as fundamental causes of disease," *Journal of Health and Social Behavior* 36 (Extra Issue): 80–94.

Lipsitz, Lewis A. and Ary L. Goldberger. 1992. "Loss of complexity and aging," *Journal of the American Medical Association* 267(13): 1806–1809.

Markides, Kyriakos S., Laura Rudkin, Ronald J. Angel, and David V. Espino. 1997. "Health status of Hispanic elderly," in L. G. Martine and B. J. Soldo (eds.), *Racial and Ethnic Differences in the Health of Older Americans*. Washington, DC: National Academy Press, pp. 285–300.

McEwen, Bruce S. 1998. "Protective and damaging effects of stress mediators," *New England Journal of Medicine* 338(3): 171–179.

McEwen, Bruce S. and Eliot Stellar. 1993. "Stress and the individual: Mechanisms leading to disease," *Archives of Internal Medicine* 338: 171–179

Molla, Michael, Jennifer H. Madans, Diane K. Wagener, and Eileen M. Crimmins. 2003. *Summary Measures of Population Health: Report of Findings on Methodologic and Data Issues.* Hyattsville, MD: National Center for Health Statistics.

Palloni, Alberto and Jeffrey D. Morenoff. 2001. "Interpreting the paradoxical in the Hispanic paradox," in Maxine Weinstein, Albert Hermalin, and Michael A. Stoto (eds.), *Population Health and Aging: Strengthening the Dialogue Between Epidemiology and Demography.* New York: New York Academy of Sciences.

Robine, Jean Marie, Carol Jagger, Eileen Crimmins, Colin Mathers, and Richard Suzman (eds.). 2003. *Determining Health Expectancies.* West Sussex, England: John Wiley & Sons.

Rogers, Richard G., Robert A. Hummer, and Charles B. Nam. 2000. *Living and Dying in the USA.* New York: Academic Press.

Rogers, Richard, Robert Hummer, Charles B. Nam, and Kimberley Peters. 1996. "Demographic, socioeconomic, and behavioral factors affecting ethnic mortality by cause," *Social Forces* 74(4): 1419–1438.

Rowe, John W. and B. R. Troen 1980. "Sympathetic nervous system and aging in man," *Endocrine Review* 1: 167–179.

Seeman, Teresa E. 1991. "Personal control and coronary artery disease: How generalized expectancies about control may influence disease risk," *Journal of Psychosomatic Research* 35: 661–669.

————. 1996. "Social ties and health," *Annals of Epidemiology* 6: 442–451.

Seeman, Teresa E., Lisa F. Berkman, Daniel Blazer, and John Rowe. 1994a. "Social ties and support and neuroendocrine function: MacArthur Studies of Successful Aging," *Annals of Behavioral Medicine* 16: 95–106.

Seeman, Teresa E., Lisa F. Berkman, Peter Charpentier, Daniel Blazer, Marilyn Albert, and Mary Tinetti. 1995. "Behavioral and psychosocial predictors of physical performance: MacArthur Studies of Successful Aging," *Journal of Gerontology Medical Sciences* 50A: M177–M183.

Seeman, Teresa E., Lisa F. Berkman, F. Kohout, A. LaCroix, Robert Glynn, and Daniel Blazer. 1993. "Intercommunity variations in the association between social ties and mortality in the elderly: A comparative analysis of three communities," *Annals of Epidemiology* 3: 325–335.

Seeman, Teresa E., Mei Hua Huang, Phillip Bretsky, Eileen Crimmins, Lenore Launer, and Jack M. Guralnik. "Education and APOE-ε4 in longitudinal cognitive decline: MacArthur Studies of Successful Aging," *Journal of Gerontology: Psychological Sciences* (in press).

Seeman, Teresa E., Peter A. Charpentier, Lisa F. Berkman, Mary E. Tinetti, Jack M. Guralnik, Marilyn Albert, Daniel Blazer, and John W. Rowe. 1994b. "Predicting changes in physical performance in a high functioning elderly cohort: MacArthur Studies of Successful Aging," *Journal of Gerontology* 49: M97–M108.

Seeman, Teresa E. and Eileen Crimmins. 2001. "Social environment effects on health and aging: Integrating epidemiological and demographic approaches and perspectives," in M. Weinstein, A. I. Hermalin, and M. A. Stoto (eds.), *Population Health and Aging: Strengthening the Dialogue Between Epidemiology and Demography. Annals of the New York Academy of Sciences* 954: 88–117.

Seeman, Teresa E., Eileen Crimmins, Alexander Bucur, Mei Hua Huang, Tara Gruenewald, Lisa F. Berkman, and David B. Reuben. 2004. "Cumulative biological risk and socio-economic differences in mortality: MacArthur Studies of Successful Aging," *Social Science and Medicine* 58: 1985–1997.

Seeman, Teresa E., George A. Kaplan, L. Knudsen, Richard Cohen, and Jack Guralnik. 1987. "Social ties and mortality in the elderly: A comparative analysis of age-dependent patterns of association," *American Journal of Epidemiology* 126: 714–723.

Seeman, Teresa E., Gail McAvay, Susan Merrill, Marilyn Albert, and Judith Rodin. 1996. "Self-efficacy beliefs and changes in cognitive performance: MacArthur Studies of Successful Aging," *Psychology and Aging* 11: 538–551.

Seeman, Teresa E. and Bruce S. McEwen. 1996. "Social environment characteristics and neuroendocrine function: The impact of social ties and support on neuroendocrine regulation," *Psychosomatic Medicine* 58: 459–471.

Seeman, Teresa E., Bruce S. McEwen, Burton Singer, Marilyn Albert, and John W. Rowe. 1997a. "Increase in urinary cortisol excretion and declines in memory: MacArthur Studies of Successful Aging," *Journal of Clinical Endocrinology & Metabolism* 82: 2458–2465.

Seeman, Teresa E. and Richard J. Robbins. 1994. "Aging and hypothalamic-pituitary-adrenal response to challenge in humans," *Endocrine Review* 15(2): 233–260.

Seeman, Teresa E., Burton Singer, John Rowe, Ralph I. Horwitz, and Bruce S. McEwen. 1997b. "The price of adaptation—Allostatic load and its health consequences: MacArthur Studies of Successful Aging," *Archives of Internal Medicine* 157: 2259–2268.

Seeman, Teresa E., Burton Singer, John Rowe, and Bruce McEwen. 2001. "Exploring a new concept of cumulative biological risk — Allostatic load and its health consequences: MacArthur Studies of Successful Aging," *Proceedings of the National Academy of Sciences USA*, 98(8): 4770–4775.

Seeman, Teresa E., Burton Singer, Carol Ryff, Gayle Dienberg Love, and Lene Levy-Storms. 2002. "Psychosocial factors and the development of allostatic load," *Psychosomatic Medicine* 64: 395–406.

Seeman, Teresa and Leonard S. Syme. 1987. "Social networks and coronary artery disease: A comparative analysis of network structural and support characteristics," *Psychosomatic Medicine* 49: 341–354.

Seeman, Teresa E., Jennifer Unger, Gail McAvay, and Mendes deLeon. 1999. "The role of self-efficacy beliefs in perceptions of functional disability: MacArthur Studies of Successful Aging," *Journal of Gerontology Psychological Sciences* 54A: P214–P222.

Shock, Nathan W. 1977. "Systems integration," in C. E. Finch and L. Hayflick (eds.), *Handbook of the Biology of Aging*. New York: Litton Educational Publishing, pp. 639–661.

Singer, Burton and Carol D. Ryff. 1999. "Hierarchies of life histories and associated health risks," *Annals of the New York Academy of Sciences* 896: 96–115.

Singer, Burton, Carol D. Ryff, and Teresa E. Seeman. 2004. "Allostasis, homeostasis, and the cost of physiological adaptation," in J. Schulkin (ed.), *Operationalizing Allostatic Load*. New York: Cambridge University Press, pp. 113–149.

Smith, James P. 1999. "Healthy bodies and thick wallets: The dual relation between health and economic status," *Journal of Economic Perspectives* 13: 145–166.

Smith, James P. and Raynard Kington. 1997. "Demographic and economic correlates of health in old age," *Demography* 34: 159–70.

Sorlie, Paul D., Eric Backlund, Norman J. Johnson, and Eugene Rogot. 1993. "Mortality by Hispanic status in the United States," *Journal of the American Medical Association* 270: 2464–2468.

Steenland, Kyle, Jane Henley, and Michael Thun. 2002. "All-cause and cause-specific death rates by educational status for 2 million people in two American Cancer Society cohorts, 1959–1996," *American Journal of Epidemiology* 156: 11–21.

Suthers, Kristen, Jung-Ki Kim, and Eileen Crimmins. 2003. "Life expectancy with cognitive impairment in the older population of the United States," *Journal of Gerontology: Social Science* 58B: S179–S186.

Trevisan, Maurizio, Jian Liu, Fadlalla B. Bahsas, and Alessandro Menotti for the Risk Factor and Life Expectancy Research Group. 1998. "Syndrome X and mortality: A population-based study," *American Journal of Epidemiology* 148: 958–966.

Unger, Jennifer, Gail McAvay, M. Bruce, Lisa F. Berkman, and Teresa E. Seeman. 1999. "Variation in the impact of social network characteristics on physical functioning in elderly persons: MacArthur Studies of Successful Aging," *Journal of Gerontology Social Science* 54B: S245–252.

Volpato Stefan, Suzanne G. Leveille, Maria-Chiara Corti, Tamara B. Harris, and Jack M. Guralnik. 2001. "The value of serum albumin and high-density lipoprotein cholesterol in defining mortality risk in older persons with low serum cholesterol," *Journal of the American Geriatrics Society* 49: 1142–1147.

Wamala, Sarah P., John Lynch, Horsten Myriam, Murray A. Mittleman, Karin Schenck-Gustafsson, and Kristina Orth-Gomer. 1999. "Education and the metabolic syndrome in women," *Diabetes Care* 22(12): 1999–2003.

Weaver, Jonathan, Mei H. Huang, Marilyn Albert, Tamara Harris, John Rowe, and Teresa E. Seeman. 2002. "Interleukin-6 as a predictor of cognitive function and cognitive decline: MacArthur Studies of Successful Aging," *Neurology* 59: 371–378.

Williams, David R. 1990. "Socioeconomic differentials in health: A review and redirection," *Social Psychology Quarterly* 53: 81–99.

Wilson, Craig J., Caleb E. Finch, and Harvey J. Cohen. 2002. "Cytokines and cognition—The case for a head-to-toe inflammatory paradigm," *Journal of the American Geriatrics Society* 50: 2041–2056.

Wilson, Peter W., Ralph B. D'Agostino, Daniel Levy, Albert M. Belanger, Halit Sibershatz, and William B. Kannel. 1998. "Prediction of coronary heart disease using risk factor categories," *Circulation* 97: 1837–1847.

Winkleby, Marilyn A., Catherine Cubbin, David K. Ahn and Helena C. Kraemer. 1999. "Pathways by which SES and ethnicity influence cardiovascular disease risk factors," *Annals of New York Academy of Science* 896: 191–209.

Winkleby, Marilyn A., Helena C. Kraemer, David K. Ahn, and Ann N. Varady. 1998. "Ethnic and socioeconomic differences in cardiovascular disease risk factors: Findings for women from the Third National Health and Nutrition Examination Survey, 1988–1994," *Journal of the American Medical Association* 280: 356–362

Wong, Melanie, and Eileen Crimmins. 2002. "Inequality in health: SES and race/ethnic patterns of biological risk," paper presented at the annual meetings of the Gerontological Society of America, November, Washington, DC.

Wong, Mitchell D., Martin F. Shapiro, W. John Boscardin, and Susan L. Ettner. 2002. "Contribution of major diseases to disparities in mortality," *New England Journal of Medicine* 347(20): 1585–1592.

Young, James B., John W. Rowe, Johanna A. Pallota, David Sparrow, Lewis Landsberg. 1980. "Enhanced plasma norepinephrine response to upright posture and oral glucose administration in elderly human subjects," *Metabolism* 29: 532–539.

Unraveling the SES–Health Connection

JAMES P. SMITH

People of lower socioeconomic status (SES) consistently appear to have much worse health outcomes.[1] No matter which measures of SES are used or how health is measured, the evidence that this association is large and pervasive across time and space is abundant (Marmot 1999; Smith 1999). To document its principal features, Figure 1 displays the main contours of the socioeconomic status health gradient in the United States by plotting at each age the fraction of people who self-report themselves in excellent or very good health by age-specific household income quartiles. Figure 2 plots the same fractions for people in poor or fair health.

Until the end of life, at each age every downward movement in income is associated with being in poorer health. Moreover, these health differences by income class can only be described as dramatically large. The fraction in excellent or very good health in the top income quartile is often 40 percentage points larger than the fraction in the lowest income quartile. In both Figures 1 and 2, there also exists a strong nonlinearity in the relation between income and health, with the largest health differences taking place between the lowest income quartile and all the others. Since this nonlinearity will prove to be important in resolving some of the key issues surrounding the SES health gradient, I return to it below. Finally, there is a distinct age pattern to the SES health gradient, with health disparities by income class expanding up to around age 50 years, after which the health gradient slowly fades away.[2] This age pattern will also be critical later in this chapter.

There is a broad consensus about the facts and about the key scientific and policy questions surrounding the SES health gradient—only the answers are controversial. Do these large differences in health by socioeconomic status indicators such as income largely reflect causation from SES to health, as many noneconomists appear to believe? Medical scientists are often convinced that the dominant situation is that variation in socioeconomic status produces large health disparities; their main debate is about why low economic status leads to poor health (Marmot 1999). Recent and often insight-

FIGURE 1   Percent reporting excellent or very good health status by age-specific household income quartiles

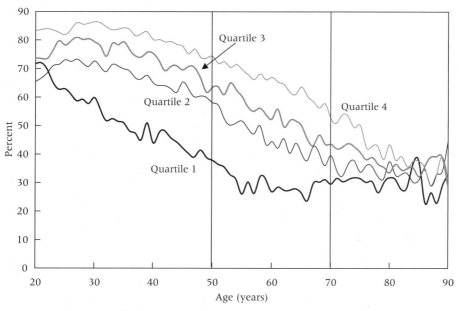

SOURCE: Calculations by author from the pooled National Health Interview Surveys 1991–96.

ful contributions by these scholars have investigated the influence of other factors besides access to high-quality health care or deleterious personal behaviors, both of which are believed to offer incomplete explanations. These contributions have instead emphasized long-term impacts of early childhood or even intrauterine environmental factors (Barker 1997), the cumulative effects of prolonged exposures to individual stressful events (Seeman et al. 1997), or reactions to macro-societal factors such as rising levels of income inequality (Wilkinson 1996) and discrimination (Krieger 1999).

While debate continues about competing reasons why SES may affect health, there is little recognition that the so-called reverse causation from health to economic status may be fundamental as well. Even if the direction of causation is that SES mainly affects health, what dimensions of SES actually matter: the financial aspects such as income or wealth, or nonfinancial dimensions like education? Finally, is there a life course component to the health gradient so that we may be misled in trying to answer these questions by looking only at people of a certain age—say those past 50?

This chapter, which is divided into four sections, provides my answers to these questions. The first section examines the issue of reverse causation or whether a new health event has a significant impact on four aspects of SES: out-of-pocket medical expenses, labor supply, household income, and household wealth. The next section switches the perspective by asking

FIGURE 2   Percent reporting fair or poor health status by age-specific household income quartiles

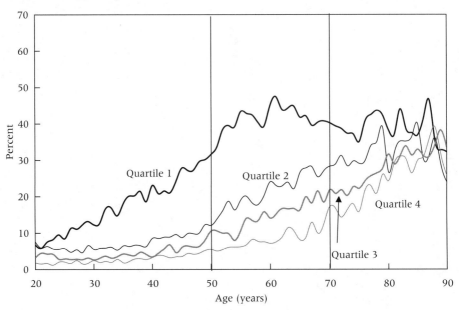

SOURCE: Calculations by author from the pooled National Health Interview Surveys 1991–96.

whether the so-called direct causation from SES to health really matters. Because the answer is yes, a subtheme in this section concerns which dimensions of SES—income, wealth, or education—matter for individual health. The answer to that question turns out to be education, and the third section deals with the much more difficult issue of why education matters so much. The evidence in these first three sections relies on data for people above age 50. Figures 1 and 2 suggest that the nature of the SES health gradient may be quite different after age 50 than before. In the final section I test the robustness of my answers to these basic questions about the meaning of the SES health gradient, using data that span the entire lifecourse.

Does health affect socioeconomic status?

The primary focus among epidemiologists and those in the health research community more generally has been on disentangling the multiple ways in which socioeconomic status may influence health outcomes. Consequently, much less is known about the possible impacts health may have on SES. But for many individuals, especially those who are middle aged, health feedbacks to labor supply, household income, or wealth may be quantitatively important. I explore this question by estimating the effect of new health events on subsequent outcomes that are both directly and indirectly related to SES. The outcomes investigated include out-of-pocket medical expenses, labor supply, household income, and wealth.

Before summarizing those results, I first outline the essential issues in estimating the effects of SES on health as well as the effects of health on SES. Current economic status and health reflect a dynamic history in which health (H_t) and SES (Y_t) are mutually affected by each other as well as by other relevant forces. Most of the relevant ideas can be summarized by the following two equations:

$$H_t = \alpha_0 + \alpha_1 H_{t-1} + \alpha_2 Y_{t-1} + \alpha_3 \Delta \hat{Y}_t + \alpha_4 X_{t-1} + u_{1t} \tag{1}$$

$$Y_t = \beta_0 + \beta_1 H_{t-1} + \beta_2 Y_{t-1} + \beta_3 \Delta \hat{H}_t + \beta_4 X_{t-1} + u_{2t} \tag{2}$$

where X_{t-1} represents a vector of other possibly nonoverlapping time- and non–time-varying factors influencing health and SES, and u_{1t} and u_{2t} are possibly correlated shocks to health and SES. The key parameters α_3 and β_3 measure the effects of new innovations of SES ($\Delta \hat{Y}_t$) on health and health on SES ($\Delta \hat{H}_t$) respectively. In this framework, we can also estimate whether past values of SES predict health ($\alpha_2 \neq 0$) or past values of health predict SES ($\beta_1 \neq 0$).[3]

While cross-sectional data can shed light on these issues, there are advantages to examining questions of causation with panel data. To estimate the "effect" of either (α_3 or β_3) on the other, we require exogenous variation in health (or SES) that is not induced by SES (health). In particular, this implies that it is not appropriate to use the complete between-period changes in health or SES to estimate these effects since such variation hopelessly confounds feedback effects.

In an earlier paper (Smith 1999), I proposed a research strategy for isolating new health events: the onset of new chronic conditions. While to some extent people may anticipate onset, much of the actual realization and especially its timing may be unanticipated. While new onsets may provide the best chance of isolating health shocks, not all new onset is a surprise. A set of behavioral risk factors and prior health or economic conditions may make some people more susceptible than others to this risk. Thus, predictors of new onsets should be included in models so as to increase one's confidence that the remaining statistical variation in new onsets is "news." I make a similar point in the next section in discussing the impact of SES on health.

A new health event in one year may affect medical expenditure, labor supply, and income not only in that year but in future years as well. For example, the onset of a new condition may induce only single-period changes in labor supply, after which labor supply may stabilize. But spillover effects of a health shock may further depress work effort in future years, or alternatively some recovery to original levels may take place. One way of estimating such patterns is to estimate a series of four equations for each of waves 2 through 5 of the Health and Retirement Study, summarizing changes in each outcome between adjacent waves (say labor supply L_t) as

$$\Delta L_t = \alpha X + \sum_{t-2}^{5} \beta_t \Delta H_t$$

where L_t is the between-wave change in labor supply and H_t the within-period health event from period t to $t-1$. Similar equations would apply for household income, out-of-pocket medical expenses, and other outcomes. If there is only a contemporaneous one-period effect of health events, all lagged values of changes in health will be zero.

The research I summarize here uses the first five waves of data on health status and transitions, medical expenses, labor supply, income, and wealth accumulation from the Health and Retirement Study (HRS). HRS is a national sample of about 7,600 American households (12,654 individuals) with at least one person in the household aged 51–61 years originally interviewed in the fall of 1992 and winter of 1993. The principal objective of HRS is to monitor economic transitions in work, income, and wealth, as well as changes in many dimensions of health status. Follow-ups of HRS respondents were fielded at two-year intervals. HRS instruments span the range of behaviors of interest: on the economic side, work, income, and wealth; on the functional side, health and functional status, disability, and medical expenditures.

In addition to its excellent array of economic variables, HRS measured many aspects of respondents' health. These included self-reports of general health status, the prevalence and incidence of many chronic conditions, the extent of functional limitations, and out-of-pocket and total health care expenditures. The chronic diseases asked about include hypertension, diabetes, cancer, chronic lung disease, heart problems (e.g., heart attack, angina, coronary heart disease, congestive heart failure), stroke, and arthritis. In addition, risk behaviors include current and past smoking, current and past drinking, self-reported height and weight (BMI), and exercise.

To calculate the impact of the onset of new health events, I estimated a parallel set of models predicting out-of-pocket medical expenses, changes in labor supply, and changes in household income. A vector of baseline attributes is included in all models, including baseline measures of birth cohort (or age), marital status, race, ethnicity, education, region of residence, quintiles of family income, and most importantly an extensive vector of measures of baseline health. These health measures include dummies for four of the five categories of self-reported health status, the presence at baseline of each chronic condition, a set of behavioral risk factors (smoking, exercise, BMI, drinking), and a scaled index of functional limitations based on the answers to the questions about activities of daily living.

I divided new health shocks into two categories—major (cancer, heart disease, and diseases of the lung) and minor (all the rest). My results for health shocks that took place between the first and second wave of HRS are summarized in Table 1.[4] The columns represent the principal outcomes of interest (medical expenses, labor supply, and household income) while the rows trace the evolving impact of this health shock across the HRS waves. The final row summarizes the full impact of the health event across all five waves.

A severe health shock that occurred between waves 1 and 2 of HRS initially increased mean out-of-pocket medical expenses by $1,720 during the two-year interval in which it happened. This same health event also produced future increases in health costs that were of progressively smaller amounts. By the fifth wave, the mean total cost was a little over $4,000 so that less than half of the incremental costs were borne around the time of the event. All of these impacts on out-of-pocket medical expenses were much smaller when the health event was minor.[5]

Similar to the time pattern of effects documented for out-of-pocket medical expenses, the onset of a new severe health shock has the immediate and large impact of reducing the probability of working, followed by diminishing ripple-like effects in subsequent waves. To illustrate, a severe health event between the first and second wave of HRS reduced the probability of work by 15 percentage points between the two waves. Since the average labor force participation rate at baseline among those who were

TABLE 1 Impacts during waves 2–5 of a new health shock occurring between waves 1 and 2

Wave	Out-of-pocket medical expenses ($)	Work probability	Household income ($)
Major health shock			
2	1,720	–.148	–4,033
3	1,037	–.054	–1,258
4	893	–.030	–658
5	503	–.036	–269
Total	4,153	–.268	–6,258
Minor health shock			
2	175	–.041	–498
3	313	–.036	–988
4	160	–.017	–44
5	567	–.013	–169
Total	1,215	–.107	–1,699

SOURCE: Calculations by author from first five waves of the US Health and Retirement Study.

about to experience this major health event was .55, the impact on work is decidedly not trivial. Once again, estimated incremental effects in subsequent years cascade downward so that by the end of HRS wave 5, the probability of work had declined by about 27 percentage points as a result of a major health shock between waves 1 and 2. Just as was reported for medical costs, estimated effects are considerably smaller if the health events come under the minor label.

Not surprisingly, given the labor force results just described, new health events also depress household income, with the reduction larger when the shock is major. There is no evidence of household income recovery in subsequent years, so that the initial income losses persist. In fact, consistent with the labor force participation effects, additional diminishing income losses occur in subsequent waves. The final row in Table 1 presents the total household income loss associated with the health event. On average, by the end of wave 5 total household income is about $6,300 lower when a major health event was experienced between the first and second waves of HRS. The comparable estimate for a minor health event was about $1,700.

Income losses that persist over time can eventually accumulate into large sums indeed. The first rows in Table 2 (for major health events) and Table 3 (for minor health events) contain my estimates of the cumulative income loss associated with the onset of health events occurring between the HRS waves. To illustrate, by wave 5 a health event that took place between the first two waves of HRS led to a total loss in household income of almost $37,000. These losses in household income are typically far larger than any cumulative out-of-pocket medical expenses associated with the health event. For example, for the wave 1–2 major health shock, the out-of-pocket medical expenses of about $4,000 are only one-ninth of the total household income loss. While lower for the severe health shocks that took place between the other waves of HRS, cumulative income losses typically

TABLE 2 Cumulative impact of a new major health event taking place between

	W1–W2 ($)	W2–W3 ($)	W3–W4 ($)	W4–W5 ($)
HRS sample				
Cumulative income loss	−36,884	−13,828	−6,856	−3,601
Cumulative income loss + out-of-pocket expenses + lost interest	−48,941	−19,388	−9,805	−5,901
AHEAD sample				
Cumulative income loss + out-of-pocket expenses + lost interest	−11,347	−3,553	−3,005	

SOURCE: Calculations by author from first five waves of the US Health and Retirement Study and the first four waves of US AHEAD Survey.

TABLE 3 Cumulative impact of new minor health event taking place
between

	W1–W2 ($)	W2–W3 ($)	W3–W4 ($)	W4–W5 ($)
HRS sample				
Cumulative income loss	–8,727	–8,811	–6,949	351
Cumulative income loss + increased expenses + lost interest	–11,544	–11,584	–8,610	–316
AHEAD sample				
Cumulative income loss + increased expenses + lost interest		5,926	–6,838	–702

SOURCE: Calculations by author from first five waves of the US Health and Retirement Study and the first four waves of US AHEAD Survey.

exceed cumulative medical expenses by a large single-digit integer. Once again, cumulative household income losses are much smaller when the health event is minor, but even in this case income losses far exceed the additional medical expenses.

Table 2 also includes the same summary measures of household income loss and cumulative medical expenses obtained from the same models estimated using the original AHEAD sample, a sample of respondents who were at least age 70 at baseline. Given the predominance of retirement and virtually universal coverage by Medicare in the AHEAD sample, not surprisingly changes in household income and out-of-pocket medical expenses triggered by a new health event, whether major or minor, are considerably smaller. There is much less possibility of income loss since most AHEAD respondents' income is annutized either through Social Security or through private pensions and thus is not contingent on changes in health status (Smith and Kington 1997). These much smaller feedbacks from health to several SES measures in AHEAD serve as a warning that the magnitude of any causal effects from health to SES may vary a good deal over the life course. I return to this issue in the penultimate section.

The lifetime budget constraint linking consumption, income, wealth, and savings implies that this sum of period-by-period income loss plus medical expenses (adjusted by the forgone interest on this money) represents one way of measuring the wealth change or dis-savings that took place across the first five waves of HRS owing to the health shocks.[6] This measure of lost wealth is listed in the second rows of Tables 2 and 3. My estimates of the reduction in wealth due to a new health event are not trivial—for a new major health shock between the first and second HRS wave it is almost $50,000. Given the much smaller income losses involved, estimated wealth losses are considerably smaller when the health events are minor and when estimated for the older AHEAD sample.

These numbers in Tables 2 and 3 can be used to illustrate the macro-economic losses due to new bad health events. In the HRS sample (those ages 51–61 at baseline), about one-fifth of respondents experienced a major health event during the next eight years and another 30 percent had a minor health event. Since there were approximately 35 million Americans in that age range, this implies that about 7 million persons will have a serious onset and 10.5 million a minor onset. The total costs in the household sector alone of the serious onsets that took place within the eight-year window would be 350 billion dollars. Since the total costs of the minor onsets would be 121 billion, the combined economic costs of these health events are a little less than 500 billion dollars. While these numbers are only illustrative, they do suggest that the economic benefits from better health among those in their 50s can translate into very large numbers, even when only the narrow dollar metric of economics is used. Moreover, these aggregate economic costs associated with new onsets of bad health will likely grow rapidly in the future as the numbers of Americans at risk for these health onsets expands with the aging of the baby boom generations.

What then have we learned? First, at least among people in their 50s, pathways from health to the financial measures of socioeconomic status are decidedly not trivial. Especially as time unfolds, new health events have a quantitatively large impact on work, income, and wealth. This pathway should not be viewed as a sideshow to the main event. Second, the principal risk people face when poor health arrives is not the medical expenses they must pay but rather the currently not fully insured loss of work and income. Finally, not all health events are alike. My estimates have produced quantitatively different effects of the health events labeled major compared to those that are minor ones.

Does socioeconomic status affect health?

Finding evidence of significant feedbacks from new health events to several key measures of socioeconomic status does not negate the likelihood that the probability of experiencing the onset of a new health event is not uniform across several SES dimensions. I explore the pathway from SES to health by examining whether the onset of new chronic conditions is related to levels of household income, wealth, and education, once one specifies a set of preexisting demographic and health conditions.[7] I also explore the extent to which innovation in economic status "causes" health.

These models again include as covariates a vector of baseline health conditions of the respondent: self-reported general health status, the presence of a chronic condition at baseline, and the extent of functional limitations scale. The models also include a standard set of behavioral risk factors (currently a smoker, number of cigarettes smoked), whether one engages in vigorous exercise, body mass index, and a standard set of demographic controls: birth cohort, race, ethnicity, sex, and region of residence. My main interest, however, lies in the SES measures that include household income, baseline levels of and changes in household wealth, and respondent's education.[8] Strictly speaking, the ability of past histories of income and wealth to predict future health onsets does not imply causality since there may remain observed factors correlated with these past histories of household financial resources and with health trajectories. However, it is likely that most of these unobserved factors are positively correlated both with higher financial resources and with better health so that the absence of any predictive effects of SES on health is very informative.

Just as one needed innovations in health that were not caused by SES to estimate the impact of health on SES, so it is necessary to isolate innovations in SES that were not caused by health to estimate the impact of SES on health. One opportunity for doing so lies in the large wealth increases that were accumulated during the stock market surge in the United States during the 1990s. Given the unusually large gains in the stock market during these years, it is reasonable to posit that a good deal of this surge was unanticipated and thus captures unanticipated exogenous wealth increases that were not caused by a person's health. If financial measures of SES do improve health, such increases in stock market wealth should be associated with better subsequent health outcomes, at least with a lag.[9]

Knowing which aspect of SES affects health is key to the policy debate that surrounds the issue of the SES health gradient. For example, consider the extreme where all pathways from SES to health operate through education and none through the primary financial measures of SES, namely income or wealth. If that were so, then policies directed at income redistribution, while perhaps desirable on their own terms, could not be justified in terms of any beneficial impact on health. Combining all dimensions of SES into a single construct basically precludes discussion of most of the policy-relevant options.[10]

The results from these models, reported in Table 4, are provided for onsets of major and minor conditions and for each chronic disease separately. A consistent generalization can be made for household income—it never predicts future onsets of either minor or major health conditions. In no single case is the estimated coefficient on household income (which vacillates in sign) statistically significant. While the coefficients on wealth lean toward negative values (5 out of 7), in only one case (stroke) is a statistically significant negative result obtained for household wealth. Finally, my best measure of an exogenous wealth change—the wealth increase from the stock market—is statistically significant in only one instance (arthritis), and there it has the incorrect sign so that an increase in stock market wealth makes the onset of arthritis more likely. In sum then, SES variables that

TABLE 4 Probits predicting the future onset of specific chronic conditions

SES indicator	Any major condition		Any minor condition	
	Estimate	Chi square	Estimate	Chi square
Income	0.0111	0.06	−0.0063	0.03
Wealth	−0.0046	2.26	−0.0005	0.05
12–15 years schooling	−0.1108	7.78	−0.0912	5.96
College or more	−0.0844	2.43	−0.1588	10.26
Change in stock wealth	−0.0004	0.44	0.0004	0.88
	Cancer		**Hypertension**	
	Estimate	Chi square	Estimate	Chi square
Income	0.0130	0.05	0.0153	0.11
Wealth	−0.0030	0.53	−0.0032	1.01
12–15 years schooling	0.0008	0.00	−0.0675	2.45
College or more	0.0567	0.61	−0.0623	1.17
Change in stock wealth	0.0003	0.32	−0.0001	0.11
	Diseases of the lung		**Diabetes**	
	Estimate	Chi square	Estimate	Chi square
Income	−0.0271	0.12	0.0382	0.40
Wealth	−0.0067	1.13	−0.0023	0.29
12–15 years schooling	−0.1920	10.32	−0.1153	4.82
College or more	−0.1432	2.67	−0.0777	1.11
Change in stock wealth	0.0006	1.13	−0.0023	1.37
	Heart disease		**Arthritis**	
	Estimate	Chi square	Estimate	Chi square
Income	−0.0447	0.64	−0.0069	0.03
Wealth	0.0015	0.19	0.0000	0.00
12–15 years schooling	−0.1086	5.10	−0.0819	4.29
College or more	−0.0519	0.62	−0.1857	12.14
Change in stock wealth	−0.0012	1.36	0.0006	2.41
	Stroke			
	Estimate	Chi square		
Income	0.0683	0.70		
Wealth	−0.0175	3.83		
12–15 years schooling	−0.0390	0.36		
College or more	−0.0746	0.59		
Change in stock wealth	−0.0017	0.57		

NOTE: Models also control for presence of baseline health (self-reported health status, functional limitations, and the existence of specific chronic conditions) and a standard set of health risk factors (smoking, drinking, and BMI). In addition, sex, race, ethnicity, and region of residence are included. Income and wealth measured in $100,000 of dollars.
SOURCE: Calculations by author from first five waves of the US Health and Retirement Study.

directly measure or proxy for family's financial resources are either not related or at best only weakly related to the future onset of disease over the time span of eight years.

This largely negative conclusion is in sharp contrast to the results obtained for the final SES measure, education. Additional schooling is strongly and statistically significantly predictive of the new onset of both major and minor disease over the first five waves of the HRS. In all cases except cancer (which looks like an equal opportunity disease), the effects of schooling are preventative against disease onset.

This moves us to the most perplexing question of all: why does education matter so much in the promotion of good health? To provide insight on this question, I ran expanded versions of these models that included proxies for some of the most frequently mentioned reasons about why education might matter. The proxies available in the HRS included measures of cognition and memory, past health behaviors such as smoking and drinking, job-related environmental hazards, early-life health outcomes and economic environments, parental education, and parental health.[11]

Within this list of expanded variables, the only ones that mattered in terms of their statistical significance and in reducing the size of the effects of education were the current self-evaluation of childhood health and economic status and parental health as measured by age of death of each parent. These results are summarized in Table 5. For the major health onsets, both self-assessed better health status and better economic status during childhood reduce the risk of incurring a serious health onset in one's 50s and early 60s even after controlling for current health and economic status. In their support for the delayed health impact of early childhood exposures, these results are consistent with the research reported by Barker (1997), although his specific hypotheses related to the intrauterine environments. In the minor onset specification in Table 5, measures of parental health make a difference. Having a living parent or having a parent who was older when he or she died tends to reduce the likelihood of the onset of new chronic conditions at these ages. Whether this association between parental health and health during one's 50s reflects genetic factors, shared household economic and health environments during childhood, or something else would be speculative at the stage of our knowledge. Since the impact of education remains after including these variables in Table 5, my overall conclusion is that collectively these additional factors explain some but by no means all of education's ability to predict the future onset of a chronic condition.

Another clue to why education may be so critical concerns the role it plays in self-management of disease (Goldman and Smith 2002). A positive trend in recent decades has been the development of many new effective therapies for disease management. While clearly beneficial, these therapies can often be complicated and difficult for patients to fully adhere to, and

TABLE 5 Probits predicting the future onset of major and minor chronic conditions

SES indicator	Major condition		Minor condition	
	Estimate	Chi square	Estimate	Chi square
Income	0.0456	0.93	−0.0044	0.00
Wealth	−0.0040	1.60	−0.0001	0.00
Change in stock wealth	−0.0008	1.06	0.0003	0.75
12–15 years schooling	−0.0783	2.66	−0.0527	1.38
College or more	−0.0483	0.52	−0.0927	2.33
Health excellent or very good as child	−0.0870	4.68	0.0042	0.01
Not poor during childhood	−0.0949	6.31	0.0155	0.20
Mother's education	0.0028	0.18	0.0004	0.00
Father's education	−0.0018	0.09	−0.0046	0.72
Father alive	−0.1362	1.34	−0.2001	3.32
Age of father at death	−0.0001	0.00	−0.0014	0.88
Mother alive	−0.0743	0.49	−0.2465	6.51
Age of mother at death	−0.0002	0.09	−0.0028	4.60

NOTE: Models also control for presence of baseline health (self-reported health status, functional limitations, and the existence of specific chronic condition) and a standard set of health risk factors (smoking, drinking, and BMI). In addition, sex, race, ethnicity, and region of residence are included. Income and wealth measured in $100,000 of dollars.
SOURCE: Calculations by author from first five waves of the US Health and Retirement Study.

consequently for treatment of many diseases adherence rates are often alarmingly low. The question Goldman and I asked was what role education played in self-management.

I illustrate our findings with one of the diseases we investigated, diabetes.[12] New treatments for diabetes are known to be efficacious, but the treatment places great demands on a patient's ability to self-monitor his or her condition. One study we did was based on a major clinical trial: the Diabetes Control and Complications Trial. In the trial, patients with type 1 diabetes were randomized into treatment and control groups. The treatment arm involved an intensive regimen in which there was close self and external monitoring of blood glucose levels and encouragement of strict adherence. In particular, patients in the treatment arm were seen weekly until a stable treatment program was achieved. While not insignificant, the treatment in the control arm consisted of a more standard regimen and far less intrusive external monitoring of patients.

Table 6 shows that before the intervention there were large differences across education groups in several measures of good behaviors. For measures such as checking blood, following insulin regimens, exercise, or smoking, those with less education were not doing as well. Given these initial but unsurprising baseline differences by education in adherence to good

TABLE 6 Educational differences in treatment adherence at Diabetes Control and Complications Trial baseline

Measure of adherence	Post-graduate degree	College graduate/ some college	HS degree/ some secondary
Number of times self-monitored blood glucose per week	8.8	7.7	6.7
Missed insulin injection at least once in past month (%)	4.3	6.0	9.2
Did not follow insulin regimen at least once in past month (%)	15.7	25.2	26.6
Did not self-test blood or urine at least one day in past month (%)	66.1	74.1	77.2
Minutes of very hard exercise per week	58.1	49.6	19.7
Currently smoking cigarettes (%)	16.5	19.2	40.8

SOURCE: Goldman and Smith (2002).

practice, we hypothesized that imposing a good behavior regimen—which is essentially what the rigorous treatment regimen did—would impart more benefits to the less educated, who were having more problems with treatment to begin with.

We used an objective health outcome measure in the trial—glycosolated hemoglobin, which measures the amount of sugar binding to the blood. Higher levels indicated worse control. The impact of enforcing a common treatment regime can be obtained by subtracting what normally would occur (the control sample) from what took place under an enforced treatment regimen (the treatment sample). The data in Table 7 demonstrate that while persons in all education groups benefited from being in the treatment arm, the benefits from enforced better adherence relative to the control group were largest for the least educated (see the final row in Table 7). Thus, a differential ability to adhere to beneficial albeit complicated medical regimens appears to be one reason for the association between education and health outcomes for the chronically ill.

In our study, Goldman and I also provided evidence on why education might matter for adherence. Once again, two factors that did not matter in promoting better adherence were household income and having a better memory. By contrast, higher-level aspects of abstract reasoning, which included the ability to internalize the future consequences of current decisions, appeared to promote adherence.

Additional research on why education matters greatly should receive high priority. One possibility is that the education experience itself is simply a marker for personal traits (reasoning ability, rates of time preference, etc.) that may lead people to acquire more education and to be healthier. But education may also help train people in decisionmaking, problem solv-

TABLE 7   Educational differences in treatment impact for diabetics

Group	Glycosolated hemoglobin		
	Post-graduate degree	College graduate/ some college	HS degree/ some secondary
Conventional therapy only (n=495)			
Baseline	8.42	8.76	8.96
End of study	8.88	9.08	9.59
Difference	0.46	0.32	0.63
Intensive treatment only (n=490)			
Baseline	8.04	8.86	8.93
End of study	7.18	7.30	7.43
Difference	−0.85	−1.56	1.51
Treatment effect[a]	−1.31	−1.88*	2.14**

*p<.10; **p<.05
[a]Treatment effect is the improvement in glycemic control among the intensive treatment group relative to conventional therapy. Significance levels are for a test of equivalence with the postgraduate category and control for duration in study, sex, marital status, and age.
SOURCE: Goldman and Smith (2002).

ing, adaptive skills, and forward-looking behavior, all of which have fairly direct applications to a healthier life. Education may well have biological effects on the brain, which result in improved cognitive function and problem-solving ability, some of which may impart benefits to choices made regarding one's health. This is similar to the argument that more active brain functioning at a young age delays the onset of dementia.

The SES health gradient and the life course

The steady negative progression in health and disease as we age is well established. Long before age 51, the minimum age entry point for the HRS samples on which the previous analyses are based, a slow but accelerating decline in average health status has taken place. Less well established is the shape of the SES health gradient across age groups. Imagine that all we knew about the SES health gradient is what the AHEAD sample (originally those over age 70) or the HRS sample (originally those aged 51–61) was able to tell us. In Figures 1 and 2, in the AHEAD sample we would only observe that portion of the graph above age 70, which is demarcated by the vertical solid line at that age. While we would begin with an income–health gradient among the youngest AHEAD respondents, what we really would be monitoring is the demise of the gradient. Indeed, among the oldest AHEAD respondents, there is hardly any income gradient to health.

Since most health differences with income are disappearing, it should not surprise us in this sample that income does not affect health. When we add the age groups contained in the other HRS cohorts so that the data consist of the age groups past 50 (indicated by another vertical solid line), the income gradient with health stands out more clearly. But all we might really have done is to add additional ages to our illustration of the demise of the health–income gradient.

We know from Figures 1 and 2 that ages before 50 are very much the mirror image (now expanding with age) of what happens subsequently. It is legitimate to ask whether conclusions drawn about the meaning of the SES health gradient over ages during which the gradient is withering away will generalize to the whole life course, especially to those ages during which it is emerging.

To address this question, I first use the Panel Study of Income Dynamics (PSID), which has gathered almost 30 years of extensive economic and demographic data on a nationally representative sample of approximately 5,000 (original) families and 35,000 members of those families. PSID is recognized as the premier general-purpose survey measuring several key aspects of SES. Details on family income and its components have been gathered in each wave since the inception of PSID in 1967. Starting in 1984 and in five-year intervals until 1999, PSID has asked a set of questions to measure household wealth.

Although not traditionally known as a health survey, PSID has been collecting information on self-reported general health status (the standard five-point scale from excellent to poor) since 1984. Starting in 1999 and for subsequent waves, PSID has obtained information on the prevalence and incidence of chronic conditions for the respondent and spouse: heart disease, stroke, heart attack, hypertension, cancer, diabetes, chronic lung disease, asthma, arthritis, and emotional, nervous, or psychiatric problems. In addition to the prevalence in 1999, individuals were asked the date of onset of the condition and whether it limited their normal daily activities. The time of the onset of a health shock can be identified (keeping in mind issues related to recall bias), and the impact of these new health events on labor supplies, income, and wealth can be estimated.[13]

PSID offers several key additions to the research agenda. First, as the data provided in Figure 1 suggest, the nature of the SES health gradient may vary considerably over the life cycle. In contrast to HRS, PSID spans all age groups, allowing us to examine behavior over the complete life cycle. Labor-supply effects induced by new health events may be particularly sensitive to life-cycle stage: for example, following shocks that occur in the late 50s or early 60s individuals may select an option they would have chosen in a few years anyway—retirement. Second, the long-term nature of PSID allows one to estimate the impact of health and SES innovations over long periods of time, even decades. It may well be that health responds to changes in financial measures of SES but only after a considerable lag.

Table 8 displays information on onset of major and minor chronic conditions in four age groups. Onsets during the previous 15 years are placed into three five-year windows—1994–99, 1989–93, and 1984–88. Both in cross-section (reading across a row) and within cohort (reading up a column) disease onset increases rapidly with age. While less common than for those in the HRS age ranges, health episodes for PSID respondents less than 50 years old are not negligible. Among those in their 40s in the 1999 wave, 13 percent had previously had a major disease onset at some time in their lives, and 39 percent have a minor chronic health condition. In the five years before 1999, 7 percent of these 40-year-olds experienced a major disease onset while 23 percent reported a new minor onset.

Table 9 lists the estimated impacts of a new major health onset that took place between 1995 and 1999 on three outcomes: the probability of continuing to work, the change in household income, and the change in household net worth. To detect the possibility of an age pattern, I present the impacts of the major health events for three age groups, all measured in 1994.[14] The most unambiguous results apply to labor supply, where the largest impact of a new severe health shock takes place among those in their 50s or early 60s. This may not be surprising since people in the preretirement years may be simply quickening the inevitable movement into retirement. While there are legitimate questions about robustness of results since income and household wealth are much harder to measure and the timing of onset given the use of retrospective data less certain, it appears that the largest impact on family income and wealth also occurs among those aged

TABLE 8   Percent experiencing an onset of major and minor conditions by age

| | Age group (years) | | | |
	Less than 41	41–50	51–61	Over 61
Major onset				
1994–99	3.9	7.2	12.9	26.0
1989–93	1.5	3.4	6.9	12.0
1984–88	0.6	1.4	4.2	6.0
1999 major prevalence	7.0	13.3	26.1	46.0
Minor onset				
1994–99	12.2	23.1	28.8	30.3
1989–93	3.9	10.4	16.7	23.7
1984–88	1.7	3.9	8.0	12.6
1999 minor prevalence	17.9	38.6	54.7	72.6

SOURCE: Calculations by author from 1999 PSID.

TABLE 9   Impacts of a new major health shock, 1995–99

Impact	Ages (years)		
	Less than 51	51–61	Over 61
Change in employment	–0.084	–0.307	–0.202
Change in family income	–488	–2,731	–107
Change in net worth	–2,889	–8,789	–1,507

SOURCE: Calculations by author from the US Panel Survey of Income Dynamics.

51–61 years. The offsetting factor to this ranking may be that disease onsets at a younger age affect people for a longer period of time so that their impacts, while smaller when measured in a set time interval, have the potential to grow over longer periods of time.

PSID can also be used to investigate the effect of SES on health across the full life course. Table 10 summarizes my results predicting future onset of major chronic conditions. Following the HRS format, I use three financial measures of SES: baseline levels of household income and household wealth and the increase in stock wealth observed over the period covered by the health shock. Consistent with the time frame allowed by the wealth

TABLE 10   Does SES predict future major disease onsets? (ages 21 years and older—PSID)

SES indicator	First 1–5 years		6–10 years		11–15 years	
1984 baseline						
Income	0.0013	(1.39)	0.0010	(0.11)	–0.0080	(1.14)
Wealth	0.0002	(0.54)	0.0001	(0.32)	0.0003	(0.97)
Change in stock wealth	0.0020	(0.74)	0.0001	(0.10)	0.0006	(2.40)
12–15 years schooling	–0.1217	(1.25)	–0.2160	(2.82)	–0.1312	(1.94)
College or more	–0.2834	(2.14)	–0.3238	(3.02)	–0.2888	(3.09)
1989 baseline						
Income	0.0016	(0.25)	–0.0030	(0.71)		
Wealth	–0.0007	(0.76)	0.0004	(1.11)		
Change in stock wealth	0.0010	(0.51)	0.0006	(2.30)		
12–15 years schooling	–0.1971	(2.73)	–0.1489	(2.30)		
College or more	–0.3170	(3.22)	–0.2743	(3.09)		
1994 baseline						
Income	–0.0089	(1.91)				
Wealth	0.0005	(1.21)				
Change in stock wealth	0.0004	(1.28)				
12–15 years schooling	–0.1387	(2.27)				
College or more	–0.1844	(2.18)				

NOTE: Financial variables expressed in $10,000. z statistics based on robust standard errors.
SOURCE: Calculations by author from the US Panel Survey of Income Dynamics.

modules, three time periods are used with alternative baseline years: 1984, 1989, and 1994. The occurrence of major health events is measured over five-year intervals.

These results closely parallel those obtained for the older populations represented by the HRS and AHEAD. Whether one looks at the relatively short horizon of the next five years or more than a decade ahead, all three financial measures of SES are very poor predictors of future health outcomes. While not shown in Table 10, this conclusion remains when longer lag structures of income are included in the model. Since these longer lag structures are an approximation to permanent income, the lack of predictability of income is not because transitory measures of income are being used. These longer-horizon PSID results on financial measures of SES are quite powerful in that they partly respond to the objection that one may have controlled for most of the indirect effects of SES by conditioning on baseline attributes. In this case, the conditioning variables are sometimes measured more than a decade earlier.

Once again, I do not imply that SES cannot predict future health events: education is a statistically significant predictor across both short and long horizons. To me it is nothing short of remarkable that even after one controls for an extensive array of current health conditions, persons with less schooling are much more likely to experience the onset of a major negative health shock—effects that persist into old age.

The basic question is whether our main conclusion about the dominance of education over financial measures of SES is sustained when we consider the complete life course. To place the issue in perspective, Figure 3 plots the education gradient for those in fair or poor health in the same manner as Figure 2 did for income. In several key dimensions, the income and education health gradients are quite similar. Whether stratified by income or education, higher SES is associated with better health, a relationship that first expands with age up to around age 50 and then contracts, and one that is highly nonlinear with the lowest SES group in much worse health than all the others. But there are some differences as well. Most important, unlike income the education health gradient is more persistent and never fully disappears at either very old or very young ages.

Given the strong correlation of income and education, the question of whether the SES health gradient is due to income or education requires examining them jointly. Those in lower SES groups are more likely not to be married, which alone produces lower family incomes. To control for this confounding factor, I limit samples in what follows to married individuals. Figure 4 displays the health gradient by income quartile among those with 0–11 years of schooling. Now the strong income effects that were present especially at younger ages—say below age 50—virtually disappear with one key exception: those in the lowest income quartile remain in much worse

FIGURE 3   Percent reporting fair or poor health status by education

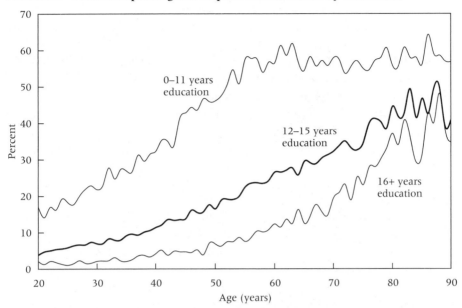

SOURCE: Calculations by author from the pooled National Health Interview Surveys 1991–96.

FIGURE 4   Percent of married male respondents with 0–11 years of education reporting fair or poor health status by age-specific income quartiles

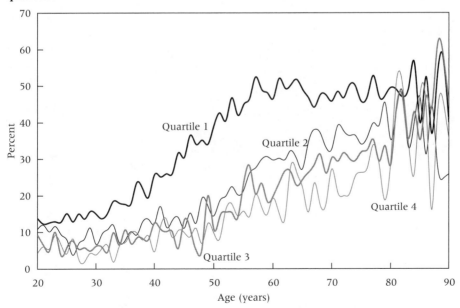

SOURCE: Calculations by author from the pooled National Health Interview Surveys 1986–96.

health. While not shown here, the same story applies to the other two education groups, those with 12–15 or 16-plus years of schooling.

Why is the bottom income quartile so distinct as a signal of poor health even after controlling for education? A clue is contained in Figure 5, which plots for those with 0–11 years of schooling the fraction who are not working within each income quartile. The basic age pattern is not surprising, with labor force participation rates declining rapidly during ages 50–65 as retirement looms. Comparing Figures 4 and 5, the patterns across income quartiles are remarkably similar. There is not much difference among the top three income quartiles, but the bottom income quartile stands apart. Even at relatively young ages—30s and 40s—a large fraction of those in the bottom income quartile are not working, strongly suggesting that their low incomes are a consequence of not working.

Why are so many people in the lowest income quartile not in the labor force even in the prime of their lives? Figure 6 completes the circle and provides the answer. This graph plots within education groups the fraction in fair or poor health by their labor force status. Those who are not working are much more likely to report being in poor or fair health. At age 50, for example, 70 percent of those not working report themselves in either poor or fair health—a figure some 40 percentage points larger than among those who are working.[15]

FIGURE 5 Percent of married male respondents with 0–11 years of education, not working in labor force, by age-specific family income quartile

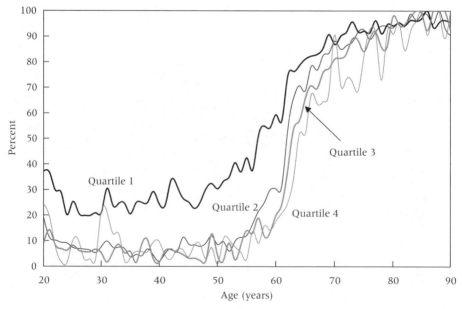

SOURCE: Calculations by author from the pooled National Health Interview Surveys 1986–96.

FIGURE 6   Percent of married male respondents in poor or fair health by whether or not they are currently working

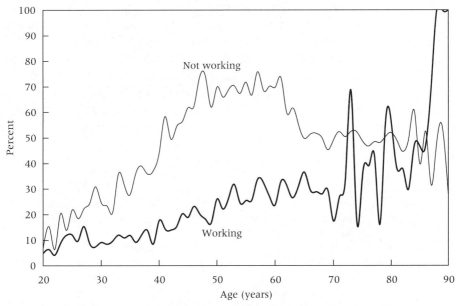

SOURCE: Calculations by author from the pooled National Health Interview Surveys 1986–96. Sample is limited to those with 0–11 years of schooling in the lowest income quartile.

Conclusion

In this chapter, I reexamined one of the most important and mysterious social science issues of the day: the substantial gradient of health according to socioeconomic status. My midterm report based on my personal voyage of discovery is this. First, I found that causal pathways from health to financial measures of SES are very important: new serious health events have a quantitatively large impact on work, income, and wealth. The current literature mistakenly tends to downplay this pathway. SES also affects future health outcomes, although the primary factor here is years of schooling and not an individual's financial resources.

Contrary to widespread and deeply held beliefs within the policy and research community, my empirical evidence demonstrated that the principal financial measures of SES—household income and household wealth— do not seem to be related to individual health outcomes. But in research, one finding always begets another puzzle. There is growing evidence, including some presented here, that measures of economic circumstances during childhood have a bearing on health outcomes later in life. Parental incomes appear to be central correlates of the onset of some critical childhood diseases, which then set the stage for the adult SES health gradient (see the excellent discussion in Case, Lubotsky, and Paxson 2002; Case, Fertig, and Paxon 2004; Smith 2004). In a more historical vein, certain months of birth that coincide with the nutritional benefits of the agricultural cycle are associated with added years of life even at older ages (Doblhammer and Vaupel 2001). Why is health apparently so sensitive to financial resources in the early years of life, an influence that then disappears as we age? While the influence of money may dissipate, the impact of how we are stratified by other aspects of SES decidedly does not. Whatever the origins of this stratification, it has profound implications for population health, where the consequences are serious and where the core reasons remain a mystery.

Notes

This research was generously supported by grants from the National Institute on Aging. This chapter was presented at seminars at the University of California, Berkeley and Princeton University, where very helpful comments were received.

1 Socioeconomic status (SES) is defined as any one of several composite measures of social rank, usually including income, education, and occupational prestige.

2 Similar conclusions were reached by Case and Deaton (2002).

3 For an insightful debate about the conditions under which coefficients that are zero or stationary also reveal something about causality, see the paper by Adams et al. (2003) and the comments on that paper in the same volume.

4 Health shocks that took place between the other HRS waves had similar types of effects and thus are not repeated here. See Smith (2003) for more details on the full set of impacts.

5 The estimates in Table 1 summarize mean impacts. Effects of new health shocks on the tails of the out-of-pocket medical expense distribution were much larger (see Smith 2003).

6 The only component not included in this wealth loss measure is any change in household consumption other than medical expenses. Smith (1999) outlines the conditions under which other total household consumption increases or decreases as the result of a new medical event.

7 A controversy that has occupied a substantial part of the recent literature has investigated the hypothesis attributed to Wilkinson (1996) that measures of societal levels such as income inequality affect individual-level health. For an excellent review and critique of the theoretical and empirical literature on this hypothesis see Deaton (2002). Deaton concludes that at least in the United States and Britain there is little empirical support for this view, at least as when it is confined to income inequality per se.

8 Since the sample is restricted to those who were in the HRS for all five waves, this analysis ignores the relationship of SES with attrition and mortality. Given the age range of HRS and PSID respondents, mortality selection is unlikely to be critical. That is clearly not the case in the AHEAD sample. For a model that incorporates mortality selection and deals with the causality issue in more detail see Adams et al. (2003).

9 One limitation of using increases in stock market wealth is that these increases are concentrated at the top of the income distribution (see Smith 2000) so that one is examining the effects of financial resources on health in that subset of the population where the impacts are likely to be smallest. In addition, the exogeneity argument is more credible in the time dimension than in the person dimension since for the latter one needs to explain why some people have accumulated so much stock in the past thereby exposing them to the possibility of larger capital gains in the future. Obtaining other believable measures of exogenous

changes in financial resources that more evenly span the entire income distribution would be very useful.

10 See Deaton (2002) for an insightful elaboration of these issues.

11 HRS data on some concepts are limited but they do record whether one smoked in the past and whether one was exposed on the job to a health hazard (and the number of years of exposure), the education of parents, whether or not each parent is alive, and, if deceased, the age of death, self-assessed general health status as a child (the same five-point scale), and an assessment of the economic environment in which one lived during childhood. The specific question for health was "Consider your health while you were growing up, from birth to age 16. Would you say that your health during that time was excel- lent, very good, good, fair, or poor?" The specific question for economic circumstances was "Now think about your family when you were growing up, from birth to age 16. Would you say your family during that time was pretty well off financially, about average, or poor?"

12 We found similar results for persons with HIV.

13 For a detailed analysis of the quality of the PSID health data, see Smith (2004).

14 Similar to the HRS findings, new minor health events had no detectable effects on any of these outcomes.

15 Similar conclusions are reached in an insightful paper by Case and Deaton (2002) where the primary focus is gender differences by SES and age.

References

Adams, Peter, Michael Hurd, Daniel McFadden, Angela Merrill, and Tiago Ribeiro. 2003. "Healthy, wealthy, and wise? Tests for direct causal paths between health and socio-economic status," *Journal of Econometrics* 112: 3–56.

Barker, David J. P. 1997. "Maternal nutrition, fetal nutrition and diseases in later life," *Nutrition* 13(9): 807–813.

Case, Anne, Angela Fertig, and Christina Paxson. 2004. "The lasting impact of childhood health and circumstance," Center for Health and Wellbeing, Princeton University, April.

Case, Anne C. and Angus Deaton. 2003. "Broken down by work and sex: How our health declines," NBER working paper 9821, July.

Case, Anne C., Darren Lubotsky, and Christina Paxson. 2002. "Economic status and health in childhood: The origins of the gradient," *American Economic Review* 92(5): 1308–1334.

Deaton, Angus. 2002. "Policy implications of the gradient of health and wealth," *Health Affairs* 21(2): 13–30.

Doblhammer, Gabriele and James Vaupel. 2001. "Lifespan depends on month of birth," *Proceedings of the National Academy of Sciences* 98: 2934–2939.

Goldman, Dana and James P. Smith. 2002. "Can patient self-management help explain the SES health gradient?" *Proceedings of the National Academy of Sciences; USA (PNAS),* August 6, 99(16): 10929–10934.

Krieger, Nancy. 1999. "Embodying inequality: A review of concepts, measures, and methods for studying health consequences of discrimination," *International Journal of Health Services* 29(2): 295–352.

Marmot, Michael. 1999. "Multi-level approaches to understanding social determinants," in Lisa Berkman and Ichiro Kawachi (eds.), *Social Epidemiology.* Oxford: Oxford University Press.

Seeman, Teresa, Burt Singer, John Rowe, Ralph Horwitz, and Bruce McEwen. 1997. "Price of adaption-allostatic load and its health consequences," *Archives of Internal Medicine* October 27: 157.

Smith James P. 1999. "Healthy bodies and thick wallets," *Journal of Economic Perspectives* 13(2): 145–166.

————. 2000. "Why is wealth inequality rising?," in Finis Welch (ed.), *Increasing Income Inequality in America: The Facts, Causes, and Consequences*. Chicago: University of Chicago Press, pp. 83–116.

————. 2003. "Consequences and predictors of new health events," Working Paper 10063 NBER and W03/22, Institute for Fiscal Studies, forthcoming in David Wise (ed.), *Analyses in the Economics of Aging*. Chicago: University of Chicago Press, 2005.

————. 2004. "The impact of SES on health over the life-course," unpublished paper, October.

Smith, James P. and Raynard Kington. 1997. "Demographic and economic correlates of health in old age," *Demography* 34(1): 159–170.

Wilkinson, Richard G. 1996. *Unhealthy Societies: The Afflictions of Inequality*. London: Routledge.

Socioeconomic Status and Coronary Heart Disease: A Psychobiological Perspective

Andrew Steptoe

Michael Marmot

The socioeconomic disparities in health are particularly striking in the case of coronary heart disease, with rates of disease being substantially higher in lower-status individuals as defined by education, occupational position, or income. Both childhood and adult socioeconomic factors contribute, and disparities are maintained in old age after retirement (Marmot and Shipley 1996; Wannamethee et al. 1996). Low socioeconomic status is associated with subclinical levels of the underlying disease (atherosclerosis) as well as with manifest heart disease (Lynch et al. 1995). Coronary heart disease has also been linked with living in deprived neighborhoods independently of individual socioeconomic characteristics (Diez Roux et al. 2001).

Several psychosocial factors are associated with increased risk of coronary heart disease as well. Authoritative reviews have concluded that the strongest evidence is for work stress, lack of social integration, depression, and depressive symptoms, with suggestive but weaker evidence for anger, hostility, and anxiety (Hemingway, Kuper, and Marmot 2003; Krantz and McCeney 2002). Other forms of chronic stress such as caregiver burden have been related to the incidence of coronary heart disease in a more limited set of studies (Lee et al. 2003). It is telling that many of these psychosocial factors are socially graded. For example, low job control, one of the most toxic elements of chronic work stress, is more prevalent among people working in lower-status jobs (Marmot et al. 1997). Social isolation is more common among less educated and less affluent individuals (Turner and Marino 1994), and there is a consistent association between lower socioeconomic position and depressive symptoms (Lorant et al. 2003).

This chapter addresses the issue of how socioeconomic position and other social and psychological factors are reflected in differences at the bio-

133

logical level. What are the pathways through which socioeconomic factors accelerate or retard the physical processes of coronary atherosclerosis, thrombosis, and impaired cardiac function? We have been working on this problem for the last several years, bringing together perspectives from epidemiology and psychobiology. Here we present a rationale for how to tackle these issues and a summary of what we have learned so far.

Pathways to coronary heart disease

Economic factors, educational attainment, social isolation, and other psychosocial factors are indirect causes of coronary heart disease. They do not affect disease pathology directly, but do so through more proximal processes. An understanding of these pathways requires some background concerning the pathology of coronary heart disease. The underlying problem in coronary heart disease is coronary atherosclerosis, a progressive disease involving the gradual thickening of the walls of the coronary arteries. Coronary atherosclerosis used to be regarded as a largely passive process resulting from the gradual accumulation of lipid (cholesterol) in the arterial wall. The last two decades have witnessed a fundamental change in knowledge about the causes of atherosclerosis and thrombosis, however, and the disease is now known to involve chronic vascular inflammation (Ross 1999). The inflammation begins in the cells lining the vessel wall and leads to progressive accumulation not only of lipid, but also of smooth muscle cells and white blood cells such as macrophages, lymphocytes, and platelets. The process is regulated in part by inflammatory cytokines such as interleukin (IL)-6 and tumor necrosis factor alpha and by molecules called acute phase proteins, notably C-reactive protein. At later stages of the disease process, plaque (clumps of atheromatous material) forms on the internal vessel walls and obtrudes in the interior through which the blood flows. These plaques can rupture, causing thrombosis (internal clot formation) and acute blockage of arteries. Blood clotting or hemostatic factors are therefore involved in this process in conjunction with inflammation of the arterial walls; molecules such as fibrinogen are important, together with small white blood cells called platelets.

Atherosclerosis starts early in life and continues for decades without clinical consequences. The disease typically comes to light at an advanced stage when the coronary arteries become partly or completely blocked and the muscle of the heart fails to be supplied with energy. The person may then experience angina pectoris, a myocardial infarction, or death.

Proximal causes

The observation that low socioeconomic position affects disease risk and is associated with subclinical atherosclerosis indicates that socioeconomic position has a long-term influence on the disease process. Thus, rather than triggering acute cardiac events in people with advanced disease, socioeconomic factors influence the underlying disease. Similarly, many prospective studies of psychosocial factors such as work stress have demonstrated effects that developed over 10 to 25 years (Kivimaki et al. 2002). These factors must therefore influence the process of vascular inflammation and accumulation of cells in the sub-endothelial layers, and also possibly plaque rupture and thrombus formation. The major determinants of atherosclerosis are the standard risk factors, namely high circulating cholesterol, high blood pressure, and cigarette smoking (Greenland et al. 2003). A second set of risk factors involves disturbed glucose metabolism, leading to insulin resistance and in some cases to diabetes. The new understanding of coronary atherosclerosis has led to the identification of inflammatory markers that also predict coronary heart disease, such as the concentration of fibrinogen and C-reactive protein in the blood (Danesh et al. 1998). Several of the factors involved in blood clotting and the formation of thrombus have also emerged through prospective epidemiological studies as risk factors, including plasma viscosity and a molecule involved in the adhesion of platelets to vessel walls called von Willebrand factor (Danesh et al. 2000).

Some of these cardiovascular risk factors are socially graded, and as such must be candidates for mediating socioeconomic disparities. Smoking has a strong social gradient in the United States and northern Europe at least, with higher rates in less affluent groups. For other risk factors, social gradation seems to be more pronounced for the newly identified inflammatory and metabolic markers than it is for the older established indexes such as high blood pressure and high cholesterol level. Thus high blood pressure has a small and inconsistent association with socioeconomic position, and social gradients in cholesterol levels are small and variable across studies (Colhoun, Hemingway, and Poulter 1998; Marmot et al. 1991; Wamala et al. 1997). By contrast, insulin resistance and fibrinogen have shown consistent socioeconomic gradients, and differences have also been recorded for C-reactive protein, IL-6, and von Willebrand factor (Brunner et al. 1996; Brunner et al. 1997; Kumari, Marmot, and Brunner 2000; Owen et al. 2003).

The issue of the mediation of socioeconomic disparities can therefore be reframed as a specific question about how social and psychological experience can induce changes in vascular, metabolic, and inflammatory processes. Our conceptual model is that low socioeconomic position is associated with greater exposure to adversity in life, coupled with lower protective resources such as social support and effective coping responses (Steptoe and Marmot 2003). These in turn affect biological responses that increase cardiovascular disease risk. The translational process is a problem of psychobiology.

Psychobiological processes

Psychobiological processes are the pathways through which psychosocial factors stimulate biological systems via central nervous system activation of autonomic, neuroendocrine, and immunological responses (Steptoe 1998). The physiological responses that are relevant to coronary heart disease are organized through central nervous stimulation of two neurobiological pathways: the hypothalamic–pituitary–adrenocortical (HPA) axis leading to release of steroid hormones such as cortisol, and the sympatho-adrenal axis, involving activation of the sympathetic branch of the autonomic nervous system in conjunction with hormones such as epinephrine (adrenaline) and norepinephrine. These pathways have a range of effects on biological systems that are adapted for vigorous physical activity and for fight-or-flight responses. For example, cortisol stimulates the production of glucose in the liver, helps release free fatty acids from fat stores, and is involved in the regulation of water balance and control of the immune system (McEwen et al. 1997). Sympathetic nervous system activation leads to increases in blood pressure and heart rate, stimulation of blood clotting processes, upregulation of immune function, and release of stored free fatty acids. These responses become maladaptive under conditions of repeated or chronic stimulation, or when they are elicited under inappropriate conditions. When this happens, either excessively high or low levels of HPA and sympatho-adrenal function occur, with adverse effects on health. This can be illustrated by rare clinical conditions such as Cushing's disease, which is characterized by prolonged heightened secretion of cortisol; victims of Cushing's disease are prone to high blood pressure (hypertension), insulin resistance, abdominal obesity, osteoporosis, gonadal dysfunction, depression, irritability, and fatigue. These factors in turn contribute to type 2 diabetes and coronary heart disease.

Psychobiological processes are studied extensively in animal experiments, where many of the specific responses leading to physical pathology have been worked out. For example, studies in nonhuman primates have demonstrated that exposure to chronic social stress can accelerate coronary artery blockage or stenosis (Kaplan et al. 1982). Furthermore, individual differences in cardiovascular stress reactivity predict the impact of social stress on stenosis (Manuck, Kaplan, and Clarkson 1983). The challenge is how to investigate the psychobiological processes related to socioeconomic disparities in humans. Epidemiological techniques provide evidence for associations between biological factors and socioeconomic status. But to understand dynamic influences of life experience on biological responses, we are limited to two principal methods: acute mental stress testing and naturalistic monitoring of biological responses in everyday life.

Mental stress testing and socioeconomic disparities

Mental stress testing involves the standardized measurement of biological responses when people are exposed to demanding situations. Participants are typically assigned tasks that they find difficult and stressful. These might include problem-solving tasks, emotionally stressful interviews, and simulated public speaking. The biological responses are recorded at baseline, during tasks, and then in the post-task recovery period.

There are two components to the psychobiological response: the size of the response and the speed of post-task recovery. One individual or group might produce larger blood pressure increases than another in response to the same standardized task. Variations in acute blood pressure reactions have been shown to predict future hypertension and the progression of subclinical atherosclerosis (Lynch et al. 1998; Treiber et al. 2003). Alternatively, two individuals might produce the same size of reaction, but differ in the rate at which they recover or return to baseline blood pressure levels. Future cardiovascular disease can also be predicted by the speed of recovery (Schuler and O'Brien 1997). The recovery component is particularly relevant to the concept of allostatic load developed by McEwen and colleagues (McEwen 1998). They argue that chronic or repeated attempts at adaptation to life's demands result in wear and tear on biological regulatory systems so that they no longer remain within optimal operating ranges, resulting in reduced ability to adapt over time (McEwen and Wingfield 2003).

Before we began our studies, the influence of socioeconomic status on psychobiological responses during mental stress testing had been investigated by a number of researchers with inconsistent results. Studies of children and adolescents showed that individuals from poorer families or those who lived in deprived neighborhoods experienced greater blood pressure reactions than more advantaged participants, but findings in adults had been variable. We have reviewed this literature elsewhere (Steptoe and Marmot 2002). Two factors might be important in explaining these inconsistencies. The first is the nature of the tasks given to people during mental stress testing. A strength of the laboratory method is that conditions are standardized, so that the same challenges are administered to everyone; any differences in response are therefore due to variations in how people react, not to what they experience. But many of the tasks used in mental stress testing might be appraised differently across the social gradient. Some tasks are intelligence tests, so that people of different intellectual capability are not challenged to the same extent. One large study of socioeconomic status used portions of an intelligence test to stimulate cardiovascular responses (Carroll et al. 1997). Simulated public speaking tasks are also popular for eliciting stress responses, but public speaking is much more familiar to people in higher socioeconomic positions who may speak to audiences as part of their regular work. Most of these tasks do not provide a fair test for comparison of socioeconomic groups, and we therefore thought it important to use stimuli that were appraised similarly by people across the social gradient. Second, the previous literature had focused exclusively on blood pressure and heart rate responses. Although these are critical, they need to be supplemented by more-direct measures of the inflammatory and hemostatic factors involved in atherosclerosis.

The Whitehall psychobiological studies

Over the last five years, we have carried out psychobiological studies to test the hypothesis that heightened biological responsivity is associated with lower socioeconomic position. The main study involved 238 middle-aged men and women who were members of the Whitehall II epidemiological cohort (Steptoe et al. 2002). Whitehall II is a sample of 10,308 London-based civil servants originally recruited in 1985–88 to investigate demographic, psychosocial, and biological risk factors for coronary heart disease (Marmot et al. 1991). The reason for using this sample is that socioeconomic status defined by occupational grade in the British civil service is known to be related to coronary heart disease, so that by systematically sampling from different grades we identified groups varying on socioeconomic characteristics that are definitely relevant to cardiovascular health. We compared individuals from higher, intermediate, and lower grades of employment. None of the participants had manifest heart disease or other cardiovascular disorders such as diabetes. Although participants were selected on the basis of occupational grade, they also varied on other common markers of socioeconomic status. For example, at the time of testing, the median personal income for the lower, intermediate, and higher grade participants was equivalent to US$38,000, $50,000, and $71,000 respectively. Three-quarters of the lower grade group had only elementary education, compared with 45 percent of the intermediate and 18 percent of the higher grade groups.

We measured blood pressure, heart rate, cortisol, and several blood anylates during and following the performance of two brief tasks that we had pre-tested for being appraised similarly across groups. These tasks were a color/word interference task and a mirror tracing task. Ratings obtained after each task confirmed that men and women in the three occupational grades found the tasks equally stressful, difficult, and uncontrollable.

One of the first fruits of this work was our discovery that many of the factors involved in vascular inflammation and in hemostatic control are sensitive to psychological stress. Thus we observed that in response to stress, increases occur in the concentration of fibrinogen and C-reactive protein, in proinflammatory cytokines such as IL-6 and tumor necrosis factor alpha, in hemostatic factors such as von Willebrand factor and plasma viscosity, and in platelet activation. These responses have quite variable time courses. For example, fibrinogen and von Willebrand factor increase acutely during tasks, and decrease in the post-task period (Steptoe et al. 2003a; Steptoe et al. 2003c). By contrast, C-reactive protein and IL-6 respond slowly, so marked changes are not observed until two hours following the tasks (Brydon et al. 2004; Steptoe et al. 2003d). These biological processes are therefore sensitive to psychosocial influence. The question is whether response patterns vary with socioeconomic position.

The analyses of blood pressure responses indicated that the tasks elicited substantial increases, but that reactivity did not vary markedly by socioeconomic status. Systolic blood pressure increased by an average of 22.5 mmHg, while diastolic pressure rose by 13.6 mmHg during tasks. But important differences emerged during the post-stress recovery period. We continued to measure blood pressure for up to 45 minutes after tasks had been completed. Blood pressure failed to return to baseline levels in a substantial proportion of participants, even though they were relaxing without any further tasks. The failure of blood pressure to return to baseline was associated with socioeconomic status. As shown in Figure 1, the likelihood of incomplete post-task recovery was greater in men and women of lower socioeconomic position. Compared with the higher occupational grades (the reference group), the odds of incomplete recovery in the lower grade group were 2.60 (95 percent C.I. 1.20–5.65) for systolic pressure and 3.85 (1.48–10.0) for diastolic pressure, adjusted for sex, age, baseline values, and the magnitude of reactions to tasks. Figure 1 also shows that there was impairment in heart rate variability recovery in the lower grade group. Heart rate variability is relevant to the autonomic control of cardiac function, and low heart rate variability is a predictor of future cardiovascular disease (La Rovere et al. 1998; Schroeder et al. 2003).

Our data suggest that socioeconomic status is associated not so much with the magnitude of cardiovascular reactions to a challenge as with the rate of recovery or duration of responses. Similar patterns were observed for some other biological measures. For example, we assessed variables involved in the processes through which blood clots and thromboses are formed, including Factor VIII and plasma viscosity. The grade of employment groups did not differ in the magnitude of reactions to tasks, but values remained significantly more elevated 45 minutes following the tasks in the lower grade compared with the high and intermediate grade participants (Steptoe et al. 2003c). These effects were independent of age, sex, and other factors that might be influential such as body mass and smoking. We also observed socioeconomic differences in the post-task increases in

FIGURE 1   Odds of incomplete recovery to baseline by 45 minutes post-stress in systolic blood pressure, diastolic blood pressure, and heart rate variability

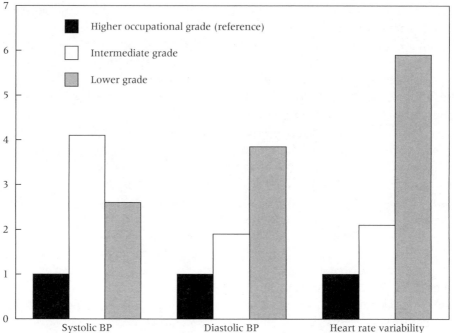

SOURCE: From Steptoe et al. (2002).

the concentration of inflammatory cytokines such as IL-6 and IL-1 receptor antagonist (Brydon et al. 2004; Owen et al. 2003).

However, not all variables show this pattern. Two examples are shown in Figure 2. Higher absolute levels of plasma fibrinogen and von Willebrand factor were recorded in the lower occupational grade groups, suggesting a contribution to heightened cardiovascular disease risk (Steptoe et al. 2003a; Steptoe et al. 2003c). But the magnitude of stress-induced increases did not differ across grades of employment, and the duration of responses was also similar. Figure 2 also indicates that the intermediate employment group was not midway between lower and higher status groups, but closer to the higher grade group in their biological profile. We have observed this pattern in a number of variables, but do not yet have a satisfactory explanation. It could be that acute mental stress testing is not the most accurate way of investigating these particular biological factors.

Although mental stress testing can help identify biological responses associated with socioeconomic status, it has two limitations. First, the responses are acute and typically subside within two to four hours. Second,

FIGURE 2   Mean concentration of plasma fibrinogen (upper panel) and von Willebrand factor (lower panel) at baseline, immediately after stressful tasks, and 45 minutes later in men and women from higher, intermediate, and lower grades of employment

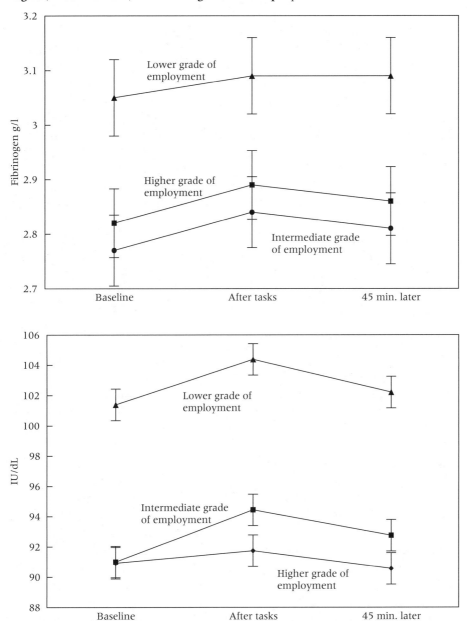

NOTE: Von Willebrand factor was log transformed before analysis, and geometric means are presented. Error bars represent standard error of the mean.
SOURCE: From Steptoe et al. (2003a and 2003c).

the stimuli used to elicit reactions are artificial and seldom encountered in real life. We therefore need to supplement these findings with investigations of biological responses to everyday experiences in people of differing socioeconomic status.

Naturalistic monitoring of biological markers

Naturalistic monitoring involves the assessment of biological function during everyday life. Clearly it is possible though difficult for health professionals or researchers to visit people in their homes or work places and obtain biological measures, but it is even more informative to study processes repeatedly as participants go about their everyday lives. This field has expanded enormously over recent years because of two advances. The first is the introduction of ambulatory blood pressure monitors. These relatively unobtrusive measurement devices can be programmed to record blood pressure and heart rate repeatedly throughout the day. The instruments are often timed to take measures every 15–20 minutes in the daytime and less frequently at night. This provides information about blood pressure under everyday as opposed to clinical conditions, and is increasingly used in the clinical management of hypertension. It is also possible to relate fluctuations in blood pressure to ongoing activities, events, and experiences during the day, so as to provide an insight into psychobiological processes. The second advance is the development of salivary assays of hormones. The main hormone that has been studied is cortisol, but it is also possible to measure dehydroepiandrosterone (DHEA), testosterone, and other substances. Before salivary measures were introduced, assessments of neuroendocrine function were limited to blood and urine sampling, both of which are invasive and may disrupt the very phenomena that are being investigated. Salivary sampling for cortisol involves having people spit into test tubes, or place dental rolls in their mouths for a few minutes until saturated. These samples are placed in labeled test tubes, which can then be sent to the laboratory for analysis. Fortunately, cortisol is relatively stable in saliva, so it can be stored at room temperature for several days without degradation.

Naturalistic methods have several limitations. One disadvantage is that the range of biological markers that can be assessed is small compared with those recorded in the laboratory, so many of the interesting biological processes involved in cardiovascular pathology cannot be measured. Additionally, the data require sophisticated statistical handling, since it is necessary to adjust for the many other factors that influence biological function in everyday life. For instance, blood pressure is affected by current and recent physical activity, posture, smoking, and drinking tea and coffee, and these need to be accounted for in the analysis.

To date only a handful of published studies have used ambulatory methods to investigate socioeconomic position. Matthews and coworkers (Matthews et al. 2000) carried out ambulatory blood pressure monitoring of 50 higher and 50 lower status men and women as defined by occupation. They found no differences in systolic or diastolic blood pressure over the working day, although heart rate was faster in lower status participants who experienced negative moods over the day. In a study of New York working men, ambulatory blood pressure was positively associated with work stress, but this effect was more marked in participants of lower occupational status (Landsbergis et al. 2003). Cortisol responses to everyday life stressors were inversely related to social status in a sample of 51-year-old Swedish men (Rosmond and Bjorntorp 2000).

We carried out ambulatory blood pressure monitoring with participants in the main Whitehall psychobiology study and obtained useful data from 199 men and women. We found that systolic blood pressure was higher in the lower occupational grade participants, but only during the morning hours (Steptoe et al. 2003b). Systolic pressure averaged 128.9 ± 15.7 mmHg in the lower grade group, compared with 122.6 ± 12.5 mmHg in the intermediate and 123.3 ± 12.7 mmHg in the higher grade participants. Differences were significant after adjusting for age, gender, smoking, alcohol intake, physical activity, and body weight. The groups did not differ over the rest of the working day or in the evening. Thus associations between socioeconomic status and disturbances of blood pressure control were most apparent early in the day. A similar conclusion is supported by our cortisol data.

Cortisol shows a strong diurnal variation, being high early in the morning and falling over the day. Recent work suggests that from the psychobiological perspective, two distinct phenomena are at work. The first is the profile of cortisol over the day itself, in terms of absolute output and pattern of decline into the evening. In our study, cortisol output over the working day was greater in men of lower than higher socioeconomic status, as we might expect from the perspective of the chronic allostatic load model developed by McEwen. But among women, the opposite pattern emerged, with greater cortisol concentrations in higher than lower status participants (Steptoe et al. 2003b). We have no explanation for this pattern, which appears to be independent of marital status, having children, and stress over the day.

The second part of the cortisol profile is the response to waking in the morning. Cortisol typically increases over the first minutes of the day, reaching a peak 20–30 minutes after waking. There is growing evidence that this cortisol awakening response is greater among individuals experiencing chronic stress from work or emotional strain (Pruessner et al. 2003; Steptoe et al. 2000). It appears to be an anticipatory response associated with the realization of the demands of the day ahead.

We persuaded most of the participants in our psychobiology study to take saliva samples on waking and then 30 minutes later both on a work day and a weekend day. We expected the cortisol awakening response to be smaller on the more relaxed weekend day and wondered whether there would be differences by occupational grade and whether these persisted on both days. The relevant results are summarized in Figure 3. Because a number of participants did not produce reliable data on both days, the three occupational grade groups were compressed into two (lower and higher). There are three interesting effects in these results. First, the level of salivary cortisol on waking was stable on the two days, and did not vary with socioeconomic position. Thus even though people were waking more than an hour later on the weekend, the cortisol level was unchanged. Second, there were significant increases in cortisol after waking on both days, but the increases were much smaller on the weekend. This is consistent with the notion that the cortisol increase on waking represents an anticipatory response to the coming day, and that this is attenuated when the pressure of commuting and working is eliminated. Third, on both days the lower socioeconomic group showed a larger cortisol awakening response than did the

FIGURE 3   Mean concentration of salivary free cortisol sampled on waking and 30 minutes later on a work day and weekend day in men and women from higher and lower grades of employment

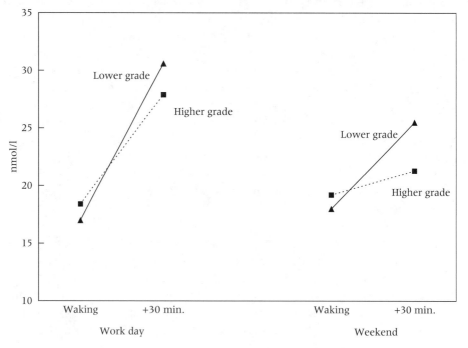

SOURCE: From Kunz-Ebrecht et al. 2004.

higher status participants. The differences were statistically highly significant, and were independent of smoking status. They represent real differences in neuroendocrine regulation associated with socioeconomic status.

It is tempting to see parallels between the results that we have obtained in standardized laboratory stress testing and naturalistic monitoring. In both cases, evidence has emerged for disturbances of psychobiological regulation in adults of lower socioeconomic status. In both cases, these disturbances are manifest less in absolute differences in reactivity to events than in the maintenance of healthy regulatory function. In the naturalistic study, the most striking differences were observed not while people were at work, when they might be most exposed to the stresses associated with their occupational status, but earlier as they prepared to face the challenges of the day. In the laboratory, the differences were most apparent during the period after exposure to challenge, as readjustment to normal equilibrium was being established. These effects may therefore be quite insidious, occurring at times of day and in situations where they are not expected.

The differences we have observed across the social gradient are quite small in absolute terms both in the laboratory and during everyday life. But the importance of these responses is that they are repeated on a regular basis for months or years of adult life. One can make an analogy with smoking. A single cigarette has an acute effect on biological function that soon dissipates without lasting consequences. But a cigarette every 30 minutes, every day, every month, every year for decades has a profound effect on health. The same may be true of these small psychobiological responses.

Additional pathways

The emphasis that we have placed on psychobiological processes should not be taken to imply that these are the only pathways through which socioeconomic status influences risk of coronary heart disease. Several other mediating mechanisms may be relevant. One that can probably be discounted is mediation through genetic differences. There is a heritable component to much of coronary heart disease and its risk factors (Nabel 2003). Although it is theoretically possible that the genetic determinants of coronary heart disease are socially graded, this is unlikely. Socioeconomic patterns of the disease have changed drastically in Britain and the United States over one or two generations, far more quickly than could sustained by any inherited process. A more plausible but untested possibility is that exposure to infection is involved. The notion that infection might in part cause coronary heart disease has stemmed from the search for the origins of coronary vascular inflammation. Inflammation of any tissue typically occurs in response to injury or infectious organisms, but studies of specific microorganisms such as *Chlamydia pneumoniae* have been inconclusive (Danesh et al. 2002). An alternative idea is that the total pathogen burden, or the number of infectious organisms to which people are exposed in their lifetimes, is relevant. Among patients with advanced atherosclerosis, those with antibodies for a larger number of common pathogens were at higher risk for future cardiac events (Espinola-Klein et al. 2002). Exposure to infection might be socially graded, with poorer people living in less hygienic conditions being at higher risk. But the possibility that such exposure accounts for socioeconomic differences in coronary heart disease is highly speculative at present. It is more likely that infectious burden is a marker of socioeconomic status, rather than a mediating pathway.

The pathway that probably makes a large contribution to the translation of socioeconomic disparities into coronary heart disease risk is lifestyle. Lifestyle factors such as smoking, food choice, alcohol consumption, and physical activity are socially graded in many countries. Indeed, the social gradient in cigarette smoking in the UK has increased markedly over recent decades, owing both to differences in uptake and more importantly to greater cessation rates in more affluent sectors (Jarvis and Wardle 1999). There is a relatively consistent social gradient in overweight and obesity, although this is much stronger in women than men (Lantz et al. 1998). Fat consumption shows no clear association with socioeconomic status in the United States and Britain, but fruit, vegetable, and fiber intake is greater in higher status groups (Bennett et al. 1995; Shimakawa et al. 1994). Vigorous leisure-time physical activity is more common in higher status groups, as is moderate alcohol consumption (Marmot 1997; Wardle and Steptoe 2003).

Several studies of social position have demonstrated that gradients in coronary heart disease persist after controlling statistically for factors such as smoking, body mass index, diet, and alcohol, so lifestyle is certainly not the complete explanation (Marmot, Kogevinas, and Elston 1987; Steenland, Henley, and Thun 2002). The question of how much of the variance in coronary heart disease is accounted for by lifestyle is difficult to gauge. In the Finnish Kuopio study, about 50 percent of the income gradient in cardiovascular mortality was accounted for by smoking, alcohol, and physical activity (Lynch et al. 1996), while in the Dutch Globe study, more than half of the educational gradient in acute myocardial infarction was accounted for by smoking, alcohol, body mass, and physical inactivity (Van Lenthe et al. 2002). In the Whitehall II study, we estimate that lifestyle factors account for only about a quarter of the socioeconomic gradient. But in a recent analysis of educational differences in blood pressure in the United States, Stamler and colleagues (Stamler et al. 2003) argued that nutritional factors account for most of the difference between better and less well educated adults. Few studies have assessed all relevant lifestyle factors in a comprehensive way, and it is likely that the importance of these factors varies with the nature of the population (urban/rural, high or low smoking countries, dietary traditions, etc.) and possibly with the way in which socioeconomic status is measured.

Conclusions

We have argued that psychobiological processes are plausible pathways through which socioeconomic disparities are translated into cardiovascular disease risk and coronary heart disease incidence. The evidence is preliminary. Although variations in psychobiological function have been associated with socioeconomic status, we do not know whether they contribute to disease end points. The quantification of the relative importance of psychobiological, lifestyle, and other mediating pathways has not yet been attempted. Nonetheless, the possibility now exists for identifying mechanisms at the most precise level of pathogenesis that are affected by social forces and psychological characteristics. The elaboration of psychobiological methods so that they can be used in large-scale population studies will further this integration of disciplines and our understanding of how socioeconomic status affects coronary heart disease risk.

Note

This research was supported by the Medical Research Council and the British Heart Foundation.

References

Bennett, N., T. Dodd, J. Flatley, S. Freeth, and K. Bolling. 1995. *Health Survey for England 1993*. London: HMSO.

Brunner, E. et al. 1996. "Childhood social circumstances and psychosocial and behavioural factors as determinants of plasma fibrinogen," *Lancet* 347: 1008–1013.

Brunner, E. J. et al. 1997. "Social inequality in coronary risk: central obesity and the metabolic syndrome: Evidence from the Whitehall II study," *Diabetologia* 40: 1341–1349.

Brydon, L., S. Edwards, V. Mohamed-Ali, and A. Steptoe. 2004. "Socioeconomic status and stress-induced increases in interleukin-6," *Brain, Behavior and Immunity* 18: 281–290.

Carroll, D., G. Davey Smith, D. Sheffield, M. J. Shipley, and M. G. Marmot. 1997. "The relationship between socioeconomic status, hostility, and blood pressure reactions to mental stress in men: Data from the Whitehall II study," *Health Psychology* 16: 131–136.

Colhoun, H. M., H. Hemingway, and N. R. Poulter. 1998. "Socio-economic status and blood pressure: An overview analysis," *Journal of Human Hypertension* 12: 91–110.

Danesh, J., R. Collins, P. Appleby, and R. Peto. 1998. "Association of fibrinogen, C-reactive protein, albumin, or leukocyte count with coronary heart disease: Meta-analyses of prospective studies," *Journal of the American Medical Association* 279: 1477–1482.

Danesh, J., R. Collins, R. Peto, and G. D. Lowe. 2000. "Haematocrit, viscosity, erythrocyte sedimentation rate: meta-analyses of prospective studies of coronary heart disease," *European Heart Journal* 21: 515–520.

Danesh, J. et al. 2002. "Chlamydia pneumoniae IgA titres and coronary heart disease; prospective study and meta-analysis," *European Heart Journal* 23: 371–375.

Diez Roux, A. V. et al. 2001. "Neighborhood of residence and incidence of coronary heart disease," *New England Journal of Medicine* 345: 99–106.

Espinola-Klein, C. et al. 2002. "Impact of infectious burden on extent and long-term prognosis of atherosclerosis," *Circulation* 105: 15–21.

Greenland, P. et al. 2003. "Major risk factors as antecedents of fatal and nonfatal coronary heart disease events," *Journal of the American Medical Association* 290: 891–897.

Hemingway, H., H. Kuper, and M. Marmot. 2003. "Psychosocial factors in the primary and secondary prevention of coronary heart disease: An updated systematic review of prospective cohort studies," in S. Yusuf, J. A. Cairns, A. J. Camm, E. L. Fallen, and B. J. Gersh (eds.), *Evidence-Based Cardiology*, Second edition. London: BMJ Books, pp. 181–218.

Jarvis, M. and J. Wardle. 1999. "Social patterning of individual health behaviours: The case of cigarette smoking," in Michael Marmot and Richard G. Wilkinson (eds.), *Social Determinants of Health*. Oxford: Oxford University Press, pp. 240–255.

Kaplan, J. R., S. B. Manuck, T. B. Clarkson, F. M. Lusso, and D. M. Taub. 1982. "Social stress, environment, and atherosclerosis in cynomolgus monkeys," *Arteriosclerosis* 2: 359–368.

Kivimaki, M. et al. 2002. "Work stress and risk of cardiovascular mortality: prospective cohort study of industrial employees," *British Medical Journal* 325: 857.

Krantz, D. S. and M. K. McCeney. 2002. "Effects of psychological and social factors on organic disease: A critical assessment of research on coronary heart disease," *Annual Review of Psychology* 53: 341–369.

Kumari, M., M. Marmot, and E. Brunner. 2000. "Social determinants of von Willebrand factor: the Whitehall II study," *Arteriosclerosis, Thrombosis and Vascular Biology* 20: 1842–1847.

Kunz-Ebrecht, S. R., C. Kirschbaum, M. Marmot, and A. Steptoe. 2004. "Differences in cortisol awakening response on work days and weekends in women and men from the Whitehall II cohort," *Psychoneuroendocrinology* 29: 516–528.

La Rovere, M. T., J. T. Bigger, F. I. Marcus, A. Mortara, and P. J. Schwartz. 1998. "Baroreflex sensitivity and heart-rate variability in prediction of total cardiac mortality after myocardial infarction," *Lancet* 351: 478–484.

Landsbergis, P. A., P. L. Schnall, T. G. Pickering, K. Warren, and J. E. Schwartz. 2003. "Lower socioeconomic status among men in relation to the association between job strain and blood pressure," *Scandinavian Journal of Work Environment and Health* 29: 206–215.

Lantz, P. M. et al. 1998. "Socioeconomic factors, health behaviors, and mortality: results from a nationally representative prospective study of US adults," *Journal of the American Medical Association* 279: 1703–1708.

Lee, S., G. A. Colditz, L. F. Berkman, and I. Kawachi. 2003. "Caregiving and risk of coronary heart disease in U.S. women: A prospective study," *American Journal of Preventive Medicine* 24: 113–119.

Lorant, V., D. Deliege, W. Eaton, A. Robert, P. Philippot, and M. Ansseau. 2003. "Socioeconomic inequalities in depression: a meta-analysis," *American Journal of Epidemiology* 157: 98–112.

Lynch, J. W., S. A. Everson, G. A. Kaplan, R. Salonen, and J. T. Salonen. 1998. "Does low socioeconomic status potentiate the effects of heightened cardiovascular responses to stress on the progression of carotid atherosclerosis?," *American Journal of Public Health* 88: 389–394.

Lynch, J. W., G. A. Kaplan, R. D. Cohen, J. Tuomilehto, and J. Salonen. 1996. "Do cardiovascular risk factors explain the relation between socio-economic status, risk of all-cause mortality, cardiovascular mortality, and acute myocardial infarction?," *American Journal of Epidemiology* 144: 934–942.

Lynch, J. W., G. A. Kaplan, R. Salonen, R. D. Cohen, and J. Salonen. 1995. "Socioeconomic status and carotid atherosclerosis," *Circulation* 92: 1786–1792.

Manuck, S. B., J. R. Kaplan, and T. B. Clarkson. 1983. "Behaviorally induced heart rate reactivity and atherosclerosis in cynomolgus monkeys," *Psychosomatic Medicine* 45: 95–102.

Marmot, M. 1997. "Income, deprivation, and alcohol use," *Addiction* 92, Suppl 1: S13–S20.

Marmot, M. G., H. Bosma, H. Hemingway, E. Brunner, and S. Stansfeld. 1997. "Contribution of job control and other risk factors to social variations in coronary heart disease incidence," *Lancet* 350: 235–239.

Marmot, M. G., M. Kogevinas, and M. A. Elston. 1987. "Social/economic status and disease," *Annual Review of Public Health* 8: 111–135.

Marmot, M. G. and M. J. Shipley. 1996. "Do socioeconomic differences in mortality persist after retirement? 25 year follow up of civil servants from the first Whitehall study," *British Medical Journal* 313: 1177–1180.

Marmot, M. G. et al. 1991. "Health inequalities among British civil servants: the Whitehall II study," *Lancet* 337: 1387–1393.

Matthews, K. A. et al. 2000. "Do the daily experiences of healthy men and women vary according to occupational prestige and work strain?," *Psychosomatic Medicine* 62: 346–353.

McEwen, B. S. 1998. "Protective and damaging effects of stress mediators," *New England Journal of Medicine* 338: 171–179.

McEwen, B. S. et al. 1997. "The role of adrenocorticoids as modulators of immune function in health and disease: Neural, endocrine and immune interactions," *Brain Research Review* 23: 79–133.

McEwen, B. S. and J. C. Wingfield. 2003. "The concept of allostasis in biology and biomedicine," *Hormones and Behavior* 43: 2–15.

Nabel, E. G. 2003. "Cardiovascular disease," *New England Journal of Medicine* 349: 60–72.

Owen, N., T. Poulton, F. C. Hay, V. Mohamed-Ali, and A. Steptoe. 2003. "Socioeconomic status, C-reactive protein, immune factors, and responses to acute mental stress," *Brain Behavior and Immunity* 17: 286–295.

Pruessner, M., D. H. Hellhammer, J. C. Pruessner, and S. J. Lupien. 2003. "Self-reported depressive symptoms and stress levels in healthy young men: Associations with the cortisol response to awakening," *Psychosomatic Medicine* 65: 92–99.

Rosmond, R. and P. Bjorntorp. 2000. "Occupational status, cortisol secretory pattern, and visceral obesity in middle-aged men," *Obesity Research* 8: 445–450.

Ross, R. 1999. "Atherosclerosis—An inflammatory disease," *New England Journal of Medicine* 340: 115–126.

Schroeder, E. B. et al. 2003. "Hypertension, blood pressure, and heart rate variability: The Atherosclerosis Risk in Communities (ARIC) Study," *Hypertension* 42: 1106–1111.

Schuler, J. L. and W. H. O'Brien. 1997. "Cardiovascular recovery from stress and hypertension risk factors: a meta-analytic review," *Psychophysiology* 34: 649–659.

Shimakawa, T. et al. 1994. "Dietary intake patterns and sociodemographic factors in the Atherosclerosis Risk in Communities Study," *Preventive Medicine* 23: 769–780.

Stamler, J. et al. 2003. "Higher blood pressure in middle-aged American adults with less education—role of multiple dietary factors: the INTERMAP study," *Journal of Human Hypertension* 17: 655–775.

Steenland, K., J. Henley, and M. Thun. 2002. "All-cause and cause-specific death rates by educational status for two million people in two American Cancer Society cohorts, 1959–1996," *American Journal of Epidemiology* 156: 11–21.

Steptoe, A. 1998. "Psychophysiological bases of disease," in M. Johnston and D. Johnston (eds.), *Comprehensive Clinical Psychology Volume 8: Health Psychology*. New York: Elsevier Science, pp. 39–78.

Steptoe, A., M. Cropley, J. Griffith, and C. Kirschbaum. 2000. "Job strain and anger expression predict early morning elevations in salivary cortisol," *Psychosomatic Medicine* 62: 286–292.

Steptoe, A., P. J. Feldman, S. Kunz, N. Owen, G. Willemsen, and M. Marmot. 2002. "Stress responsivity and socioeconomic status: A mechanism for increased cardiovascular disease risk?," *European Heart Journal* 23: 1757–1763.

Steptoe, A. and M. Marmot. 2003. "The burden of psychosocial adversity and vulnerability in middle age," *Psychosomatic Medicine* 65: 1029–1037.

———. 2002. "The role of psychobiological pathways in socio-economic inequalities in cardiovascular disease risk," *European Heart Journal* 23: 13–25.

Steptoe, A., S. Kunz-Ebrecht, N. Owen, P. J. Feldman, A. Rumley, G. D. Lowe, and M. Marmot. 2003a. "Influence of socioeconomic status and job control on plasma fibrinogen responses to acute mental stress," *Psychosomatic Medicine* 65: 137–144.

Steptoe, A., S. Kunz-Ebrecht, N. Owen, P. J. Feldman, G. Willemsen, C. Kirschbaum, and M. Marmot. 2003b. "Socioeconomic status and stress-related biological responses over the working day," *Psychosomatic Medicine* 65: 461–470.

Steptoe, A., S. Kunz-Ebrecht, A. Rumley, and G. D. Lowe. 2003c. "Prolonged elevations in haemostatic and rheological responses following psychological stress in low socioeconomic status men and women," *Thrombosis and Haemostasis* 89: 83–90.

Steptoe, A., P. Strike, K. Magid, L. Brydon, S. Edwards, J. Erusalimsky, and J. McEwan. 2003d. "Mental stress-induced platelet activation and increases in C-reactive protein concentration in coronary artery disease," in B. S. Lewis, D. A. Halon, M. Y. Flugelman, and G. F. Gensini (eds.), *Frontiers in Coronary Artery Disease*. Bologna: Monduzzi Editore, pp. 429–432.

Treiber, F. A. et al. 2003. "Cardiovascular reactivity and development of preclinical and clinical disease states," *Psychosomatic Medicine* 65: 46–62.

Turner, R. J. and F. Marino. 1994. "Social support and social structure: a descriptive epidemiology," *Journal of Health and Social Behavior* 35: 193–212.

Van Lenthe, F. J., E. Gevers, I. M. Joung, H. Bosma, and J. P. Mackenbach. 2002. "Material and behavioral factors in the explanation of educational differences in incidence of acute myocardial infarction: The Globe Study," *Annals of Epidemiology* 12: 535–542.

Wamala, S. P., A. Wolk, K. Schenck-Gustafsson, and K. Orth-Gomér. 1997. "Lipid profile and socioeconomic status in healthy middle aged women in Sweden," *Journal of Epidemiology & Community Health* 51: 400–407.

Wannamethee, S. G., P. H. Whincup, G. Shaper, and M. Walker. 1996. "Influence of fathers' social class on cardiovascular disease in middle-aged men," *Lancet* 348: 1259–1263.

Wardle, J. and A. Steptoe. 2003. "Socioeconomic differences in attitudes and beliefs about healthy lifestyles," *Journal of Epidemiology and Community Health* 57: 440–443.

III. AGING, WORK, AND PUBLIC POLICY

Quantifying Our Ignorance: Stochastic Forecasts of Population and Public Budgets

RONALD LEE

A good deal of demographic research is justified on the grounds that it may lead to improved population forecasts. However, most researchers have never made a forecast, and actual projections are usually done by some form of trend extrapolation with little mention of theory. I believe that most demographers view forecasting as a mechanical exercise having little intellectual content. And indeed much forecasting, including good forecasts and my own forecasts, could be fairly characterized in this way. But nonetheless forecasting is one of the most important tasks demographers perform, and it is important that it be done well and to high professional standards. We need forecasts to anticipate population aging, for example, and as inputs for economic, fiscal, environmental, and social service planning. And we need forecasts simply to be able to visualize our collective future. Some kinds of planning depend on demographic patterns many decades in the future, and because of the long-term demographic consequences of current population age distribution, demographers sometimes make useful predictions of these. However, like most kinds of forecasts, population forecasts often turn out to be quite mistaken. It is also a task of demographic forecasters to provide indications of the kinds of errors they may make and the probabilities of such errors.

Demographers use accounting identities to translate assumptions about the time path of age-specific fertility, mortality, and migration into the future population sizes and age distributions they imply. However, demographic rates are only probabilities at the individual level. If a fertility rate for a 27-year-old women is 0.5 per year, that means there is a 50 percent probability that a particular woman will give birth within a year, and a 50 percent chance that she will not, and similarly for probabilities of death and survival, and migration. This intrinsic uncertainty at the individual level is diminished when we talk about larger groups of women, because it tends to average out, but it never disappears completely. Even if the true rates were known with certainty ex ante, the outcomes could not be predicted with certainty. Early researchers looked here for the source of uncertainty in population forecasts. However, simple calculations showed that this source of uncertainty became vanishingly small in the larger national populations, yet forecasts for large populations were little more successful than for small ones. Then it was recognized that the main source of uncertainty was that the vital rates (that is, the probabilities) themselves change over time, and that we make errors in forecasting these changes (Sykes 1969).

Unfortunately, the analytic tools of pure demography are of little use for the task of forecasting changes in vital rates. The principal analytic technique available is to place current rates in a longer run context through skilled disaggregation—for example, by parity and length of open birth interval for fertility, or by cause of death for mortality. But disaggregations of this kind are useful mainly when the underlying, disaggregated probabilities are in fact unchanging and the changes in outcomes are due to changing structures, that is to changing distributions of the population across the different relevant disaggregated categories of risk. However, there is an underlying weakness with this approach: If the distributions are not changing, then the disaggregation is not helpful. On the other hand, if the distributions are irregular and changing, this must reflect past variations in the disaggregated rates. But if the rates have been changing in the past, then they are likely to change in the future, and we are back to the problem of trying to forecast their changes. Faced with the need to forecast the disaggregated rates, demographers tend to extrapolate their most recently observed levels. Thus for the most part, classic demographic methods are of limited use in a changing world.

For the past 35 years, I have been working on the problem of demographic forecasting under uncertainty. My goal has been partly intellectual, to figure out how to think about the processes at work. But it has also been to develop new forecasting methods that would be more than illustrative and that might be good enough to inform real-world planning.

In this article, I will explain how this work developed over the years, what directions I tried, and why some failed and some succeeded. I will not try to provide a comprehensive overview of this large topic, which I attempted to do in Lee (1999) and Lee and Tuljapurkar (2000). However, I will give some indication of the contributions of others, and the directions they have taken.

Fundamental issues

As a graduate student, my interest in forecasting stemmed from an attempt to understand how and why populations grew and declined, and how the process was related to economic change, age distribution, and accident. In thinking about these questions, I was troubled by a number of questions:

1) Theories of Malthus, Easterlin, ecologists, and others tell us that population size and age distribution should themselves have an influence

on current vital rates, which implies that population processes should be subject to negative feedback. Yet in practice this is generally ignored in projections. What should we make of this?

2) Some analysts have viewed population change as an independent force, itself explaining economic and social changes. Others have viewed population change as endogenous, responding passively to economic change. How can we reconcile the interplay of random and systematic influences on vital rates and population growth?

3) How can variations over age and time in vital rates such as fertility or mortality be represented parsimoniously yet realistically?

Regardless of how forecasting is actually carried out, it explicitly or implicitly involves deep theoretical and empirical assumptions and judgments. Can we ignore feedback? Do more people in the reproductive ages mean more births or fewer births? Will environmental pressures be increased by population growth and in turn retard that growth? Will mortality rise as population density increases? Does a larger population lead to more rapid technological progress, or to poverty? If, in the end, most population forecasts say nothing about these questions, that outcome reflects an assumption on the part of the forecasters that demographic trends can continue without encountering such feedback, not proof that such economic and environmental interactions with population do not matter. The potential role of such factors is discussed in Lee (1990) and Cohen (1995).

Modeling variation in demographic rates over age and time

There is a tradition in mathematical demography of modeling variation over age and time, closely related to the demographic tradition of constructing model age schedules for fertility, nuptiality, and mortality. One approach involves fitting nonlinear parametric functions to the observed age schedules and then letting some or all of the parameters vary over time. For example, Gompertz or gamma functions have been used for fertility, and the Heligman–Pollard nine-parameter function has been used to extrapolate mortality rates (McNown and Rogers 1989). Another approach generates new age schedules by transforming an existing one, or a standard; this is sometimes called a relational approach. For example, one simple model assumes an equal additive change to mortality at every age, which is the simplest and most tractable model of all, but which fits actual change only poorly. Another example, this time more realistic but less tractable, assumes that mortality at every age changes by the same proportion. Still more realistic is Brass's logit transform.

The approach I developed was still very simple but, like the logit, both flexible and realistic. It lets each age-specific rate have its own additive or multiplicative pattern of change, with the relative sizes of these changes fixed across age:

$$m(x,k) = a(x) + k*b(x).$$

Here $m(x,k)$ can represent either a vital rate at age x for parameter value k, or the logarithm of the rate for the multiplicative version. As k varies, the model generates a family of age schedules of the vital rates m or $\exp(m)$. The model can be fit to a matrix of historical rates varying over age and time, resulting in estimates of the $a(x)$, $b(x)$ schedules, and a time series of the parameter k, call it $k(t)$. We can hold $a(x)$ and $b(x)$ fixed and then focus on analyzing, modeling, and forecasting $k(t)$ without having to worry about the age-specific details. The model has been used mainly for mortality, but also for fertility and migration.

This model also makes it easy to incorporate stochastic disturbances in a natural way, by treating k as a random variable. Then k, for fertility or mortality, can be projected using standard statistical methods, together with its probability distributions. From these, probability distributions for age-specific fertility and mortality can be calculated. Other sources of uncertainty, resulting from imperfect fit of the model given above, or from uncertainty about the parameters of the time series models used to forecast k, can also be incorporated.

The framework

Figure 1 gives a very large-scale schematic framework for this multi-decade undertaking, showing fertility and mortality as processes to be modeled, then showing them as inputs to a stochastic population forecast, and finally showing the use of the stochastic population forecast as an input to stochastic fiscal projections of various kinds. The vertical arrangement in Figures 1, 3, and 4 is both temporal, with the earlier work higher up, and logical, with the earlier entries providing inputs for entries lower down in the figures. The remainder of the article takes a close look at each of these legs of the journey, showing the blind alleys as well as the final route.

Forecasting mortality: Development of the Lee–Carter model

Since US life expectancy was widely believed to have reached its natural upper limit in the mid-1960s while I was a graduate student in demography, I didn't pay much attention to it at the time. Subsequently, mortality began to decline rapidly, and mortality caused larger errors in Census Bureau projections in the 1970s than fertility, so the picture changed. In the late 1980s, Lawrence Carter spent a semester visiting at Berkeley. We had collaborated

FIGURE 1 The development of demographic and fiscal stochastic forecasting: A schematic view

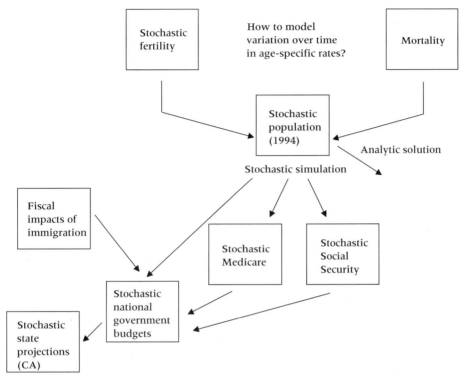

earlier on a model of population renewal based on birth-to-marriage and marriage-to-birth transitions. This time, we decided to use the simple age-time model I had developed for historical work to model and forecast mortality. The single parameter $k(t)$ indexed the intensity of mortality, and we estimated it for the United States from 1900 to 1989, as shown in Figure 2. Remarkably, the trajectory of $k(t)$ was quite linear, unlike life expectancy, which rose at a slowing pace throughout the century. This linearity was striking, because it persisted through important changes like the development of antibiotics and the emergence of the AIDS epidemic. We modeled $k(t)$ as a random walk with drift, and forecasted it along with its probability distribution. From this, we derived the forecasts and probability distributions of age-specific death rates and life expectancy. While we were developing this method, McNown and Rogers (1989, 1992) were developing an approach based on fitting the Heligman–Pollard model mentioned above to the historical mortality data, and then using time series methods to forecast a subset of the estimated parameters. There were lively debates about the relative merits of the two methods. Figure 3 charts this and subsequent efforts to model and forecast mortality. The path ultimately followed is shown by the continuing main line, while the spurs branching off to the sides represent paths tried but abandoned.

FIGURE 2   Lee–Carter mortality index $k(t)$, fitted (1990–96) and forecasted (1997–2096)

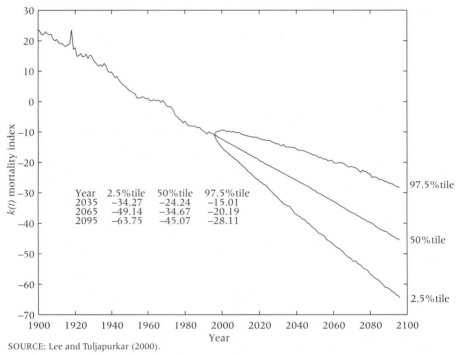

Year	2.5%tile	50%tile	97.5%tile
2035	−34.27	−24.24	−15.01
2065	−49.14	−34.67	−20.19
2095	−63.75	−45.07	−28.11

SOURCE: Lee and Tuljapurkar (2000).

FIGURE 3   False starts and promising paths for modeling mortality change

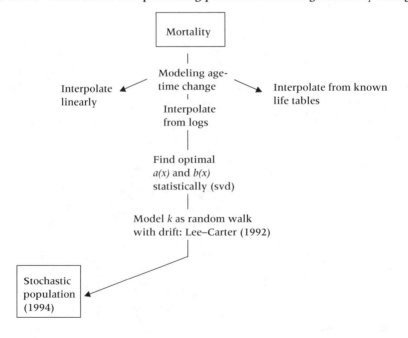

Even before our article (Lee and Carter 1992) was published, Statistics Canada invited us to apply our method to Canadian data, at Nathan Keyfitz's suggestion (Lee and Nault 1993), and they began to use it partially in their projections. Since then, the model has gradually gained acceptance, and is now also used in some respects by the US Census Bureau, Japan, and the United Nations. Tuljapurkar, Li, and Boe (2000) applied it to the G7 countries and found that, as for the United States, it predicted life expectancy gains by 2050 that were two to four years greater than the official projections, and for Japan, eight or nine years greater. Lee and Miller (2001) investigated hypothetically how the method would have worked had it been applied in earlier years. We found that the forecasting errors would have been quite well described by the probability distributions generated by the method. We also found that longer term forecasts tended to understate the future gains in life expectancy, in the United States and in a number of other countries. Recently, Li, Lee, and Tuljapurkar (2004) have extended the method for use in countries with mortality data available for only a few irregularly spaced periods.

Forecasting fertility

For fertility forecasts, I reasoned that once the fertility transition was over, we really had no clue about which way fertility would move, and the best we could do was to model its level as a trendless (covariance stationary) stochastic process (Lee 1974a). I then modeled births as an autoregressive time series, with net maternity rates as the autoregressive parameters, and derived the variance of the best linear forecast of the number of births in relation to the uncertainty of the fertility process by analyzing the renewal equation. From this I saw that the uncertainty in the forecast of births grew linearly with time to a good approximation, and that it was a moving average of past fertility shocks with weights equal to the progeny of a birth cohort at each lag. This work was my first presentation at the Michigan brown bag seminar series as a starting assistant professor there, and it was not well received, to say the least. The sociologists thought it was blasphemous to model fertility as a random process. Twenty years later, I got a very similar reaction when I submitted a related paper to *Demography*, which was rejected. The work appeared elsewhere (Lee 1993) and is a key component of the full-scale stochastic population forecasts.

In between my first paper and this elaborated model twenty years later, I had tried many other approaches to forecasting fertility. One line of work modeled an Easterlin-style effect of population age distribution on fertility (Lee 1974b and 1976). In this approach, I used the same kind of autoregressive birth equation, but now fertility was a function of the numbers of earlier births at each lag—that is, it depended on the contemporary population age distribution. Unfortunately, the future did not oblige by conforming to the predictions of the model; no new baby boom occurred, although a brief up-swing between 1988 and 1992 looked promising. I also wrote a series of papers on the use of birth expectations data from surveys (Lee 1981), which led to a paper on "Aiming at a moving target" (Lee 1980), but in the end proved of little use for forecasting. In other work, I considered using New Home Economics type fertility models for forecasting, but did not see how that approach could lead to useful predictions, since it seemed to imply fertility decline without limit as income and female wages rose. Finally, with Carter, I developed a time series model of the joint evolution of births and marriages, each feeding into the other (Carter and Lee 1986). It was an elegant paper, but with the rise in extramarital fertility, marriage became less important as a fundamental force driving fertility, and that approach was abandoned. It was a defeat to come back to treating fertility as a stochastic process, with model forecasts heavily conditioned by imposed assumptions for central tendency and, perhaps, for upper and lower bounds (e.g., total fertility rate between 0 and 4). But sometimes it is best to acknowledge defeat, and make peace on the best available terms; that was what I did in Lee (1993). This long journey of discovery for fertility modeling is portrayed in Figure 4.

FIGURE 4   False starts and promising paths for modeling fertility change

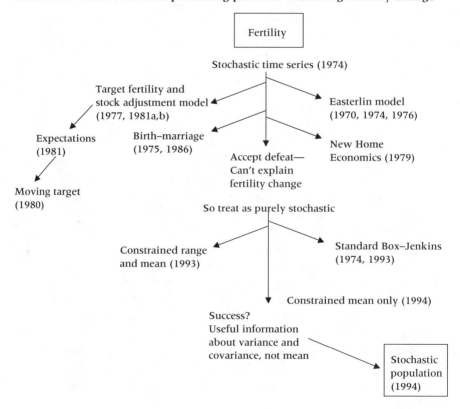

FIGURE 5   Total fertility rate, historical values (1917–96) and forecasted (1997–2096), with 95 percent probability intervals for annual values and for the cumulative average up to each horizon

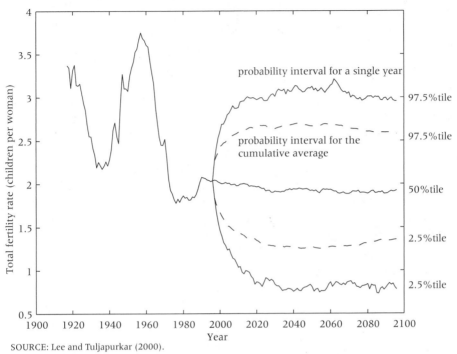

SOURCE: Lee and Tuljapurkar (2000).

Figure 5 shows a fertility forecast for the United States treating fertility as a stochastic process. The probability fan seems too wide, with the 95 percent probability bounds ranging from a TFR of .8 to 3.0. However, those bounds are intended to cover annual ups and downs. If we instead ask for central tendencies, by computing the probability interval for the average TFR along stochastic trajectories up to each horizon, we get a narrower 95 percent bound ranging from 1.4 to 2.6 for long-run forecasts.

The traditional treatment of uncertainty in population forecasts

The traditional approach to estimating and communicating the uncertainty of population forecasts is through the construction of scenarios. First, the analyst constructs high, medium, and low projections for each of the rates, typically fertility, mortality, and net immigration. The high and low trajectories do not have any probabilistic interpretation, but are chosen to span a range that the analyst believes to be plausible. The next step is to bundle these trajectories together to form high, medium, and low scenarios. This is done in different ways, depending on the purpose of the projections. For example, in the United States, the Census Bureau bundles together high fertility and low mortality (and high immigration) to form the high scenario, yielding the highest rate of population growth, and similarly for the low scenario. But the Social Security Administration bundles together high fertility with high mortality (and immigration), because these generate the lowest old-age dependency ratio (OADR), which is the key demographic variable for their financial projections. The Census Bureau's choice of bundles minimizes the high–low range of the OADR, because high fertility tends to make the population young, while low mortality tends to make the population old, and these effects cancel. The Social Security Administration's bundles minimize variations in the population growth rate, because high fertility makes the growth rate high, while high mortality makes it low, and these effects cancel.

This problem is illustrated by the 1992 Social Security population projections (Board of Trustees 1992). For 2070, the high–low range for the population aged 0–19 years is ±34 percent; for the population 20–64, the range is ±20 percent; and for 65+ it is ±9 percent. Yet for the total dependency ratio, which is the sum of the first and the third divided by the second, the range is only ±5 percent, whereas we would expect it to be many times this large. The scenario method inevitably gives probabilistically inconsistent indications of uncertainty for different population variables in the same forecast.

The arbitrariness of the choice of bundles is one of the problems with the scenario approach. Another is that no probabilities can be attached to the high–low range of the projections. Still another is that along the scenario trajectories, fertility is always high, medium, or low, and mortality likewise. It is therefore implicitly assumed that forecasting errors for fertility and mortality are perfectly correlated over time, so that fluctuations such as the baby boom are ruled out by assumption. In addition, errors in fertility and mortality are implicitly assumed to be perfectly correlated with one another, in the sense that high fertility is always associated with low mortality (or always with high mortality). A final problem is that the high–low bounds cannot have any consistent probabilistic interpretation across different measures, since true uncertainties tend to cancel in larger aggregates like total population, relative to their constituent parts like numbers of births in certain years or the sizes of particular age groups. In the scenario approach, no such cancellation can take place.

From this point, I will focus on the main direction taken in the research, with less attention to the side routes that turned out to be deadends.

Stochastic population forecasts

As a graduate student, I wanted to develop more genuinely probabilistic population forecasts. I realized that most population forecasting errors derived from errors in forecasting the vital rates rather than from individual-level uncertainty, as discussed earlier. At first I thought that the answer lay in formulating stochastic models of fertility and mortality, and then using the probability intervals from their fertility and mortality forecasts to set the upper and lower 95 percent probability bounds for the projection scenarios. However, it soon became clear that this would not do, for all the reasons given above: scenarios do not and cannot work probabilistically. Probabilistic projections required a population projection matrix with stochastic rates that could vary after every projection step, with the probability distribution of the projected population derived from the sequence of matrixes.

I could write down the equations for the stochastic vital rates, perhaps, but I did not know how to derive their implications. A few years later, I began seeing a series of papers by Shripad Tuljapurkar (Tulja), on population renewal in random environments. He was interested in the population dynamics of all species, and he explicitly developed the probability distributions of population variables when reproduction and survival were disturbed by climate, predation, and other partially natural influences (Tuljapurkar 1990). Later, Tulja spent some time at Berkeley and we joined forces to tackle the problem of stochastic population forecasts, combining my work on modeling the vital rates as stochastic processes and his work on population renewal in random environments.

After several years of work, and improvements due to referees, the results were published in Lee and Tuljapurkar (1994). The paper contained analytic approximations for the actual probability distributions, derived at great cost. In order to check on these analytic results, Tulja also carried out stochastic simulations, which confirmed their accuracy. This exercise taught us that while the explicit mathematical solutions were intellectually satisfying and yielded some insights, the stochastic simulations were far simpler and could be used to estimate probability distributions for any desired functions of the age distributions. We reluctantly abandoned the analytic solutions in our subsequent work. This work, finally brought to a successful resolution, drew on earlier deep theoretical research by Tulja in mathematical population biology, and by me in historical demography.

Figure 6 shows forecasts from 1999 to 2080 of the old-age dependency ratio, here defined as (population 65+)/(population 20–64), with 95 percent probability intervals and comparisons to the Census and Social Security (SSA) projections and ranges. The central forecasts of all three are quite similar, although ours are slightly higher because we forecast more rapid mortality decline. Our 95 percent interval is much broader than the high–low interval of Social Security, which is in turn substantially broader than that of Census, because of the bundling choices for defining their trajectories, as discussed earlier. We find that the high Social Security trajectory is just above the 75th probability bound, and far below the 97.5 percent probability bound. According to our forecasts, there is a considerable possibility

FIGURE 6 Old-age dependency ratio forecasts: 1999 to 2080

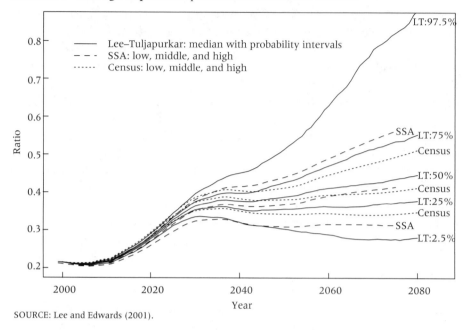

SOURCE: Lee and Edwards (2001).

that population aging may be much more severe than that considered by Social Security and Census.

I have emphasized the contributions of Tuljapurkar and myself, but at the same time Juha Alho and his collaborators (Alho and Spencer 1985; Alho 1990, 1997) were working along similar lines and making important contributions. Keyfitz, in unpublished work, suggested a different approach: randomly sampling rates of mortality change from the past, and independently randomly sampling levels of fertility, as a basis for developing a stochastic forecast. Stoto (1983) and Keyfitz (1981) developed methods for attaching probability intervals to forecasts of population growth rates and population size by analyzing ex post forecasting errors, an approach extensively developed and discussed in National Research Council (2000). Pflaumer (1988) made stochastic population forecasts by randomly sampling vital rates from the high–low range in official forecasts. Lutz, Sanderson, and Scherbov (1996) have elaborated on this approach in a series of papers, an approach criticized by Lee (1999) and Tuljapurkar, Lee, and Li (in press). Vigorous debates at several international meetings have explored the relative merits of these approaches.

But what are these good for? Stochastic Social Security forecasts

We had achieved an important goal, one I had started working on 27 years earlier. But we soon realized that nobody really understood these new projections, or what they were good for. Yes, we could now provide a probability distribution for the forecast of any demographic quantity, simply by examining our stochastic simulation results. But how did, say, the 95 percent probability bounds differ from the standard high, medium, and low scenarios? In fact they differed profoundly, but this was difficult to convey.

After trying to explain all this to practitioners who were accustomed to the traditional scenarios, and failing to get the point across, we decided that we would need to work out an application ourselves, to illustrate the power of the new stochastic population forecasts. Social Security finances seemed the best place to start, because the Trustees projected over a 75-year horizon every year, and because demography and population aging played key roles in these projections. Furthermore, the Social Security Trust Fund was the cumulation of net surpluses, and so it should depend on the sum of functions of the demography. Along any stochastic trajectory, there should tend to be some degree of cancellation of errors in our projections, but not in the traditional high-low scenarios used by the Social Security Actuaries.

Tulja and I initially developed simulations of the Trust Fund, with only the demography stochastic. Michael Anderson, who at the time was a graduate student in demography and statistics at Berkeley, programmed the stochastic simulations. Soon, however, we moved on to model productivity growth rates and real interest rates as stochastic processes, and for some purposes we similarly modeled stock market returns. Our stochastic forecasts for the Trust Fund typically reflected four stochastic inputs out of the eight or ten inputs that were usually viewed as uncertain. The inputs we did *not* treat as stochastic included inflation, disability, and immigration. We believed that the four we included were the most important sources of uncertainty and would capture most of the overall uncertainty.

Figure 7 shows histograms for the date of exhaustion of the Social Security Trust Fund assuming no change in the payroll tax rate, no investment of the fund in equities, and no change in the currently legislated increase in the normal age of retirement to 67, based on the central assumptions contained in the Trustees' Report of 1998 (somewhat more pessimistic than the more recent Trustees' assumptions). The median date of exhaustion was then 2032, with 2.5 percent probability of exhaustion by 2022 and 97.5 percent by 2072. We consistently find that even the most favorable 2.5 percent bound shows exhaustion in less than 75 years, in contrast to the Trustees' "Low Cost" forecasts, which suggested that if we were lucky the system would be able to continue robustly in the future.

At the same time we were developing our stochastic forecasts for the Social Security Administration, the Congressional Budget Office (CBO) had noted our 1994 paper on stochastic population forecasts and asked whether they could use our stochastic population trajectories as the basis for stochastic Social Security projections of their own. We sent them a set of a thousand stochastic population simulations, and they did indeed develop

FIGURE 7   Histograms of 1,000 dates of exhaustion for the Social Security Trust Fund

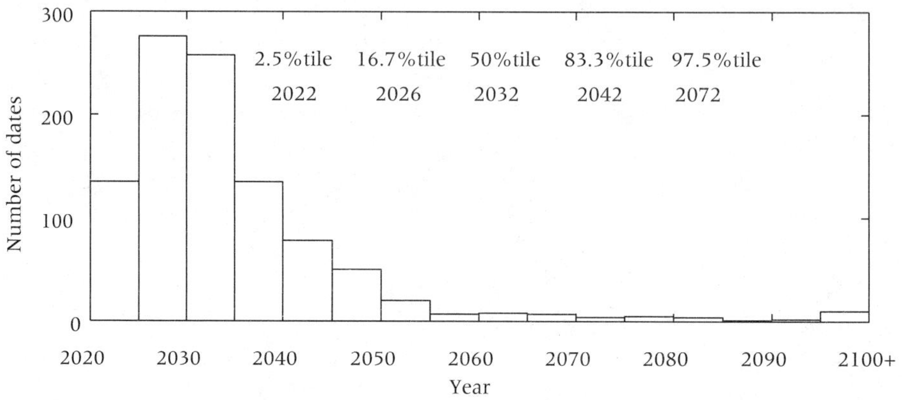

	2.5%tile	16.7%tile	50%tile	83.3%tile	97.5%tile
	2022	2026	2032	2042	2072

SOURCE: Lee and Tuljapurkar (2000).

stochastic forecasts that they published annually for a number of years. In 2001 they published a more elaborate stochastic forecast for SSA, this time developing their own stochastic population model from scratch. I believe that this effort benefited from the short class we taught in Washington, DC for three summers, which I will describe later.

In 1999–2000, I served on the Technical Advisory Panel for Social Security, and I presented our results there. The Trustees and Actuaries had already been advised by earlier committees that they should do stochastic forecasting, so our efforts fit well with those recommendations. Although nothing happened at the time, in 2003 SSA did develop and publish its own stochastic forecasts for the first time, using methods closely related to ours. They also published comparisons of their stochastic projections to ours and to a set developed by CBO. The three were remarkably consistent.

Stochastic fiscal projections

When President Bush began arguing for tax cuts in early 2001, the Congressional Budget Office was projecting large surpluses over the next decade, and Alan Greenspan, Chairman of the Federal Reserve, was worrying about what would be done once all the government debt had been paid back. A probabilistic forecast would have shown that not much confidence should have been placed in those projections, and indeed the Congressional Budget Office had included probability intervals based on its own analysis of the past performance of its projections, and these showed that it was quite possible that the surpluses would turn to deficits within a few years. I was invited to testify to the Senate Budget Committee about the uncertainties in the fiscal outlook and on the impact of population aging on the federal budget. My testimony was received with interest, but I doubt that it had much impact. Here is the story of how the probabilistic fiscal forecasts were developed.

In 1995, I served on a panel organized by the Committee on Population of the National Academy of Sciences, chaired by James Smith, to assess the economic and demographic consequences of immigration to the United States for a special bipartisan Congressional Commission. My task was to estimate the fiscal impact of immigrants using a longitudinal design which required that I prepare long-run projections of US government budgets at the federal, state, and local levels. I had developed relevant methods during earlier work on estimating the externalities to childbearing, involving the estimation of age profiles of government benefits and taxation and shifting these over time with productivity growth. Figure 8 illustrates cross-sectional age profiles of this sort for the year 2000, showing the dominating importance of public education, Social Security benefits, Medicare, and institutional Medicaid. Similar age profiles were estimated for various kinds of taxes.

I received advice on modeling government budgets from Alan Auerbach and Robert Inman, two leading public finance economists also on the immigration panel. I hired Ryan Edwards, then a graduate student in Economics, to work on the budgetary side of these projections. Tim Miller, a demographic

FIGURE 8   How the value of benefits received from government programs varies by age of individual in the US in 2000 (lines show cumulative totals)

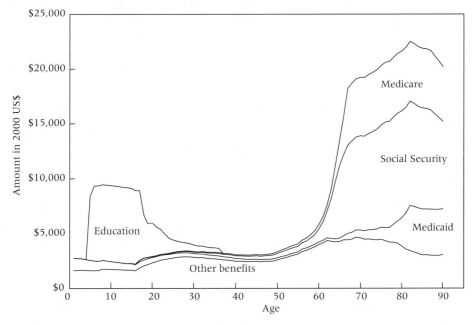

SOURCE: Lee and Edwards (2001).

researcher at Berkeley, did most of the necessary estimation. With NIA support, this research team worked for a year and brought the project to an interesting and successful conclusion. As a byproduct, we had developed the expertise to make long-run deterministic budget projections for all levels of government. If we could do it for one set of demographic and economic assumptions, then we could do it for others, so we had the machinery in place to construct stochastic budget forecasts for all government programs and total taxes and expenditures, exploiting detailed population age distributions and schedules of benefits and costs by age, as driven by productivity growth rates. We were able to draw on both the stochastic population projection methods and the methods for stochastic projections of SSA. It seemed only natural to take advantage of the situation to construct probabilistic forecasts of federal, state, and local taxes and expenditures. We did this, based on seven kinds of taxes and 25 age-specific government programs. The results were published in Lee and Edwards (2001 and 2002).

Figure 9 shows probabilistic forecasts of government spending as a share of gross domestic product at all levels (federal, state, and local) combined, but disaggregated by age group in the first three panels and in total in the last panel. These forecasts are conditional on the assumption that current program structures remain constant or vary only according to currently legislated plans such as the increase in the normal retirement age. Panel C shows that no change is projected for the share of age-neutral programs, consisting mainly of such items as defense expenditures, police, fire, and research: expenditures that cannot be assigned to recipients of any particular age. The flat line with no probability dispersion reflects the assumption made, following assumptions of the Congressional Budget Office, that such expenditures will be a constant share of GDP in the future. Panel B shows that expenditures on the young (defined on a programmatic basis and including expenditures on higher education) are also expected to be flat over the coming decades, although in this case there is substantial uncertainty, reflecting uncertainty about fertility and therefore the share of children in the population. Panel A shows that expenditures on the elderly (again defined by program) are expected to rise strongly, nearly tripling in 80 years, owing primarily to the effect of population aging on Social Security, Medicare, and institutional Medicaid (that is, for long-term care). The probability distribution is narrow for the first 25 years or so, reflecting mainly uncertainty about mortality and survival. After this point, however, the much greater uncertainty about fertility begins to affect the projected size of the working age population, which drives projections of GDP and therefore strongly influences expenditures on the elderly as a share of GDP. Panel D shows the forecast for expenditures for all age groups combined. We would expect a negative correlation between expenditures on children and the elderly as a share of GDP, since variations in fertility would affect these

FIGURE 9 Projected government spending as a share of GDP by broad age group of recipient, 1994–2070 (mean and 95% probability intervals)

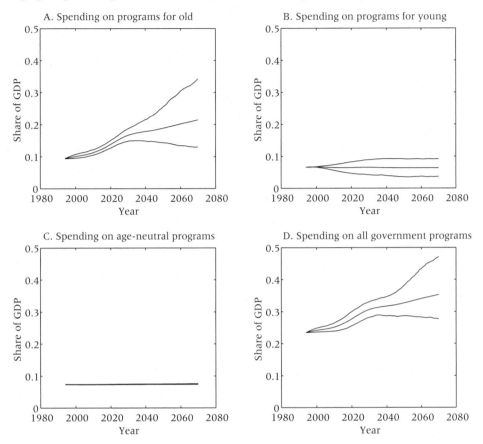

SOURCE: Lee and Tuljapurkar (2000).

expenditures in opposite directions. This correlation is implicitly taken into account in the probability intervals in Panel D. The central forecast shows that total governmental expenditures as a share of GDP would rise by more than 50 percent over the next 75 years, which we have seen is due entirely to expenditures on the elderly. The 95 percent probability interval extends from about 28 percent of GDP to about 48 percent of GDP, with uncertainty in the upward direction being greater than downward.

Health care costs: The joker in the deck

Medicare expenditures were one piece of the federal projections reported above about which we had reservations. However, based on earlier research by actuaries of the Health Care Financing Administration, Tim Miller (2001) published a paper showing how data on Medicare costs by time until death could be used in projections of Medicare costs. In these projections, as mortality falls, there are two effects on costs. First, there are more old people at every age, so costs tend to rise. Second, at any given age a smaller proportion of people is near death, so costs tend to fall. These two effects largely cancel, as it happens, so it makes little difference to costs whether mortality declines rapidly or slowly. Miller's work paved the way for a subsequent paper on stochastic forecasts of Medicare expenditures (Lee and Miller 2002). In these forecasts, we estimated a stochastic time series model for the growth in Medicare expenditures per enrollee in excess of per capita income growth. This was used as a multiplicative shifter for a schedule relating Medicare costs to years until death. Along each stochastic trajectory, we knew the distribution of deaths by age, so we could apply this schedule to the distribution of deaths to find the Medicare costs implied.

Figure 10 contrasts our probabilistic time-until-death-based forecasts of Medicare costs with the official government projections. Here, probability deciles are indicated by the darkness of the fan. The probability is 10 percent that Medicare hospital insurance spending will fall in the darkest area and 90 percent that it will fall within the whole shaded area. The lines represent the

FIGURE 10   Medicare Hospital Insurance Program as a percent of GDP: Lee–Miller probability deciles and Trustees' scenarios (excludes Medicare's Supplementary Medical Insurance Program)

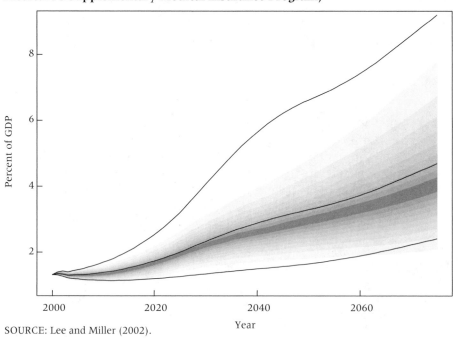

SOURCE: Lee and Miller (2002).

Trustees' low, intermediate, and high cost scenarios. It turns out that probabilistic projections are not always more gloomy than deterministic ones. First, taking time until death into account leads to projections of Medicare costs that are substantially lower than the official projections by the Medicare Trustees, because our forecasts implicitly assume improving health at every age as mortality falls. Second, we see that while our lower probability decile corresponds closely to the Trustees' low projection, their high projection is far more pessimistic than our upper 97.5 percent bound: we find it very unlikely that their high scenario will come to pass.

Population and fiscal projections for California

In 2001, I was asked to prepare projections of population aging in California for the state legislature, and I took advantage of the opportunity to enlist Tim Miller and Ryan Edwards in the effort, and to prepare stochastic projections for the population of California and for its budget through 2050. Miller developed stochastic immigration and internal migration projections, which we incorporated in the demographic forecasts. Figure 11 shows our projections of the state budget, again assuming current program structure. In contrast to the federal and general government projections, we find almost no systematic tendency for expenditures to rise relative to gross state product, because for the most part the state does not provide benefits tar-

FIGURE 11   Projections of California's general fund revenues and expenditures as shares of gross state product

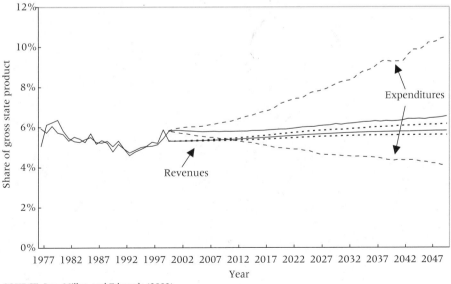

SOURCE: Lee, Miller, and Edwards (2003).

geted to the elderly and therefore is not affected by the projected population aging. Revenues are almost flat with almost no uncertainty, since they are expressed as a share of gross state product and are not much affected by population age distribution. These projections attracted considerable interest in Sacramento, and point toward the application of these methods at the state and local level.

Proselytizing and training

In the summers of 1998 to 2001, Tulja, Edwards, Anderson, and I taught a short intensive class in Washington, DC on our new methods for stochastic forecasting, with funding from the Social Security Administration. We pitched it to professional government forecasters, and people attended from many government agencies, including Social Security, Census, Congressional Budget Office, Office of Management and Budget, General Accounting Office, and Veterans Affairs. Some graduate students, academics, and government forecasters from other countries attended as well. The lectures seemed to generate a great deal of interest. It is difficult for us to assess the impact of these classes, but in 2001 CBO published its own stochastic forecast for Social Security, and in 2003 SSA published its own version, as discussed earlier.

Where next for stochastic forecasting?

These general methods for making stochastic forecasts of mortality, fertility, population, Pay-As-You-Go pension systems, health care costs, and full government budgets appear to be reasonably well established, although there is plenty of room for improving each, and for trying completely different strategies. Many questions remain about the best way to handle various details, and work on these questions is ongoing. Doubtless problems will be discovered and the methods will evolve. For example, a book by Tabeau, Jeths, and Heathcoate (2001) discusses many approaches to forecasting mortality including Lee–Carter, and an unpublished manuscript by Girosi and King (2004) contains a searching critical analysis of the Lee–Carter method and develops an alternative approach based on covariates and smoothness priors. Denton and Spencer in Canada, and CBO and the Social Security Actuaries are all exploring alternative approaches. Li Nan and I are working on modifying and extending Lee–Carter for use by the United Nations in the mortality component of their global population projections.

I would like to see government agencies develop and use stochastic long-run budget projections. This seems particularly important, given the great stresses that population aging will put on the budgets of the industrial world through public pension programs, health care, and long-term care. Policy changes today should be undertaken in light of this sobering long-term outlook, but also with a full appreciation of the degree of uncertainty about these pressures. In recent years, both the Bush administration tax cuts and the Iraq war illustrate the importance for good decisionmaking of taking into account not only the best guess forecast, but also a careful assessment of the degree of uncertainty about that guess, and the expected cost of errors.

One of the most challenging questions in this area is just how policymakers should take uncertainty into account: by acting quickly to build up buffer funds or to contain a situation that might deteriorate if no action is taken, or by postponing action until we have a clearer idea of which direction the cat is going to jump. A useful start has been made on this question by Auerbach and Hassett (2000). But posing the problem as I just did suggests that once the cat jumps, we will know how the future will unfold—rapid versus slow gains in life expectancy, deficits versus surpluses, and so on. In reality it is much more likely that the future will be no more certain in ten years or twenty or fifty than it is now. The world is not going to choose a direction and then adhere to it thereafter. There is uncertainty about big changes and at every step of the way, without end. We must live and act in the face of this uncertainty as we have always done, but understanding it better should lead to better decisions.

Note

Research described in this chapter was funded by a grant from NIA, R37-AG11761. Tim Miller made valuable contributions to the analysis. I am particularly grateful to my collaborators over the years in this work: first, Lawrence Carter and Shripad Tuljapurkar; and later, Tim Miller, Ryan Edwards, Michael Anderson, and Nan Li.

References

Alho, Juha M. 1990. "Stochastic methods in population forecasting," *International Journal of Forecasting* 6:.521–530.

———. 1997. "Scenarios, uncertainty, and conditional forecasts of the world population," *Journal of the Royal Statistical Society, Series A* 160: 71–85.

Alho, Juha M. and Bruce D. Spencer. 1985. "Uncertain population forecasting," *Journal of the American Statistical Association* 80(390): 306–314.

Auerbach, Alan and Kevin Hassett. 2000. "Uncertainty and the design of long-run fiscal policy" in Alan Auerbach and Ronald Lee (eds.), *Demography and Fiscal Policy*. Cambridge: Cambridge University Press, pp. 73–92.

Board of Trustees, Federal Old-Age and Survivors Insurance and Disability Insurance Trust Funds. 1992. *The 1992 Annual Report*. Washington, DC: US Government Printing Office.

———. 1998. *The 1998 Annual Report*. Washington, DC: US Government Printing Office.

Carter, Lawrence and Ronald Lee. 1986. "Joint forecasts of U.S. marital fertility, nuptiality, births and marriages using time series models," *Journal of the American Statistical Association*.

————. 1992. "Modeling and forecasting U.S. mortality: Differentials in life expectancy by sex," in Dennis Ahlburg and Kenneth Land (eds.), *Population Forecasting*, a Special Issue of the *International Journal of Forecasting* 8(3): 393–412.

Cohen, Joel E. 1995. *How Many People Can the Earth Support?* New York: W. W. Norton & Co.

Girosi, Federico and Gary King. 2004. "Demographic forecasting," unpublished book manuscript. Downloadable at «http://gking.harvard.edu/files/smooth.pdf».

Keyfitz, Nathan. 1981. "The limits of population forecasting," *Population and Development Review* 7(4): 579–593.

Lee, Ronald D. 1974a. "Forecasting births in post-transitional populations: Stochastic renewal with serially correlated fertility," *Journal of the American Statistical Association* 69(247): 607–617.

————. 1974b. "The formal dynamics of controlled populations and the echo, the boom, and the bust," *Demography* 11(4): 563–585.

————. 1976. "Demographic forecasting and the Easterlin hypothesis," *Population and Development Review* 2: 459–468.

————. 1980. "Aiming at a moving target: Period fertility and changing reproductive goals," *Population Studies* 34(2): 205–226.

————. 1981. "Model for forecasting fertility from birth expectations data," in Gerry Hendershot and Paul Placek (eds.), *Predicting Fertility: Demographic Studies of Birth Expectations*. Lexington, MA: Lexington Books.

————. 1990. "Longrun global population forecasts: A critical appraisal," in Kinglsey Davis and Michail Bernstam (eds.), *Resources, Environment, and Population: Present Knowledge, Future Options*, a supplement to *Population and Development Review* 16: 44–71.

————. 1992. "Stochastic demographic forecasting," in Dennis Ahlburg and Kenneth Land (eds.), *Population Forecasting*, a special issue of the *International Journal of Forecasting* 8(3): 315–328.

————. 1993. "Modeling and forecasting the time series of US fertility: Age patterns, range, and ultimate level," *International Journal of Forecasting* 9: 187–202.

————. 1999. "Probabilistic approaches to population forecasting," in Wolfgang Lutz, James Vaupel, and Dennis Ahlburg (eds.), *Frontiers of Population Forecasting*, supplement to *Population and Development Review* 24: 156–190.

Lee, Ronald D. and Lawrence Carter. 1992. "Modeling and forecasting the time series of U.S. mortality," *Journal of the American Statistical Association* 87(419): 659–671.

Lee, Ronald and Ryan Edwards. 2001. "The fiscal impact of population change," in Jane Sneddon Little and Robert K. Triest (eds.), *Seismic Shifts: The Economic Impact of Demographic Change*. Federal Reserve Bank of Boston Conference Series No. 46, pp. 220–237.

————. 2002. "The fiscal effects of population aging in the US: Assessing the uncertainties," James M. Poterba (ed.), *Tax Policy and Economy* 16. Cambridge, MA: MIT Press, pp. 141–181.

Lee, Ronald and Timothy Miller. 2001. "Evaluating the performance of the Lee–Carter approach to modeling and forecasting mortality," *Demography* 38(4): 537–549.

————. 2002. "An approach to forecasting health expenditures, with application to the US Medicare system," *Health Services Research* 37(5): 1365–1386.

Lee, Ronald, Timothy Miller, and Ryan Edwards. 2003. *A Special Report: The Growth and Aging of California's Population: Demographic and Fiscal Projections, Characteristics and Service Needs*. Berkeley: California Policy Research Center, Technical Assistance Program, University of California.

Lee, Ronald D. and Francois Nault. 1993. "Modeling and forecasting Canadian mortality: An application of the Lee–Carter approach, with extensions," presented at World Congress of the IUSSP, Montreal, August.

Lee, Ronald and Shripad Tuljapurkar. 1994. "Stochastic population projections for the United

States: Beyond high, medium and low," *Journal of the American Statistical Association*, 89(428): 1175–1189.

———. 2000. "Population forecasting for fiscal planning: Issues and innovations" in Alan Auerbach and Ronald Lee (eds.), *Demography and Fiscal Policy*. Cambridge: Cambridge University Press, pp. 7–57.

Li, Nan, Ronald Lee, and Shripad Tuljapurkar. 2004. "Using the Lee–Carter method to forecast mortality for populations with limited data," *International Statistical Review* 72(1): 19–36.

Lutz, Wolfgang, Warren Sanderson, and Sergei Scherbov. 1996. "Probabilistic population projections based on expert opinion," in Wolfgang Lutz (ed.), *The Future Population of the World: What Can We Assume Today?*," revised 1996 edition. London: Earthscan Publications.

McNown, Robert and Andrei Rogers. 1989. "Forecasting mortality: A parameterized time series approach," *Demography* 26(4): 645–660.

———. 1992. "Forecasting cause-specific mortality using time series methods," *International Journal of Forecasting* 8: 413–432.

Miller, Tim. 2001. "Increasing longevity and Medicare expenditures," *Demography* 38(2): 215–226.

National Research Council. 2000. *Beyond Six Billion: Forecasting the World's Population. Panel on Population Projections*, John Bongaarts and Rodolfo Bulatao (eds.). Committee on Population, Commission on Behavioral and Social Sciences and Education, Washington, DC: National Academy Press.

Pflaumer, Peter. 1988. "Confidence intervals for population projections based on Monte Carlo methods," *International Journal of Forecasting* 4: 135–142.

Stoto, Michael. 1983. "The accuracy of population projections," *Journal of the American Statistical Association* 78(381): 13–20.

Sykes, Z. M. 1969. "Some stochastic versions of the matrix model for population dynamics," *Journal of the American Statistical Association* 44: 111–130.

Tabeau, Ewa, Anneke Van Den Berg Jeths, and Christopher Heathcote. 2001. *Forecasting Mortality in Developed Countries*. Dordrecht, The Netherlands: Kluwer Academic Publishers.

Tuljapurkar, Shripad. 1990. *Population Dynamics in Variable Environments*. Springer-Verlag, Lecture Notes in Biomathematics no. 85.

Tuljapurkar, Shripad, Ronald Lee, and Qi Li. 2004. "Random scenario forecasts versus stochastic forecasts," *International Statistical Review* 72(2): 185–199.

Tuljapurkar, S., N. Li, and C. Boe. 2000. "A universal pattern of mortality change in the G7 countries," *Nature* 405: 789–792.

U.S. Bureau of the Census. 1989. "Current Population Reports," Series P-25, No. 1018, *Projections for the Population of the United States, by Age, Sex, and Race: 1988 to 2080*, by Gregory Spencer. Washington, DC: U.S. Government Printing Office.

———. 1992. "Current Population Reports," Series P25 No. 1092, *Population Projections of the United States, by Age, Sex, Race, and Hispanic Origin: 1992 to 2050*, by Jennifer Cheeseman Day. Washington, DC: U.S. Government Printing Office.

Wade, Virginia. 1989. *Social Security Area Population Projections: 1989*, Actuarial Study No. 105. Washington, DC: Office of the Actuary, Social Security Administration.

Social Security Provisions and the Labor Force Participation of Older Workers

DAVID A. WISE

One of the most striking economic trends in the United States over the past three decades has been the withdrawal of older persons from the labor force. This trend is common to almost all other industrialized countries as well, although in planning the analysis explained below I did not know that. There had been a great deal of work in the United States aimed at understanding the relationship between the provisions of the Social Security system and the retirement of older workers. I had participated in some of that work.[1] The United States Social Security system began in 1935 and expanded over the next four decades.

There was a concurrent trend in the United States. The adoption of employer-provided pension plans was spurred by the Revenue Act of 1942, which clarified the tax incentives to employers who established pension plans. These plans grew rapidly over the 1950s, 1960s, and 1970s. Most of these were so-called defined benefit plans, in which the employee pension benefit at retirement depended on years of service with the employer and earnings, typically earnings in the last years of employment. The first description (of which I am aware) of the incentives inherent in the plan provisions was by Jeremy Bulow (1981). Edward Lazear (1983) also wrote an influential paper proposing that the incentives were intended to induce older workers to leave the labor force, based on the proposition that, when old, they were paid more than their marginal product.

In a series of articles, Laurence Kotlikoff and I (Kotlikoff and Wise 1985, 1987, 1988, 1989a) used data from the Bureau of Labor Statistics—which published information on the precise provisions of a large sample of employer-provided plans—to describe the incentive effects over a broad range of pension plans in the United States, and we emphasized the enormous variation across plans. These data, however, contained no information on

176

the retirement decisions of individuals covered by the plans. To obtain plan provisions together with data on individual retirement choices, we examined firm personnel records. These data included information on individuals' retirement decisions and their earnings histories, in addition to a precise description of their firms' pension plan provisions. Again we (Kotlikoff and Wise 1989b) used such data to describe the striking relationship between pension plan provisions in a firm and retirement from that firm.

James Stock and I (Stock and Wise 1990a, 1990b) used firm data in the development and estimation of the option value retirement model. The central feature of this method is recognition of the important effect on retirement of the future accrual pattern of pension benefits. That is, retirement benefits could be much larger, or much smaller, if retirement is delayed, and thus the "option value" of delaying retirement can have an important effect on individual retirement decisions. Subsequent analyses by Lumsdaine, Stock, and Wise (1992) of the option value model in comparison with a stochastic dynamic programming specification were also based on firm data. Our conclusion was that the option value model seemed to capture the retirement decisions of employees just as well as or perhaps better than the closely related, but more complex, dynamic programming model. This result was confirmed by Ausink and Wise (1996). Several other articles by Lumsdaine, Stock, and Wise (1990, 1991, 1994, 1996, 1997) compared results from several firms, for men and women, and for different types of employees. We found very similar behavioral response to pension plan incentives by men and women and by different types of employees.

Although this work was directed to the retirement incentive effects of employer-provided pension plans, it was clear that the same framework could be used to analyze the incentive effects of public social security plans, which were also typically based on a defined benefit formulation of retirement benefits.

While this work establishing a new framework for analyzing the incentive effects of plan provisions was progressing, there was growing interest in the financial liability of social security systems in the United States, as well as in other countries. Feldstein (1998), for example, focused on this issue. There were three interrelated issues: one was that pay-as-you-go social security systems were under financial pressure in most industrialized countries, a second was that labor force participation rates were falling in many counties, and a third was that the provisions of the plans themselves could be contributing to the decline in labor force participation. The juxtaposition of these three issues led me to believe that by comparing social security systems across countries, it might be possible to learn much more about the retirement incentive effects of plan provisions than was possible from studying one system in isolation. Considering social security systems in different countries would be analogous to considering the effects of different employer-provided pension plans—with varying provisions—in the United States.

Thus I set out to organize such a study. Jonathan Gruber agreed to work with me on the project and we have been collaborators in this project ever since. At the outset I wrote the following letter to economists in other countries, most of whom I had known from past contacts and many of whom were friends of long standing.

> I am organizing an international project on Social Security and I would like to entice you to participate....
>
> Social Security provisions and benefits vary widely from country to country. Yet in virtually every developed country, population aging has placed increased financial pressure on the social security system. At the same time, labor force participation rates of older people are falling in many countries. Indeed, in some countries at least, incentives inherent in the social security system and employer-provided pensions provide inducement to retire early. Policy discussions and academic deliberations in many countries, including the United States, have considered ways that the financial viability of the systems might be addressed. For example, in the United States, current plans call for an increase in the Social Security retirement age from 65 to 67 and other changes in the calculation of benefits. Because the issue is so widespread, it seems to me that the topic provides a natural opportunity to learn from the experience in different countries.
>
> I have in mind a project that would include papers pertaining to the system in each participating country. The papers would include two components: The first component would describe the system in each country and would present consistent calculations that would allow comparisons between counties. In particular, we would want to describe analytically the benefit generosity, labor force participation incentives, and possibly other features inherent in the provisions of each country. To do this will require precise calculations based on the benefit formulas in each country.... We may also need to describe how the public social security system interacts with employer-provided pensions. We would develop a template that would describe the calculations that would be made for each country.
>
> The second component would be country specific and could bring out empirical or conceptual issues specific to a particular country. For example, it could discuss reform proposals and how they are intended to change the incentives or other features described in the first component....
>
> Jon Gruber has agreed to help me set up the project and in particular will help to develop a template that can be used to provide comparable cross-country comparisons.

This invitation was sent to individuals in ten countries, in addition to the United States. Almost every recipient agreed to participate and in one or two cases where the recipient was unable to do so, the recipient directed me to another likely participant. By early 1996 we had the team established. (An additional country, Denmark, was added after the first phase of the project.)

From the beginning, the key feature of the project was to prepare papers in each country according to a common template that Gruber and I developed, so that results could be compared across countries.

Three phases of the ongoing project have been completed and we are now working on the fourth. I will describe the results of the first three phases and then comment on plans for the fourth and future phases. For each phase, the country team prepared a paper for that country. The country papers for each phase are grouped into a single volume. An important component of each volume is the summary chapter that Gruber and I prepared. The intent of the summary chapters is to combine the key findings from each of the country papers in a way that facilitates comparison of the findings across countries. The results reported below are drawn largely from these summary chapters.

Phase I: Plan provisions, incentives to retire, and labor force participation of older workers

By the time work began, it had become clear that under pay-as-you-go social security systems, governments around the world had made promises they could not keep. The systems were not sustainable. Social reform discussions were ongoing, and continue, in almost all developed countries. Some proposals sought fundamental reform, often calling for funding through personal social security accounts. Other proposals called for "incremental" reform, suggesting increases in retirement ages and other changes without altering the basic pay-as-you-go structure of the systems.

It has been commonly assumed that the problem of unsustainable systems was caused by population aging. The number of retirees is now increasing very rapidly relative to the number of younger persons in the workforce. In addition, people are living longer, so that workers who reach retirement age will be receiving benefits longer than they used to. The ratio of the number of people aged 65 and older to the number 20 to 64—based on data available at the time this study was begun—is shown in Figure 1, now (in the 1990s) and in future years, for ten countries. The increase is striking in almost every country. In Japan, with the most rapid population aging, the ratio will more than double by 2020 and will almost triple by 2050. These demographic trends have placed enormous pressure on the financial viability of the social security systems in these countries, increasing the number of retirees relative to the number of employees who must pay for the benefits for retirees.

The financial pressure caused by population aging was compounded by another trend. In virtually every country employees were leaving the

FIGURE 1   Population aged 65+ years to population aged 20–64

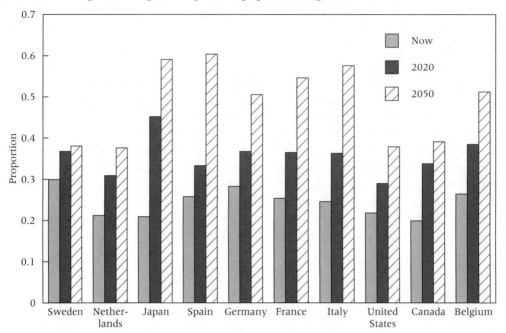

NOTE: Figure for Japan is the ratio of persons aged 65+ to those 15–64. German data for "Now" is based on the average of the ratio in 1990 and the projected ratio in 2000. Canada data shown for 2020 are for 2025.
SOURCE: Gruber and Wise (1999b).

labor force at younger and younger ages, further increasing the ratio of retirees to labor force participants who must pay for the benefits. The labor force participation rates of men aged 60 to 64 for the years 1960 to 1996 are shown for each of the ten countries in the two panels of Figure 2. The decline was substantial in each of the countries, but was much greater in some countries than in others. In the early 1960s, the participation rates were above 70 percent in all but one of the countries and above 80 percent in several. By the mid-1990s, the rate had fallen to below 20 percent in Belgium, France, and the Netherlands. It had fallen to about 32 percent in Italy, about 35 percent in Germany, and 40 percent in Spain. Although analysts in the United States have often emphasized the "dramatic" fall in that country, the US decline from 82 percent to 53 percent was modest in comparison to the much more precipitous declines in European countries. The decline to 57 percent in Sweden was also large, but modest when compared to the fall in other countries. Japan stands out with the smallest decline of all the countries, from about 83 percent to 75 percent. Labor force participation rates of 45–59-year-old men, as well as those 60 and older, have also declined substantially.[2]

FIGURE 2 Trends in labor force participation for men aged 60–64 years

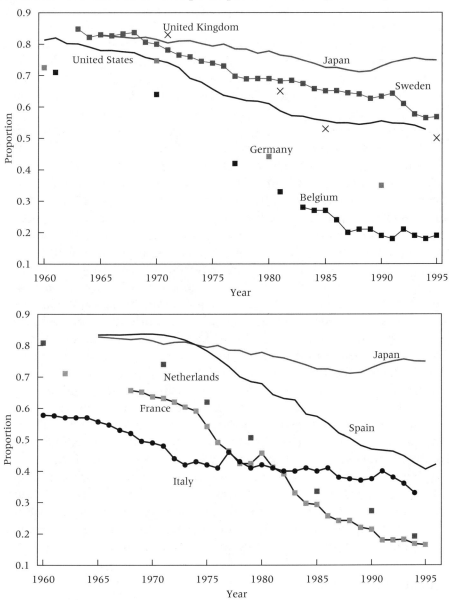

SOURCE: Gruber and Wise (1999b: 3).

What had gone largely unappreciated was that, like the retirement incentives built into employer-provided defined benefit plans in the United States, defined benefit social security programs could also induce older workers to leave the labor force. Thus the provisions of the programs could contribute to their own financial insolvency. The goal of the first phase of the project was to describe the incentives inherent in the social security provisions in the project countries and to relate the incentives to the labor force participation of older workers. The template for this phase asked that each country paper begin with a description of the historical evolution of labor force participation and then present data on the current age-specific activities and income sources of men and women. The template further asked that each country paper present data for men and women on: (1) labor force participation rates by age interval between 1960 and the present, (2) the proportion of employees covered by the public pension system and the proportion of persons over age 55 receiving public pensions from 1960 to the present, (3) replacement rates (the ratio of social security benefits to earnings just before retirement) under the public pension system from 1960 to the present, (4) current labor force participation rates by age, (5) labor force status—employed, unemployed, disabled, retired—by age, (6) proportion receiving various public "pensions"—e.g., old age, disability, survivor—by age, (7) proportions receiving employer-provided pensions by age, (8) source of household income by age, (9) retirement and public pension hazard rates by age. We asked that each paper then describe the institutional features of the country's social security system, highlighting any interactions with other public and private programs that might also influence retirement behavior.

The core of each paper is a detailed analysis of the retirement incentives inherent in the provisions of that country's retirement income system. By making the same analytic calculations and by presenting the same simulations in each of the countries, the individual studies could provide a means of comparing the retirement incentives among the countries.

Each of the country papers in this phase and in the second phase presents parallel labor force participation and other data for men and women. To simplify the exposition in what follows, I discuss only data for men. But the effect of the social security incentives on leaving the labor force, as discussed below, appears to be at least as important for women as for men. This finding is consistent with the aforementioned finding of very similar responses to employer-provided pension plan incentives by men and women, and by different types of employees, in the United States.

Unused labor force capacity

The proportion of men out of the labor force between ages 55 and 65 is shown in Figure 3 for 11 countries. The term "unused labor force capacity" is intended to emphasize that incentives to induce older persons to leave the labor force reduce national economic production, recognizing of course that not all persons in these age ranges want to work or are able to work. For the 55 to 65 age group the proportion ranges from close to 0.7 in Belgium to about 0.2 in Japan. Subsequent results will show the relationship between social security plan provisions for leaving the labor force and this

FIGURE 3   Unused labor force capacity: Men aged 55 to 65

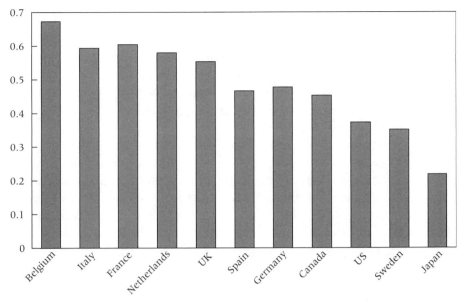

SOURCE: Gruber and Wise (1999b: 7).

measure of unused labor force capacity. I first describe the measurement of incentives to retire.

Measuring incentives to retire

Three key features of social security systems have important effects on incentives to exit the labor force. The first is the age at which benefits become available. This is called the early retirement age, or the age of first eligibility. Across the countries participating in this study, the first eligibility age ranges from about 53 for some employee groups in Italy to 62 in the United States. The "normal" retirement age—e.g., 65 in the United States—is also important, but typically much less so than the early retirement age. Now in most countries, few people work until the "normal" retirement age.

The second feature of plan provisions, which is strongly related to the extent to which people continue to work after the early retirement age, is the pattern of benefit accrual after the age of first eligibility. The idea can be explained this way: Consider two components of total compensation for working an additional year. One component is current wage earnings. The other is the "increase" in future promised social security benefits. Consider a person who has reached the social security early retirement age and suppose that a person is debating whether to work for an additional year. It is natural to suppose that if benefit receipt is delayed by a year, benefits when they are received might be increased, to offset the receipt of benefits for one less year. But in most countries this is not the case. Once benefits are available, a person who continues to work for an additional year will receive less in social security benefits over his lifetime than if he quit work and started to receive benefits at the first opportunity. That is, the present-value expected social security benefits decline. In many countries, this loss of social security benefits can offset a large fraction of the wage earnings a person would receive from continued work. Thus there is an implicit tax on work, and total compensation can be much less than net wage earnings.

More formally, consider the difference between the expected discounted value of social security benefits (social security wealth) if retirement is age $a+1$ and the present value if retirement is at age a, namely $SSW(a+1) - SSW(a)$. This difference is called the accrual of benefits between age a and age $a+1$. This value is often negative. If the accrual is positive, it adds to total compensation from working the additional year; if the accrual is negative, it reduces total compensation. The ratio of the accrual to net wage earnings is an implicit tax on earnings if the accrual is negative and an implicit subsidy to earnings if the accrual is positive. Thus a negative accrual discourages continuation in the labor force and a positive accrual encourages continued participation. This accrual rate, and the associated tax rate, form a key calculation that was made in the same way for each of the countries. As it turns out, the pension accrual is typically negative at older ages: continuation in the labor force means a loss in pension benefits, which imposes an implicit tax on work and provides an incentive to leave the labor force. In many countries the implicit tax on work is 80 percent or more the first year after benefit eligibility.

This feature of plan provisions is related to a technical term called "actuarial adjustment." In the United States, for example, if benefits are taken at age 64 instead of 65, they are reduced just enough to offset the receipt of benefits for one additional year. If they are taken at 63 instead of 65, they are reduced just enough to offset the receipt of benefits for two additional years, and so forth.[3]

A third important feature of social security systems is that in many European countries disability insurance and special unemployment programs essentially provide early retirement benefits before the official early retirement age. Where these programs are prevalent they are incorporated in our social security incentive calculations. For example in Germany, many employees retire as early as age 57 under a "disability" program.

In Germany there was no actuarial adjustment before the 1992 reform legislation, and until recently most employees still retired under provisions that did not include actuarial adjustment. The magnitude of the combined effect of early retirement under the German disability program and no actuarial adjustment is illustrated conceptually in Figure 4. The official

FIGURE 4 Germany: Base and actuarial adjustment

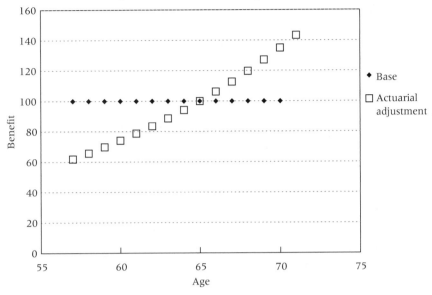

social security normal retirement age in Germany is 65. Suppose that at that age, benefits would be 100 units per year. Many employees can receive benefits at age 57 through the disability program. The disability benefits at 57 are essentially the same as normal retirement benefits at age 65. That is, a person eligible for disability benefits at age 57 who did not take the benefits at that age would forego 100 units per year. On the other hand, suppose benefits were reduced actuarially if taken before age 65 and increased actuarially if taken after age 65. Then benefits taken at 57 would be about 60 units instead of 100. And if receipt of benefits were delayed for a year (to age 58), annual benefits would be increased just enough to offset their receipt for one less year. And if the receipt of benefits were delayed past age 65 they would be increased actuarially. Benefits if taken at 70 would be about 140 units instead of 100. There would be no incentive to take benefits early. Indeed there would be no social security incentive to take benefits at any specific age, once benefits were available.

Retirement incentives and labor force participation

To summarize the social security incentive to retire in each country, we propose a simple measure. At each age, beginning with the early retirement age, the implicit tax on work was calculated in each country. These implicit tax rates on work were then summed beginning with the early retirement age and running through age 69. This measure we called the "tax force" to retire. The sum is shown for each of the countries in Figure

5. This tax force to retire ranges from more than 9 in Italy to about 1.5 in the United States.

The tax force to retire and unused labor force capacity

The key finding from this phase of the analysis is shown in Figures 6 and 7. Figure 6 shows the relationship between the tax force to retire and unused labor force capacity—the proportion of men between ages 55 and 65 who are out of the labor force. It is clear that there is a very strong correspondence between the two. Figure 7 shows the same data for all of the countries except Japan, and rescales the tax force measure to achieve a linear relationship between the tax force to retire and unused labor force capacity. The relationship between the two is even more evident. The proportion of variation in unused labor force capacity that is explained by the tax force to retire is 86 percent (as indicated by the R-squared value).

The results of the first phase were reported in Gruber and Wise (1999a). The summary to the volume (Gruber and Wise 1999b) concluded as follows:

> ... This decline in labor force participation magnifies population trends, further increasing the number of retirees relative to the number of persons who

FIGURE 5   Sum of tax rates on work, from early retirement age to 69

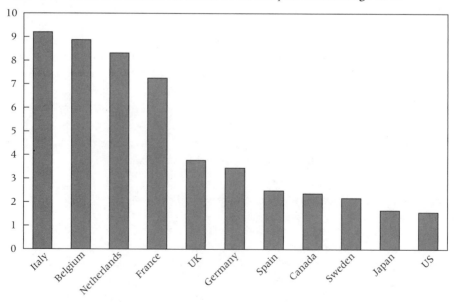

SOURCE: Gruber and Wise (1999b).

FIGURE 6   Unused labor force capacity vs. tax force to retire

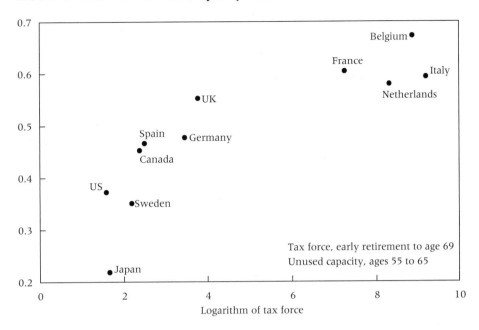

SOURCE: Gruber and Wise (1999b: 32–33, Figure 17).

FIGURE 7   Unused labor force capacity vs. tax force to retire

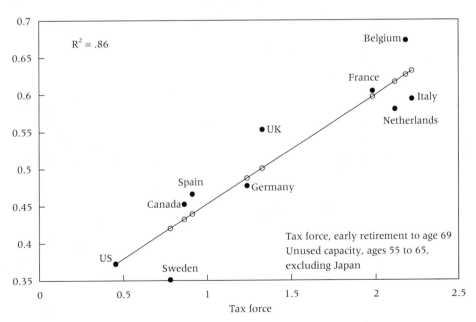

SOURCE: Gruber and Wise (1999b: 32–33, Figure 17).

are working. Together these trends have put enormous pressure on the financial solvency of social security systems around the world. Ironically, we argue, the provisions of the social security systems themselves typically contribute to the labor force withdrawal.

... We conclude that social security program provisions have indeed contributed to the decline in the labor force participation of older persons, substantially reducing the potential productive capacity of the labor force. It seems evident that if the trend to early retirement is to be reversed, as will almost surely be dictated by demographic trends, changing the provisions of social security programs that induce early retirement will play a key role. (Gruber and Wise 1999b: 34–35)

Phase II: Estimation of the effect of plan provisions on retirement

The first phase of the project established two key results: (1) that the social security systems in many countries provide enormous incentives to leave the labor force at older ages; and (2) that there is a strong correspondence between social security incentives to retire and the withdrawal of older workers from the labor force.

Building on the correspondence between incentives to retire and labor force participation, we wanted to develop estimates of the effect of changes in plan provisions on labor force participation. Thus, in the second phase of the project, we set out a template to estimate how much the retirement age would change if social security provisions were changed, based on within-country analysis of the determinants of retirement. The analysis was to be based on the micro data within each country, considering the relationship between retirement and the incentives faced by individual employees. That is, rather than considering system-wide incentives for representative persons (such as those with median earning histories) and comparing these incentives with aggregate labor force participation across countries, we now turned to micro-econometric analyses within countries. The results of these analyses are based on differences in individual circumstances within a given country.

For this phase, the investigators in each country assembled large micro data files combining information on individual retirement decisions with retirement incentives (together with other individual data). Individual measures of social security retirement incentives—which vary substantially across persons within a country—were calculated on the basis of the methods developed for the first phase of the project. The key incentive measure was the "option value" of delayed retirement. This measure is based on the potential gain (or loss) in social security wealth if receipt of benefits is delayed. That is, this constructed economic variable describes the financial gain

or loss from continuing to work. Estimation using this measure goes back
to the Stock and Wise (1990a, 1990b) procedure we used to analyze the
effect on retirement of employer-provided defined benefit pension plans in
the United States, as discussed above. Results based on this measure are
reported below. Estimates were also obtained based on the peak value measure proposed by Coile and Gruber (2001).

As in the first volume, the analysis in each country followed a detailed
template, so that results could be compared across countries. The micro analysis in each country was based on a sample of individuals. In some cases,
the data come largely from administrative records. In other cases, they were
obtained from special surveys. It was possible to estimate the same models
in each country, even though the population covered by the country data
sets differed in some respects.

The key advantage of the micro estimation is that in each country the
effects of changes in plan provisions can be predicted. The first striking feature of the collective analyses based on within-country micro data is that
social security retirement incentives have very similar effects on labor force
participation in all countries. In particular, the results strongly confirm that
the relationship between labor force participation and retirement across
countries is not the result of cultural differences that could, for example,
yield different norms, or "taste" for work, at older ages. The within-country
analyses show similar responses to retirement incentive effects, even though
the countries differ with respect to cultural histories and institutions.

The second feature of the micro analyses is that they allow consideration of several features of social security systems, as well as individual attributes, that may simultaneously affect retirement decisions. In particular,
the micro estimation results allow us to estimate jointly the effect on retirement of the age at which benefits are first available and the incentive to
retire once benefits are available. Both of these features were shown in the
first phase of the project to be key determinants of retirement.

Effect of plan provisions demonstrated by simulation

To demonstrate the effect of plan provisions on retirement, we used the
estimates for each country to simulate the effect of three illustrative changes
in plan provisions. Actually, only two illustrative plan changes were simulated in the second phase of the project, but a third was added in the third
phase. Thus all three are described here.

(1) Three-year increment in eligibility ages: This simulation increases all eligibility ages by three years, specifically the early retirement age, the normal retirement age, and the ages of receipt of disability benefits. In countries in which
disability, unemployment, or other retirement pathways are important, the eligibility age for *each* of the programs is delayed by three years.

(2) Actuarially fair reform: This reform reduces benefits actuarially if taken before the normal retirement age and increases benefits actuarially if taken after the normal retirement age.

(3) Common reform: This illustrative simulation is intended to predict the effect of the same reform (the "common reform") in each country. Under the common reform, the early retirement age is set at age 60 and the normal retirement age at 65. Benefits taken before age 65 are reduced "actuarially," by 6 percent for each year before age 65. Benefits taken after age 65 are increased by 6 percent for each year the receipt of benefits is delayed. In addition, the replacement rate at age 65 is set at 60 percent of (projected) earnings at age 60.

The potential implication of the reforms can be made clear with reference to Figure 4 above and by two additional figures. As in Figure 4, I continue to use a conceptual representation of social security provisions in Germany as an example. Figure 8 shows the effect of a three-year increment in eligibility ages. The assumption is that the first age of eligibility in Germany (for receipt of benefits from the disability program) is 57. Under this illustrative reform, benefits would be zero at ages 57, 58, and 59. Benefits would first be available at age 60. In the United States, for example, this illustrative reform would increase the age of first eligibility from 62 to 65.

Figure 4 illustrated the effect of actuarial reform in Germany. As explained above, such reform in Germany can be very important. On the other hand, actuarial reform in the United States would have little effect since the system is already actuarially fair between 62 and 65, although the de-

FIGURE 8   Germany: Base and 3-year increment

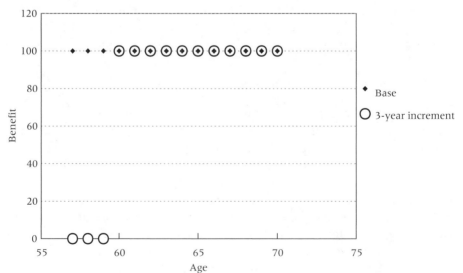

layed retirement increase is not yet quite actuarially fair. In other countries, the actuarial adjustment could in fact increase average benefits. In France, for example, the normal retirement age is 60, without actuarial adjustment in cases where retirement is delayed. But the actuarial reform would increase benefits taken after age 60.

Figure 9 shows the effect of the common reform in Germany, and, for comparison, shows the three-year increment and the actuarial reforms as well. Since the common reform in Germany would increase the age of first eligibility by three years, the common reform incorporates the three-year increment in eligibility. In addition the common reform incorporates actuarial reduction in benefits before and actuarial increase in benefits after the normal retirement age. Finally, the common reform in Germany implies a substantial reduction in benefits at the normal retirement age of 65. In short, the receipt of benefits is delayed by three years—from 57 to 60 in the conceptual illustration—benefits at the normal retirement age are reduced from 100 to 75 percent, and normal retirement age benefits are adjusted actuarially if taken before or after the normal retirement age. As Figure 9 suggests, the combined effect of these changes can be large in Germany. Benefits before age 60 are no longer available. When they become available at age 60 there is no financial incentive to take benefits then as opposed to some later age. And, when the normal retirement age is reached there is no financial incentive to take benefits at that age as opposed to some later age.

FIGURE 9 Germany: Base, 3-year increment, actuarial adjustment, and common reform

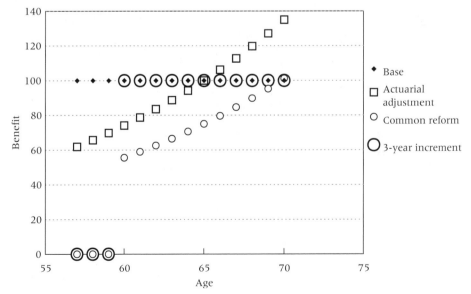

As our work progressed it became clear that we could not rely on a single estimation method or a single simulation method to obtain results. Thus based on the findings for each of the countries, and based on collective discussions with all of the participants, we concluded that we should make calculations on the basis of two principal estimation specifications and three simulation methods. The goal was to provide estimates that were likely to bracket the actual responses that might be expected if plan provisions were changed. With only one exception, all of the results summarized below are based on the option value estimation method (OV) and are based on the simulation method that I believe gives the most reliable long-run effects of the illustrative changes in plan provisions in most countries.

Three-year increment in eligibility ages and labor force participation

The basic findings can be illustrated in two figures. Figure 10 shows the effect of the three-year increment in eligibility ages, based on the method that we believe is most likely to reflect the long-run effect of such a reform. To help standardize for the wide variation across countries in the age at which retirement begins, each bar shows the reduction in the frac-

FIGURE 10   Out of labor force percent change, 25% age + 4 years, base versus 3-year delay

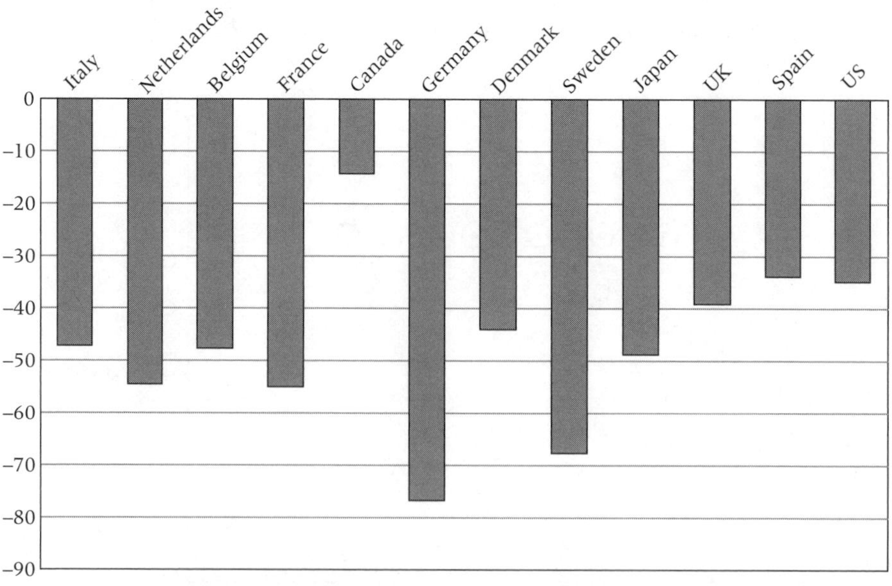

SOURCE: Gruber and Wise (2004b: 28, Figure 15).

tion of the population out of the labor force (OLF) four years after the age at which a quarter of the population has retired (which is an "effective retirement age"). There are two notable features of this figure. The first is that the average reduction in the proportion OLF—47 percent—is very large. The second notable feature is the similarity across countries. The reduction is between 34 and 55 percent in nine of the 12 countries. In Germany and Sweden, the reductions are 77 and 68 percent respectively. (The average reduction is 28 percent using the simulation method that we believe is likely on average to substantially underestimate the response to the three-year increment.)

The common reform and labor force participation

Figure 11 shows the effect on the proportion out of the labor force under the common reform. In this figure, it is clear that the greatest reductions in the proportion OLF under the common reform are realized in the countries with the youngest effective retirement ages. For the six countries with sub-stantial retirement before age 60, the average *reduction* in the proportion OLF is 44 percent. For the six countries in which most retirement is after age 60, there is a 4 percent average *increase* in the proportion OLF.

FIGURE 11   Out of labor force percent change, 25% age + 4 years, base versus common reform

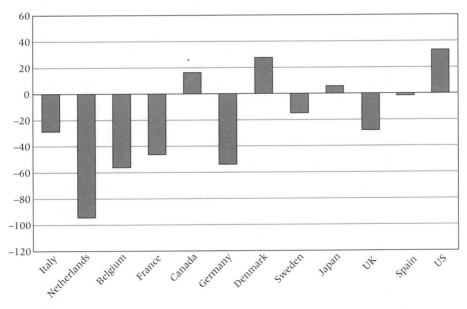

SOURCE: Gruber and Wise (2004b: 32, Figure 19).

The systematic pattern of these results shows a strong correspondence with intuition. For the six countries with the youngest effective retirement ages, the common reform represents a substantial increase in the youngest eligibility age, and the actuarial reduction means that benefits at this age are much lower than under the base country plans. Thus, for these countries, the proportion out of the labor force should decline under the reform, and that is the case for every country except Canada. But for the six countries with older retirement ages, the common reform may reduce the earliest eligibility age—as in the United States—and may provide a greater incentive to leave the labor force. In addition, the 60 percent replacement rate at the normal retirement age represents an increase in the replacement rate for some countries, such as the United States, and a reduction in the rate for other countries. Consequently, in three of these six countries, there is an increase in the proportion OLF under the common reform simulation.

A key reason for simulating the common reform was to determine whether the results would correspond with intuition based on current plan provisions. That the correspondence is close adds credence to the estimation and simulation methods and to the overall results.

We concluded the summary of this phase of the project (Gruber and Wise 2004b) with these comments:

> In short: the results in this volume provide an important complement to the first volume. The results leave no doubt that social security incentives have a strong effect on retirement decisions. And the estimates show that the effect is similar in countries with very different cultural histories, labor market institutions, and other social characteristics. While countries may differ in many respects, the employees in all countries react similarly to social security retirement incentives. The simulated effects of illustrative reforms reported in the country papers make clear that changes in the provisions of social security programs would have very large effects on the labor force participation of older employees. (Gruber and Wise 2004b: 36)

Phase III: The fiscal effects of changes in plan provisions

The third phase of the project focused on estimation of the fiscal effects of changes in the provisions of social security systems. The results in this phase rely on the retirement model estimates obtained in the second phase. We simulate the fiscal effects of the three illustrative reforms.

Our goal was not to calculate the long-run balance sheets of social security systems, as the US Social Security Administration does, for example. Rather the approach we chose was designed to illustrate the fiscal implications by calculating the implications of reform for a specific cohort or for a group of cohorts. For example, in the United States, the calculations show what the fiscal implications would have been had the social security provisions been changed for the cohort born between 1931 and 1941 (reaching age 65 between 1996 and 2006). As with the first two phases, the calculations were made according to a detailed template so that the results could be compared across countries.

An example for Germany

To help to understand the calculations that were made, I first describe the fiscal implications of actuarial reform in Germany, as reported in Börsch-Supan, Kohnz, and Schnabel (2003, working paper). Germany has a generous social security system, with strong incentives to retire early. In addition to the social security program per se, a large fraction of workers in Germany retire through disability and unemployment programs. These programs essentially provide early retirement benefits before the social security early retirement age of 60. Indeed, these programs provide the principal path to retirement in Germany. In addition, as noted above, once benefits are available, there is no actuarial reduction in benefits taken before the age 65 "normal" retirement age (although reforms in 1992 and more recently have introduced some actuarial reduction). For example, early retirement benefits taken at age 60, or benefits from the disability program taken at age 57, are the same as the age 65 normal retirement benefits. This provides an enormous incentive to take benefits when they are first available. If they are not taken, they are simply lost; there is no offsetting increase in benefits if they are received for fewer years.

Suppose that benefits in Germany were actuarially fair, so that benefits received prior to age 65 were reduced by 6 percent per year, and benefits received after 65 were increased by 6 percent per year. Table 1 shows the effect of this change on the mean retirement age for the sample of workers used in the analysis. The mean retirement age for men under the base (current provisions) is 62. The base simulation yields a mean retirement age very close to the sample mean. Actuarially fair reduction in

TABLE 1   German illustration: Effect of actuarially fair reduction in benefits on retirement age for men and women (based on OV model)

Model	Men	Women
Sample frequencies	61.9	61.7
Base simulation	62.1	62.0
Actuarially fair simulation	65.2	64.6

SOURCE: Börsch-Supan, Kohnz, and Schnabel (2003, working paper).

FIGURE 12   **Germany: Distribution of retirement ages, actuarially fair reform, OV**

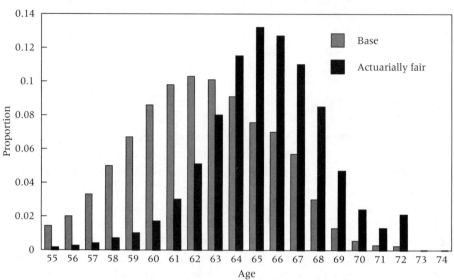

SOURCE: Börsch-Supan, Kohnz, and Schnabel (2003, working paper).

benefits would increase the retirement age by about three years for both men and women. Figure 12 shows the change in the distribution of retirement ages for men; there is a clear shift to older ages throughout the distribution.

The fiscal implications of this change are shown in Table 2. The total effect of the reform is decomposed into two parts—the "mechanical" effect that would exist if retirement ages did not change, and the behavioral effect that is attributable to change in retirement ages. Benefits received at any age before 65 are reduced actuarially, and benefits received after age 65 are increased ac-

TABLE 2   **German illustration: Fiscal implications of actuarially fair reform: Change in present discounted value, euros per worker (based on OV model with dummies shifted)**

	Mechanical effect	Behavioral effect	Total effect
Benefits	−37,056	19,632	−17,423
Contribution	0	16,766	16,766
All taxes	−1,558	50,608	49,049
Net change	−35,497	−47,741	−83,238
Percent change	−18.3	−24.6	−42.9

SOURCE: Börsch-Supan, Kohnz, and Schnabel (2003, working paper).

tuarially—in each case by 6 percent annually. If there were no change in retirement ages, the average benefit per worker would be reduced by some 37,000 euros. But the behavioral response to the reform increases the average retirement age, as shown in Table 1 and Figure 12. This increases the average benefit by nearly 20,000 euros. The total (net) effect on benefits is a reduction of around 17,000 euros.

In addition to the change in benefits, the reform has further fiscal implications. Contributions to the social security system are increased if employees continue to work. This behavioral effect is an increase of nearly 17,000 euros. In addition, if employees work longer, they pay more in other taxes. The total increase in taxes is 49,000 euros per worker (including taxes for health and other insurance programs, income taxes, and VAT tax). The net change in benefits minus the change in contributions and minus the change in taxes is a decrease of about 83,000 euros. This net reduction in the total government expenditures minus revenues is equivalent to 43 percent of base benefits under the current system, entered as negative to indicate that net government expenditures minus revenues have been reduced by an amount equivalent to 43 percent of the base cost of the social security program.

FIGURE 13   Fiscal implications of actuarially fair reform
(net): % of GDP 2001

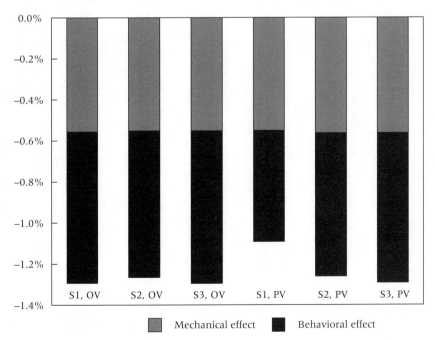

SOURCE: Börsch-Supan, Kohnz, and Schnabel (2003, working paper).

The fiscal effect of the actuarial reform in Germany as a percent of gross domestic product (GDP) is shown in Figure 13. This figure shows the estimated effect for each of six estimation and simulation methods. On balance, the reduction in benefits minus all taxes is about 1.2 percent of GDP.

Across all countries

Similar calculations were made for each country for each of the three illustrative reforms. The effect of the reforms depends of course on the current system in each country. An increase in eligibility ages will reduce expenditures and raise tax revenues in all countries. The actuarial reform, which has large effects in Germany, should have little effect in countries such as the United States and Canada where the system is already actuarially fair.

Results across all countries are shown in the next four figures. As with the results for the first two phases of the project, these results are also taken from the individual country papers. The volume containing the third phase results has not yet been published, however, so these results are taken from the working papers from each country (see the papers referenced under Phase III Working Papers).

FIGURE 14 Total fiscal effect of 3-year increment, as % of base cost

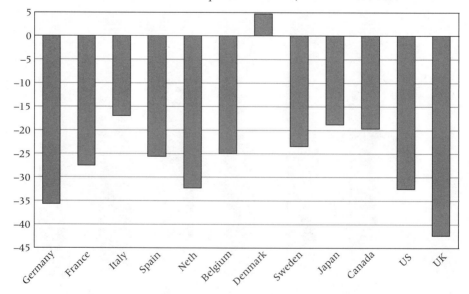

NOTE: The anomalous positive value of 4.9% for Denmark arises because of an unusual provision of the Danish system that would increase the number of persons receiving benefits from a more generous program when the eligibility ages are increased.

SOURCE: Gruber and Wise (forthcoming).

Figure 14 shows the total fiscal effect of the three-year increment in eligibility ages. For example, in Germany, the increase in government revenue resulting from a three-year increment in all eligibility ages would equal about 36 percent of the current cost of the program. Across all countries, the average increase in revenue is equivalent to 27 percent of current program cost—reported as a reduction in government expenditures minus revenues.

Figure 15 shows the increase in government revenue resulting from the three-year increment as a percent of gross domestic product. The average increase in revenue over all countries is equivalent to 0.72 percent of GDP—again reported as a reduction in government revenues minus expenditures. The result for the UK is not available.

Figure 16 shows the fiscal effect of actuarial adjustment, as a percent of base cost. As expected, there is large variation across countries. In the United States and Canada, for example, where adjustment is close to actuarial already, the effect is small. In Germany, where until recently there was no actuarial adjustment, the effect is very large, as explained in detail above. In France, actuarial increase in benefits after the age 60 normal retirement age would increase costs of the program. The same is true in the United Kingdom. On average the decrease in government expenditure minus revenue is equivalent to 2.8 percent of the base cost across all countries. Excluding the United Kingdom, the average is about 26 percent—reported as a reduction in government expenditures minus revenues.

FIGURE 15 Total fiscal effect of 3-year increment, as % of GDP

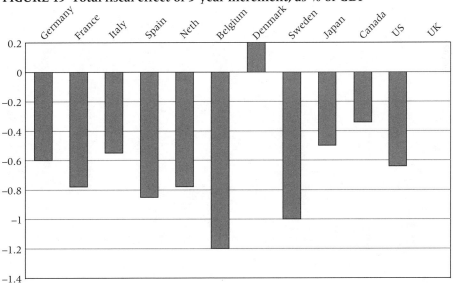

NOTE: The value for UK is not available.
SOURCE: Gruber and Wise (forthcoming).

FIGURE 16 Total fiscal effect of actuarial reform, as % of base cost

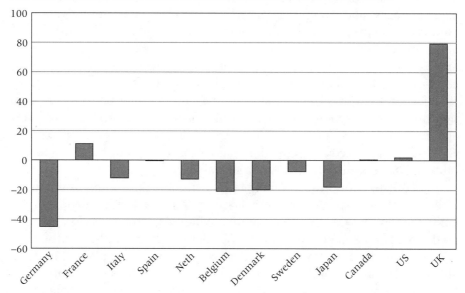

SOURCE: Gruber and Wise (forthcoming).

Figure 17 shows the fiscal effect of the common reform, as a percent of base cost. In accord with intuition, the total net government revenue as a percent of program base cost varies greatly. In the United States and Canada for example, benefits under the common reform are more generous than

FIGURE 17 Total fiscal effect of common reform, as % of base cost

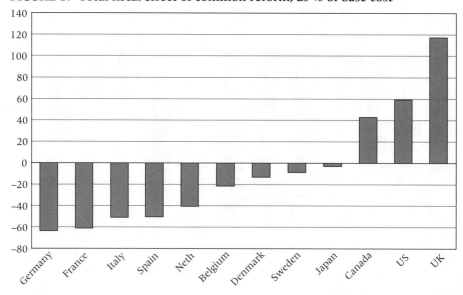

SOURCE: Gruber and Wise (forthcoming).

current benefits and they are available at age 60 instead of the current age 62 early retirement age. In the United Kingdom as well, the common reform benefits are much more generous than current benefits and the age 60 early retirement age is younger than the current early retirement age for some participants.

This phase of the project makes clear that reforms such as those considered here can have very large fiscal implications for the cost of social security benefits as well as for government revenues generated by changes in the labor force participation of older workers. Some combination of increases in the early retirement age, actuarial adjustment of benefits, and change in the benefit level can change net government revenue substantially. In many countries, the illustrative reforms simulated in this project yield increases in government revenue minus expenditures equivalent to 20 to 50 percent of current program cost. In accord with intuition, the common reform yields both increases and reductions in government revenue equivalent to a large fraction of current program costs.

The advantage of cross-country comparison

The project analysis to date has provided a much greater understanding of the economic costs of current social security policy than could have been provided by individual country-level analysis. Our estimates of the implications of changes in plan provisions are likely to inform policy decisions in all of the countries included here. And, understanding what has occurred in one country may help to redirect policy in another country. To date, the results of our analysis have been widely cited and we believe have already played an important role in policy discussions. More generally, analysis such as described here can promote the methodological advantages of cross-country comparisons.

Going forward

Social security is the largest social insurance program in most developed countries. The vast differences in program provisions have provided a natural laboratory for this ongoing international project to study the influence of program provisions on individual behavior. The findings have made clear that social security provisions in most countries induce older workers to leave the labor force early and that the substantial difference in retirement behavior across countries can be explained largely by the provisions of these programs. The findings also show that much of the inducement to retire comes through programs nominally labeled "disability insurance," although it is evident that in many countries these programs essentially serve as routes to early retirement before the social security early retirement age.

The finding that social security provisions penalize the decision to continue working and thus distort retirement decisions is a critical foundation for understanding the effects of social security provisions and in particular the implications of system reform. But a comprehensive assessment of the implications of reform also requires an understanding of the relationship between social security provisions and the well-being of both the elderly and the young. If reform to prolong years of work also reduces income, this tradeoff must be considered in evaluation of the reform. If, on the other hand, lower benefits are completely offset by other forms of support such as labor income or greater personal saving, reform may have little detrimental effect on the well-being of the elderly.

Assessment of reform also requires evaluation of the implications of reform for the employment of the young. Indeed, a common explanation of provisions that induce the elderly to retire, and a common argument in opposition to reform, is that the departure of older persons from the labor force will improve the employment prospects of younger workers. To what extent do labor markets operate in this "boxed" fashion?

In addition, to understand the implications of reforming disability insurance programs, one must understand how the genuinely disabled would be affected by such changes. In particular, how do program provisions affect the relationship between health status and employment?

The prospect of comparable longitudinal data for the study of the health and retirement of older persons—through the nexus of the Health and Retirement Study, the English Longitudinal Study of Ageing, and the forthcoming Survey of Health, Ageing and Retirement in Europe—makes such analysis especially timely. Thus we have turned attention to these other issues. In particular, we hope:

—To understand the relationship between social security system provisions and the well-being of the elderly and the young.

—To understand the relationship between social security system provisions and the employment of the young.

—To understand how the relationship between health status and retirement varies with the provisions of social security (including disability insurance) programs, and to understand how the well-being of the disabled and the healthy elderly depends on program provisions.

Notes

This chapter explains the route to discovery of the relationship between Social Security provision and the labor force participation of older workers, through the ongoing project that I am directing with Jonathan Gruber through the National Bureau of Economic Research. The project has been funded through grants P20-AG12810 and P30-AG12810 as well as grant P01-AG05842, from the National Institute on Aging. I draw freely and heavily from the results of our project. I also describe the "near" background to this project, emphasizing how I was drawn to this effort. I do not attempt to summarize the vast amount of related work.

The country participants—most of whom have been active in the project from the beginning while a few have changed over time—are:

Belgium: Arnaud Dellis, Raphaël Desmet, Alain Jousten, Sergio Perelman, Pierre Pestieau, and Jean-Philippe Stijns

Canada: Michael Baker, Jonathan Gruber, and Kevin Milligan

Denmark: Paul Bingley, Nabanita Datta Gupta, and Peder J. Pedersen

France: Didier Blanchet, Ronan Mahieu, Louis-Paul Pelé, and Emmanuelle Walraet

Germany: Axel Börsch-Supan, Simone Kohnz, Giovanni Mastrobuoni, and Reinhold Schnabel

Italy: Agar Brugiavini and Franco Peracchi

Japan: Takashi Oshio, Akiko Sato Oishi, and Naohiro Yashiro

Netherlands: Arie Kapteyn and Klaas de Vos

Spain: Michele Boldrin, Sergio Jiménez-Martín, and Franco Peracchi

Sweden: Mårten Palme and Ingemar Svensson

United Kingdom: Richard Blundell, Carl Emmerson, Paul Johnson, Costas Meghir, and Sarah Smith

United States: Courtney Coile, Peter Diamond, and Jonathan Gruber

1 Hausman and Wise 1985, for example.

2 In many countries, the aging population and early retirement trends come on top of very generous retirement benefits, further compounding the financial consequences of the these trends. For example, in Belgium, France, Italy, and the Netherlands the social security replacement rates at the early retirement age—the benefit relative to final earnings—average 77 percent, 91 percent, 75 percent, and 91 percent respectively. In contrast the replacement rate at the early retirement age in Canada is only about 20 percent; in the United States it is about 41 percent.

3 Benefits in the United States are actuarial between 62 and 65, but are increased less than actuarially if the receipt of benefits is delayed beyond age 65, thus providing an incentive to leave the labor force at 65. Under current law benefits at all retirement ages will eventually slowly become actuarial.

References

Ausink, John and David A. Wise. 1996. "The military pension, compensation, and retirement of U.S. Air Force pilots," in D. A. Wise (ed.), *Advances in the Economics of Aging*. Chicago: University of Chicago Press.

Bulow, Jeremy I. 1981. "Early retirement pension benefits," NBER Working Paper #0654.

Coile, Courtney C. and Jonathan Gruber. 2001. "Social Security incentives for retirement," in D. A. Wise (ed.), *Themes in the Economics of Aging*. Chicago: University of Chicago Press.

Feldstein, Martin (ed.). 1998. *Privatizing Social Security*. Chicago: University of Chicago Press.

Gruber, Jonathan and David A. Wise (eds.). 1999a. *Social Security and Retirement Around the World*. Chicago: University of Chicago Press.

————. 1999b. "Social Security and retirement around the world: Introduction and summary," in Jonathan Gruber and David A. Wise (eds.), 1999a. Also published as "Social Security programs and retirement around the world," *Research in Labor Economics*, Volume 18, 1999.

———— (eds.). 2004a. *Social Security and Retirement Around the World: Micro-Estimation*. Chicago: University of Chicago Press.

————. 2004b. "Introduction and summary," in J. Gruber and D. A. Wise (eds.), 2004a.

————. Forthcoming. "Social security and retirement around the world: Fiscal implications: Introduction and summary," in Jonathan Gruber and David A. Wise, eds., *Social Security and Retirement Around the World: Micro Estimation*. University of Chicago Press.

Hausman, Jerry A. and David A. Wise. 1985. "Social Security, health status, and retirement," in D. A. Wise (ed.), *Pensions, Labor and Individual Choice*. Chicago: University of Chicago Press.

Kotlikoff, Laurence and David A. Wise, 1985. "Labor compensation and the structure of private pension plans: Evidence for contractual versus spot labor markets," in D. A. Wise (ed.), *Pensions, Labor and Individual Choice*. Chicago: University of Chicago Press.

————. 1987. "The incentive effects of private pension plans," in Z. Bodie, J. B. Shoven, and D. A. Wise (eds.), *Issues in Pension Economics*. Chicago: University of Chicago Press.

————. 1988. "Pension backloading, wage taxes, and work disincentives," in L. Summers (ed.), *Tax Policy and the Economy, Volume 2*. Cambridge, MA: MIT Press.

————. 1989a. *The Wage Carrot and the Pension Stick*. Kalamazoo, MI: W. E. Upjohn Institute.

————. 1989b. "Employee retirement and a firm's pension plan," *The Economics of Aging*. Chicago: University of Chicago Press.

Lazear, E. 1983. "Pensions as severance pay," in Z. Bodie and J. Shoven (eds.), *Financial Aspects of the United States Pension System*. Chicago: University of Chicago Press.

Lumsdaine, Robin, James H. Stock, and David A. Wise. 1990. "Efficient windows and labor force reduction," *Journal of Public Economics* 43(2): 131–159.

————. 1991. "Fenêtres et retraites (Windows and retirement)," *Annales d'Economie et de Statitistique*, Issue 20-21: 219–242.

————. 1992. "Three models of retirement: Computational complexity versus predictive validity," in D. A. Wise (ed.), *Topics in the Economics of Aging*. Chicago: University of Chicago Press.

————. 1994. "Pension plan provisions and retirement: Men and women, Medicare, and models," in D. A. Wise, (ed.), *Studies in the Economics of Aging*. Chicago: University of Chicago Press.

————. 1996. "Why are retirement rates so high at age 65?," in D. A. Wise (ed.), *Advances in the Economics of Aging*. Chicago: University of Chicago Press.

————. 1997. "Retirement incentives: The interaction between employer-provided pension plans, Social Security, and retiree health benefits," in M. D. Hurd and N. Yashiro (eds.), *The Economic Effects of Aging in the United States and Japan*. Chicago: University of Chicago Press.

Stock, James H. and David A. Wise. 1990a. "The pension inducement to retire: An option value analysis," *Issues in the Economics of Aging*. Chicago: University of Chicago Press.

————. 1990b. "Pensions, the option value of work, and retirement," *Econometrica* 58(5): 1151–1180.

Phase III Working Papers

Baker, Michael, Jonathan Gruber, and Kevin Milligan. "Simulating the response to reform of Canada's income security programs," *NBER Working Paper* #9455, January 2003.

Bingley, Paul, Nabanita Datta Gupta, and Peder J. Pedersen. "Fiscal implications of reforms in retirement systems in Denmark," January 2003.

Blundell, Richard and Carl Emmerson. "Fiscal effects of reforming the UK state pension system," October 2003.

Boldrin, Michele and Sergio Jiménez-Martín. "Evaluating Spanish pension expenditure under alternative reform scenarios," September 2003.

Börsch-Supan, Axel, Simone Kohnz, and Reinhold Schnabel. "The budget impact of reduced early retirement incentives on the German public pension system," November 2003.

Brugiavini, Agar and Franco Peracchi. "Fiscal implications of pension reforms in Italy," January 2003.

Coile, Courtney and Jonathan Gruber. "Fiscal effects of Social Security reform in the United States," March 2003.

Desmet, Raphaël, Alain Jousten, Sergio Perelman, and Pierre Pestieau. "Micro-simulation of Social Security reforms in Belgium," September 2003.

Kapteyn, Arie and Klaas de Vos. "Simulation of pension reforms in the Netherlands," February 2004.

Oishi, Akiko Sato and Takashi Oshio. "Financial implications of social security reforms in Japan," November 2002.

Palme, Mårten and Ingemar Svensson. "Financial implication of income security reforms in Sweden," December 2003.

Walraet, Emmanuelle and Ronan Mahieu. "Simulating retirement behavior: The case of France," November 2002.

IV. DATA AND STATISTICS

Survey Design and Methodology in the Health and Retirement Study and the Wisconsin Longitudinal Study

ROBERT M. HAUSER
ROBERT J. WILLIS

Large-scale data collection has become the kernel of the growth of knowledge in the social sciences. Nowhere is this more evident than in research in the demography of aging and the life course, where scientific progress has been stimulated and sustained by complementary longitudinal studies of aging populations. In this chapter, we review the history, organization, and design of two of these public resources, the Wisconsin Longitudinal Study (WLS) and the Health and Retirement Study (HRS). Recent innovations in each of these studies hold promise for major advances in knowledge about the demography, economics, sociology, and epidemiology of aging. The stories of the WLS and HRS highlight important clues about the creation of systems of continuing surveys to inform science and public policy.

Sample design

There are many ways to collect information about populations, ranging from journalistic observation to full enumerations and from sparse data, like those in a census, to detailed histories of individuals, families, or communities. While demographers take probability sampling for granted, there are alternatives, some of which are chosen regularly and on a scale as large as or larger than the best-designed probability surveys. Depending on the availability of appropriate lists or sample frames, it may be more or less costly to establish a probability sample for longitudinal study.

Almost five decades ago, when a professor of education at the University of Wisconsin-Madison carried out a survey of high school seniors to assess the demand for postsecondary schooling, no one would have imagined that it would create the foundation for a major study of the life course and aging. The WLS began in large part because that survey provided a complete, identifiable list of the population. In the early 1960s, sociologist William H. Sewell learned that the questionnaires from a 1957 survey of all Wisconsin high school seniors were stored in the basement of the University of Wisconsin administration building (Sewell et al. 2003). When he examined the instruments, he learned that each questionnaire contained the name of the student and the name and address of the parents of the student. From a list of those schedules, Sewell chose a simple one-third random sample of more than 10,000 persons for further study.[1] That sample was followed up successfully in 1964 and 1975—and expanded to include randomly selected siblings in that wave. Only in 1992 to 1993, when the graduates were 53 and 54 years old, was the content of the surveys expanded to shift the focus of the study from education, careers, and family to health and aging. At present, the fourth wave of the WLS is in the field, as the graduates reach retirement age, and the sample has again been expanded to include the spouses or widows of graduates and their siblings.

In contrast, the Health and Retirement Study was created in a deliberate effort to establish a longitudinal observatory for multi- and interdisciplinary studies of aging populations (Juster and Suzman 1995), but its design and coverage, also, have evolved across time. The HRS design began with a decision to represent the US population in 1992 at ages 51 to 61 (and their spouses of whatever age). Because only 16.6 percent of households contained people in this age range, a large screening survey was undertaken by the Survey Research Center at the University of Michigan. As opportunities arose, coverage was first increased at older ages by incorporation of participants in a companion study, Assets and Health Dynamics of the Oldest Old (AHEAD), which covered cohorts born in 1890 to 1923, who were 70 and older in 1993 (Soldo et al. 1997). A decision was made to integrate the HRS and AHEAD questionnaires in 1995 and to combine the field periods in 1998. At that time, the HRS committed to a steady state design by adding two new cohorts, the "Children of the Depression" (born in 1924 to 1930) and the "War Babies" (born in 1942 to 1947). By 1998 the HRS became cross-sectionally representative of the US population older than 50, and a decision was made to maintain the steady state by adding a new six-year cohort every six years (Willis 1999).

Thus, in 2004, a fresh screening sample is being drawn to add a cohort of "Early Boomers" born in 1948 to 1953, who will then be 51 to 56 years old;[2] here the household eligibility rate is expected to be even lower, about 12.4 percent. This effort will generate a random sample of younger cohorts that will be used in the 2010 wave of the HRS, and those in older cohorts will be selected for another NIA-supported study, "Social Life, Health, and Illness at Older Ages," conducted by Linda Waite and colleagues. Other older participants in the screening sample may be asked to join a proposed project on measurement of cognition that will be used to "reengineer" HRS cognitive measures using state-of-the-art ability tests and psychometric methods. Finally, a small number of cases will be retained for use by the HRS as a "test bed" sample.

Whatever else may be problematic in the repertoire of aging surveys that are sponsored in whole or part by NIA, they all start with probability samples. This has great advantages. One can generalize to each of the populations that has been sampled, whether it is national or regional, or representative of the whole adult population or of specific age cohorts.[3] Moreover, if they are large enough, these population samples may be used as frames for the study of special populations. For example, ADAMS (Aging, Demographics, and Memory Study) has identified for intensive study a stratified random sample of about 850 persons from the Health and Retirement Study, based on survey measures of cognitive impairment. These individuals have had in-home visits by a trained nurse and psychometric technician to obtain clinically valid measures of dementia.

Similarly, Marsha Seltzer and Jan Greenberg's component of the Wisconsin Longitudinal Study is identifying several hundred participants (high school graduates or their siblings) for intensive study if one or more of their children have a developmental disability or severe mental illness. In each of these cases, the base samples are large enough to generate more cases for intensive study than one often finds in clinical research, but the subpopulations are also representative of all instances meeting the definition of the special subpopulation. Another example of this is simply that the baseline samples, both in the HRS and the WLS, are of populations large enough to yield a substantial sample, many years later, of participants at advanced ages.

Longitudinal observation of the same individuals is necessary but not sufficient to provide a useful base for analyses of change in the process of aging. Thus, while studies of unique cohorts, like the WLS graduates, are of great scientific value, they do not provide a sound basis for studies of interperiod change, nor do they permit accumulation of age-specific data for scientifically significant subpopulations in different cohorts.[4] Moreover, unique cohort studies are likely to become obsolete as the world changes and as policy issues and scientific methods evolve.

An important advantage of the repeated longitudinal cohort design is the ability to cumulate rare cases across cohorts. For example, in order to obtain an adequate sample size, the most impaired stratum of ADAMS participants has been recruited from both the 2000 and 2002 rounds of the HRS.

To be sure, repeated longitudinal studies are complemented by other research designs. Repeated cross-section surveys, including the Census, Current Population Survey, Survey of Consumer Finances, National Health Interview Survey, Medical Expenditure Survey, and the National Health and Nutrition Examination Survey, provide important trend assessments with large numbers of cases and without the large added costs of longitudinal coverage. Also, despite and perhaps because of their distinctly nonrepresentative design, Snowdon's studies of aging nuns (Snowdon et al. 1996; Snowdon 2001) have made uniquely important scientific contributions to our understanding of the precursors of longevity and of Alzheimer's disease. Likewise, Robert Fogel's studies of Union Army veterans are providing unique insights into the epidemiological transition. In an earlier period, the NBER-Thorndike data—from a study of men who volunteered to become pilots, navigators, and bombardiers in the Army Air Force in World War II—provided the first major longitudinal data on the relationship between early-ability test scores and later educational and economic success (Thorndike and Hagen 1959; Taubman and Wales 1973) and enabled researchers to address issues such as lifetime inequality in human wealth (Lillard 1977) and the relationship between ability and self-selection in educational choice (Willis and Rosen 1979).

Creating surveys: Serendipity and institutional support

What has led to continuing, large-scale data creation? In our opinion, the successes are marked by the combination of policy relevance and scientific design and control. This combination is not easily achieved. Aside from the constitutionally mandated US Census, there is no institutional structure to create and maintain a complementary system of demographic, social, economic, or health surveys. Indeed, there is no centralized statistical system in the United States, such as exists in Canada and some other countries. Rather, America's national statistical "system" is an agglomeration of activities that are housed in line agencies with responsibilities to execute policies, such as the Department of Labor, combined with the ongoing activities of scientific agencies, interest groups, and individual investigators. The decentralization of statistical activities has both disadvantages and advantages.

Many key statistical series exist through historical accident. The Current Population Survey, which now serves many purposes and audiences, was created for the sole purpose of measuring unemployment. Sharing of samples and data across statistical agencies has been severely restricted by laws that have only recently been modernized. For many decades, agency interests and mandates have reduced or precluded the use of exceptionally valuable samples. Surveys that fall under the purview of the Office of Management and Budget (OMB), because they are conducted by federal agencies or under federal contract, are more restricted in content, design, and procedure than surveys conducted with grant support by nonfederal agencies.

Despite problems like these, the decentralized US research and statistical systems have yielded excellent and innovative data for research on aging. First, the diversity of academic institutions in the United States has allowed for innovation and for open competition among research agendas and designs. Second, federal support for investigator-initiated research, notably at the National Institutes of Health and the National Science Foundation, but also at the Social Security Administration, the Department of Education, the Department of Labor, and the Department of Health and Human Services, has permitted innovative and sustained large-scale data collection and analysis. Third, unlike countries in which a central statistical agency has a monopoly on data collection, the United States has developed numerous independent survey organizations, including several that are capable of large-scale operations.

Chance, if not sheer luck, has played an important part in the development of current data resources on aging. As we mentioned earlier, in the 1950s and 1960s no one anticipated that the Wisconsin Longitudinal Study would evolve into a major longitudinal survey of health and aging. In retrospect, some of its design elements seem more valuable now than at the time they were introduced. These include the baseline measures of cognition and academic performance (from 1957) and the introduction of parallel surveys of sisters and brothers of the graduates (in 1977). However, sponsorship of the WLS shifted across time as the sample aged, and there were low points when the project might easily have been abandoned. From the inception of the 1964 follow-up through the mid-1970s, most support came from the National Institute of Mental Health, but a grant from the Spencer Foundation facilitated creation of the sibling sample. The 1990s brought initial sponsorship from the National Institute on Aging—again supplemented by the Spencer Foundation—which facilitated the shift to aging as the focus of the study and supported the latest two waves of data collection.

In contrast, the institutional framework for the HRS represents an innovative approach for the design and sustained support of a scientific and policy-relevant data collection effort (Juster and Suzman 1995). The HRS is supported through a cooperative agreement between NIA and the University of Michigan that provides extraordinary resources to allow the involvement of a broad range of scientists in the design and conduct of the study. For example, NIA provided over $1 million and 18 months of time to prepare the baseline questionnaire and sample design for the original HRS baseline survey fielded in 1992. An important part of the motivation for the HRS arose from concern about the implications of the aging of the US population for the health and economic well-being of Americans during the latter part of life and the costs that will be borne by younger portions of the population to support the elderly through public programs such as Social Security, Medicare, and Medicaid. Planning for the HRS took place with a set of working groups with expertise in economics, demography, sociology, psychology, medicine, epidemiology, health services, and survey methodology. The experts developed measures, usually by truncating or streamlining state-of-the-art measures from their fields. These working groups were overseen by an interdisciplinary group of co-investigators and advisory committees who made decisions on priorities across topical areas. These decisions were based on the potential of a given measure to contribute to the goals and theoretical framework of the HRS rather than their contribution to particular disciplinary concerns. The HRS has continued to obtain expert advice from diverse specialties as cohorts have been added and as new scientific and policy issues have arisen. For example, during 2002 some one dozen review papers were commissioned by the HRS Data Monitoring Board to assess the strengths and weaknesses of the HRS in a variety of research areas and to suggest ways of improving the quality and coverage of the survey.

Sustained support for a single data collection activity, however well designed, is not sufficient to inform public policy and the scientific enterprise. Thus, we need multiple data collection activities: to cross-validate findings, to exploit unique analytic opportunities, to support competing explanatory frameworks, and to expand content without overburdening research participants. We should prefer to see substantial overlap, comparability, and complementarities in content, along with collaboration among the users of multiple survey vehicles.

For example, in the 1992 round of the WLS, many of the economic measures were drawn from those used in the first round of the HRS. The same measures of psychological well-being have deliberately been used in the WLS, the National Survey of Families and Households (NSFH), and the survey of Midlife in the United States (MIDUS). The HRS has been employed as a model for the development of many other surveys, including the English Longitudinal Study of Ageing (ELSA), the Mexican Health and Aging Study (MHAS), and the Survey of Health, Ageing and Retirement (SHARE) in nine European countries. Similar efforts are now under discussion in Canada, Australia, and Israel. The scientific and policy rationale for developing comparable, multinational longitudinal studies of aging has been well argued in the US National Research Council's (2001) report, *Preparing for an Aging World*.

Public responsibility

Along with innovation and entrepreneurship, and beyond the relevance of research to policy, public responsibility also plays a growing part in large-scale survey research. Surveys are successful only when members of the population are willing to join with funding organizations and researchers in adding to the society's knowledge. The WLS and HRS, along with other long-term studies, bear a special burden in this regard, not only because of the large public subsidies required to sustain them, but because the scientific uses of the studies should warrant the periodic time and effort of research participants and the risks, however small, of harm to them.

Why do people become research participants? Individual motives are surely heterogeneous, and research participants have no collective voice except through the political process (Groves and Couper 1998; Hill and Willis 2001). Researchers seek to behave as if participants were behaving altruistically, by informing them of the purposes and importance of each study, even though pre-survey monetary incentives are increasingly common and are sometimes effective in securing participation (Rodgers 2002).

In the case of the WLS, the recruitment appeal to research participants goes beyond altruism and seeks to take advantage of their identification with the state, its university, and their high school class. In the past, participants were never compensated. In the 2004 round of the survey, following the completion of a 75-minute telephone interview, each respondent receives a self-administered questionnaire. Two crisp five dollar bills are attached to the front cover of the instrument with a red paper clip, but many participants have returned the money. At present, among 85 percent of participants who complete the telephone interview, 89 percent also complete the 50-page self-administered questionnaire.

Even in good times, research support is a scarce and largely public good, and respondents' time, effort, and willingness to risk disclosure of private information are of critical importance. Thus, the WLS and the HRS attempt to minimize respondent burden and risk in several ways.

First, despite some risk of disclosure, data-sharing is becoming the rule. If research participation is a public contribution, then data so obtained should be a public good. Given the growing emphasis on protecting data in secure enclaves, through licensing agreements with researchers, and with other technologies for guaranteeing privacy, we think it is fair to say that the protection of research participants provides no rationale for the unwillingness of investigators to share primary data. We believe that researchers have a responsibility, not merely to share data, but to encourage their use by the research community. Thus, rather than relying on traditional data archives for dissemination, the WLS and HRS projects have created websites designed to inform potential data uses, to register active users, and to permit downloading of data and documentation: «http://dpls.dacc.wisc.edu/wls/ (WLS)» and «http://hrsonline.isr.umich.edu/ (HRS)».

Second, while linking data from multiple sources potentially increases disclosure risks, it also increases the value of existing observations without increasing respondent burden. For example, the HRS has linked its survey data files to administrative records from the Social Security Administration, from Medicare, from employer pension plans, and to the National Death Index, while the WLS data include some of the same administrative record data. These make both sets of data much more valuable to a community of users that extends well beyond the primary investigators to include other researchers and the participating agencies. However, from the perspective of the agencies as well as the research participants, possible violations of privacy and confidentiality loom large as threats to their partnership in the research enterprise. It is thus highly significant that the Social Security Administration is contributing additional resources to the HRS in its 2004 wave for personal household interviews that will improve the chances of obtaining informed consent for links from SSA records to the HRS.

Third, one common type of data link, namely geocoding, deserves special mention because it presents serious risks of re-identification of research participants, but it often does not require partnership with a third party. For example, detailed addresses are easily obtained and are sufficient to create links with many types of public data. Indeed, it was the potential identifiability of deaths of individuals for whom only the date of death and city of residence were known that led to the controversial Shelby Amendment, mandating disclosure of some research data through the Freedom of Information Act (National Academy of Sciences (US), Science, Technology, and Law Panel, National Academy of Sciences (US), Policy and Global Affairs, and National Research Council (US) 2002). Because of the threat of disclosure, we believe that researchers should provide access to geocoded data under the same restrictions as apply to linked administrative data for individuals.

With the risks of identifiability in mind, the HRS and the WLS have each created special licensing arrangements for exceptionally detailed data extracts and linked administrative data within secure data enclaves. These make it possible to analyze sensitive data statistically without direct access to individual and actually or potentially identifying information.

Fourth, although violations of privacy and confidentiality are the main source of risk and harm to research participants in the social, economic, and behavioral sciences (National Research Council, Panel on Institutional Review Boards, Surveys, and Social Science Research 2003), researchers also have a continuing responsibility to avoid other potential risks. This is an issue of growing importance as social surveys are increasingly combined with other forms of potentially sensitive data collection, for example of biomarkers (National Research Council, Committee on Population 2001).

Interdisciplinary innovations in survey methodology

Aging is a process whose study is not the property of any given discipline. Gerontology must inherently be interdisciplinary. Aging also, by definition, proceeds through biological, demographic, social, and economic stages of the life course. As described earlier, the planning and oversight of the HRS is one positive example of multidisciplinary collaboration in the study of aging, and the new international studies are following the same model. The WLS is also a case in point. That study was dominated by sociological interests in its first 35 years, but since the early 1990s its content and direction have shifted to incorporate psychological, economic, and biomedical concerns.

The importance of cross-disciplinary partnership is well illustrated by growing interest in the ubiquitous correlation between socioeconomic status and health. Traditional epidemiology sees this correlation as dominated by the effects of economic and social resources and stresses on health, while economists have tended to view health as a form of human capital (Grossman 1972) that in part reflects deliberate choice and in part is influenced by third factors such as time discounting (Farrell and Fuchs 1982). In the past, surveys with good health measures have had poor economic measures, and vice versa, and surveys with both measures have been cross-sectional. This has hampered serious investigation. The availability of longitudinal observations with high-quality data on both health and socioeconomic status has stimulated analysis and discussion by leaders in several disciplines of the interactions between health and social and economic standing across the life course (Adams et al. 2003a, 2003b; Adda, Chandola, and Marmot 2003; Florens 2003; Geweke 2003; Granger 2003; Hausman 2003; Heckman 2003; Hoover 2003; Mealli and Rubin 2003; Poterba 2003; Robins 2003). This collaboration is discussed in more detail by James Smith in this volume.

Some of the best examples of interdisciplinary progress have come in the area of measurement. In the following paragraphs, we discuss several instances in which methods, variables, or motivating ideas cross the boundaries of economics, sociology, psychology, and medicine. This is not merely a matter of bringing "the state of the art" to bear on specific topics. Rather, in the context of large-scale data collection, the problem is often to modify specialized disciplinary measures in order to obtain valid measures within the knowledge base of respondents, without excessive intrusion, and within the time constraints of a multipurpose survey.

Sources of nonresponse

The knowledge and information-processing capacity of respondents plays a dual role in studies of aging. On the one hand, it is an object of study because it is a major determinant of health and decisionmaking behavior. On the other hand, it influences the quality and type of information that may be obtained in a survey. The latter effects range from overall survey response to specific patterns of response error, such as item nonresponse, age-heaping, and systematic mismarking of questionnaires.

For example, in the Wisconsin Longitudinal Study, there were essentially no systematic ability gradients in refusals from 1957 through 1975.

Beginning with the 1992 telephone survey, there was a modest gradient in refusal, such that 93.2 percent of persons in the top 10th of adolescent IQ responded, while only 77.7 percent of persons in the bottom 10th of IQ responded. This gradient was equally steep in the 1992 self-administered mail questionnaire, which ranged from 20 to 24 pages in length. Among graduates who completed the telephone interview, 89.8 percent of persons in the top 10th of IQ responded, compared with 68.0 percent of persons in the bottom 10th. We speculate that less able respondents may have failed to understand the purposes of the study and found it difficult and tiresome to read and respond to a long series of questions. [5] Adolescent ability also affected item response patterns. For example, in the case of Carol Ryff's measures of psychological well-being (Ryff 1989; Ryff and Keyes 1995), 11.8 percent of individuals in the bottom 10th of IQ used the same response category more than half of the time in a series of 42 items, as compared to 3.2 percent of individuals in the top 10th of IQ.[6]

The role of cognitive functioning in survey measurement is nicely illustrated by progress that has been made in the measurement of income and wealth. Traditionally, economic surveys have asked about the ownership and value of assets in a separate part of the questionnaire from questions about the flow of income from assets. Typically, these methods have yielded dramatic underreporting of income from assets, relative to estimates derived from administrative data sources. Beginning with the AHEAD cohort in 1995, this discrepancy was eliminated in the HRS in a very simple way: For each type of asset, the questionnaire asked about ownership, value, and income in that sequence (Juster and Suzman 1995).

Measuring economic quantities

A more general issue in the measurement of income and wealth arises from the problem of item nonresponse in conjunction with the fact that the most widely used measures of income and wealth are equal to sums of individual measures. For example, wealth is the sum of the value of checking accounts, house value, stock ownership, 401(k) balances, and so on. In most surveys, for example, many individuals answer "don't know" or "refuse" in response to at least part of the sequence of questions about the value of individual wealth components. In order to compute the desired aggregate measure of wealth, the analyst must impute some value to the missing items.

Traditionally, surveys have used hot-deck (borrowing values from similar cases) or regression methods for imputation, using observed individual and household characteristics to capture variation in the value of each component. However, wealth is distributed quite unequally across households, with a long right tail, and observed characteristics account for minuscule proportions of the variance of wealth. Moreover, the missing data are not missing at random, but in rather complex ways. For instance, missingness may be negatively correlated with some components of wealth—since persons who fail to report the value of wealth may be those with poor cognition—while it is positively correlated with other components—because high wealth persons are particularly sensitive to privacy concerns.

The HRS has made a major advance, both in reducing the proportion of item nonresponse and in improving the quality of the imputations for nonresponses by employing bracketing techniques (Juster and Suzman 1995). The technique itself is very simple. After getting a response of "don't know" or "refuse" in response to a question about, for example, the amount of money in a checking, savings, or money market account, most surveys simply record a missing value. Instead, in the 1992 wave, the HRS interviewer immediately asked whether the value of the account is more than a given bracket amount, say $5000. If the person answers "yes," he or she is asked whether it would be $10,000 or more; if "no," whether it would be $1,000 or more. If the answer to the $10,000 or more bracket is "yes," a final question is asked about whether the account has $50,000 or more; no further question is asked if there is a "no" answer to $1,000 or more.

The effects of using the bracketing technique are striking. Juster and Suzman (1995) report that about 90 percent of people who say "don't know" are willing to respond to the bracket questions, while about 50 percent who "refuse" to give a continuous amount such as $2,034 are willing to give a bracket amount. This results in a reduction of the item missing response rate from double-digit to low single-digit rates. Moreover, the brackets are extremely informative. For example, the checking and savings account value for a participant who completes the bracketing sequence described above is determined to be in one of the following intervals: 0–$999, $1,000–$4,999, $5,000–$9,999, $10,000–$49,999, or $50,000 or more. Within each interval, the HRS imputes a continuous value, using a hot-deck technique based on the distribution of continuous responses within the interval. Imputed values based on brackets typically explain about 80 percent of the variance (in logs) of continuous reports, as compared to only about 20 percent of the variance for an imputation based on observed characteristics of the respondent (Hurd 1999). In addition, Juster and Suzman (1995) argue that an unbiased estimate of asset values cannot be obtained from respondent characteristics because those who respond "don't know" or "refuse" are often a highly select subsample of participants with given observed characteristics. For example, Juster and Smith (1997) find that item nonresponse for asset questions is reduced by 75 percent and the estimate of housing wealth is increased by 18 percent through the use of unfolding brackets in the HRS. The success of the bracketing technique in improving asset information in 1992 led the HRS to apply brackets to almost all income, wealth, and other quantitative questions in subsequent waves, with bracket values optimized to maximize their explanatory power (Heeringa, Hill, and Howell 1995). In its current round of surveys, the WLS has followed the lead of the HRS in bracketing economic amounts, with similar success in reducing nonresponse. Also, the WLS has extended the HRS procedure by conditioning bracket points on certain characteristics of participants, for example, by sex in the case of current earnings from employment.

Why does the bracket technique reduce nonresponse to income and asset questions? There appear to be two main answers to this question, both psychological in nature. First, people who respond "don't know" may be uncertain about the value of an asset at the level of accuracy they presume the interviewer desires. The use of brackets signals that an approximate answer is all that is needed. Second, people who refuse to answer may do so because they regard the details of their economic situation to be personal information that they do not wish to disclose to a stranger. In addition, despite assurances of confidentiality, they may worry that this information might fall into the hands of the government or others who could use it to their disadvantage. By allowing them to give rough approximations, the bracketing technique appears to reassure a significant number of participants who have these concerns.

Psychological and other determinants of survey response increasingly command the attention of economists, sociologists, psychologists, and health researchers. Cognitive capacity, personality, physical abilities, motivation, and other factors influence the willingness of individuals to participate in surveys, their willingness to answer any given question, and the quality of the information they provide in their answers. Survey designers attempt to minimize survey and item nonresponse and to ask questions in a way that will elicit "true" answers. One should also recognize that many of the factors that influence the quality of an individual's survey responses may also influence his or her behavior in general. Because of this, researchers need to develop theories of survey response that provide a link between observed responses and the underlying true values. In addition, it may be useful to model an individual's behavior in the real world and his or her behavior as a survey respondent simultaneously.

We illustrate these points with several examples, beginning with further analysis of the quality of data in the HRS generated by bracketing. Soon after introducing brackets and despite their apparent success in reducing nonresponse and overcoming bias, the HRS investigators became concerned about the potential influence of bracketing due to anchoring and acquiescence bias (Hurd 1999). As discussed above, the bracketing technique is successful in obtaining information from individuals who are uncertain about the true value of a given asset or income amount. However, beginning with Tversky and Kahneman (1974), psychologists have established a robust finding of anchoring effects in questions of the form "Would it be greater or less than X?"

where "it" might be the length of the Amazon River and X is the anchor. Moreover, these effects have been shown to be largest for items about which a subject is most uncertain of the true value. In the context of the HRS, the issue is whether, for example, the entry point of $5,000 in the bracketing sequence on the value of checking and savings accounts has an influence on the final category in which a respondent ends up as compared to a bracketing sequence that began with an entry point of $1,000 or $10,000. Similarly, psychologists have found that a one-sided bracketing question—"Would it be more than $5,000?"—may lead a respondent to agree, causing an upward acquiescence bias in the HRS question format.

The HRS investigators began a set of experiments over several waves of HRS and AHEAD that were designed to determine the degree to which anchoring and acquiescence are of empirical importance. The history of this effort and findings are described in Hurd (1999). An informal Bayesian theory of anchoring bias might involve interaction between the precision of an individual's knowledge about the quantity in question and the amount of information about this quantity that the person believes to be contained in the anchor, X. The individual's knowledge is given by a subjective distribution that is concentrated about a single value if knowledge is precise but spread over a considerable interval if it is imprecise. In responding to a bracketing sequence, the individual chooses, perhaps unconsciously, a weighted average of the central tendency of his prior subjective distribution—say, the mean, the median, or the mode—and the anchor, where the weight is inversely related to the precision of his prior distribution and positively related to the perceived relevance of the anchor. For example, people usually have precise knowledge of their height and thus their answers would be unlikely to be influenced by whether a bracketing sequence began by asking whether they were "five feet or more" or "six feet or more." However, a person might be uncertain about the market value of his house and might believe that the anchor conveyed some information about the value of homes in his neighborhood. In this case, the final bracket might be sensitive to the choice of entry point unless the entry point was very far from market values in the neighborhood and hence was viewed as not relevant. The propensity to select into a bracketing sequence by answering "don't know" or "refuse" to a request for an exact answer is likely to be negatively correlated with precision of beliefs, and, conditional on selection, the anchoring bias is also likely to be negatively correlated with precision.

The importance of anchoring bias for income and assets in a survey like the HRS is an empirical question. It is likely to vary across particular items, to vary across people with different degrees of knowledge and cognitive ability, and to depend on the distance between the anchor and the true value of the item in question. Hurd (1999) describes a number of experiments, both deliberate and inadvertent, in the HRS that enable measurement of the empirical magnitude of anchoring and acquiescence effects. Qualitatively, his findings are consistent with the theoretical expectations described above. Quantitatively, the effects were sufficiently important that the HRS survey designers decided, after consultation with an expert working group, to randomize the entry points for all bracketing sequences and to replace the unbalanced format ("Would it be more than X?") with the more verbose balanced format ("Would it amount to less than $X, more than $X, or what?").

Expectations: Measuring subjective probabilities

Another example of interrelationships between the behavior of individuals as survey participants and as actors in the real world is afforded by the innovative attempt in the HRS to measure subjective probability beliefs on a wide variety of topics. These questions depart from the conventional approach to expectations in economics. Specifically, as Dominitz and Manski (1999: 16) argue, "Economists have typically assumed that expectation formation is homogeneous, all persons condition their beliefs on the same variables and process their information in the same way." Within the conventional approach, probability beliefs are treated as unobservable, and assumptions about beliefs, such as rational expectations, along with assumptions about unobservable preference parameters, such as risk aversion or time preference, are embedded in optimizing models from which testable relations between observable variables may be derived. An important motivation for asking directly about subjective probabilities is to relax the assumption of homogeneous expectations by converting probabilities from an unobservable to an observable quantity that may vary across respondents and thus capture individual heterogeneity in expectations.

The probability questions in the HRS follow an approach pioneered by Juster (1966) and Manski (1990) by asking a participant directly about the likelihood of various events by giving the interviewer a number from 0 to 100, where "0" means no chance and "100" means that the event is sure to happen. The questions cover a variety of topics that can be usefully classified into three types: (1) general events such as the chance of a severe economic depression in the next ten years, the chance that social security will become more generous, or the chance that the value of a mutual fund held in stocks will be higher at this time next year; (2) events with personal information such as the chance of surviving to age 75 or the chance that one's income will increase faster than inflation over the next ten years; and (3) events under personal control such as the chance of working past age 62 or 65 or the chance of leaving an inheritance of a given size. As this classification implies, subjective probabilities may vary across people at a moment in time or over time for a given person because of external exogenous factors such as prices or aggregate income; because of personal knowledge of idiosyncratic factors such as health or promotion possibilities at work; because of internal psychological factors such as optimism or pessimism; or because of choices about controlled stochastic processes such as work or saving that reflect the interaction of preferences and constraints that may depend on the realization of random variables such as a spouse's survival, an employer's offer of an early retirement window, and so on.

The first analyses of the HRS probability questions focused on whether the answers made sense. Striking evidence for the value of these questions came in early analysis of the survival probabilities by Hurd and McGarry (1995), who showed that, on average, there is surprising agreement between these subjective reports and life table estimates of survival, including covariation with health status and health behaviors such as smoking.

Although the subjective probability responses in HRS seem to "work well" when averaged across respondents, individual responses appear to contain considerable noise and are often heaped on "focal values" of "0", "50," and "100." The existence of focal answers raises questions about what aspects of the probability beliefs of respondents are revealed by their answers to survey questions. Some psychologists, especially Fischhoff, de Bruin, and their colleagues, have argued that focal answers at "50" often reflect "epistemic uncertainty"; that is, a failure to have any probability belief at all about the event in question or, at least, to have no clear idea of what the probability could be (Fischhoff and de Bruin 1999; de Bruin et al. 2000). Alternatively, of course, an answer of "50" might reflect a very precise belief about the probability that a fair coin will come up heads or perhaps a less precise belief that a given event is about equally likely to occur or not occur.

There has been much less emphasis in the psychological literature on focal answers at "0" or "100." When a probability question concerns a general event such as the HRS question "What is the percent chance that mutual fund shares invested in blue chip stocks like those in the Dow Jones Industrial Average will be worth more this time next year than they are today?," it does not seem credible to assume that a respondent who gives a particular answer, such as 65 percent, is completely certain that such an event will or will not take place. Such an interpretation is more plausible for questions about events with personal control such as, "What do you think the chances are that you will be working full-time after you reach age 62?" Answers at "0" or "100" may simply indicate that the respondent feels that he has already made a decision. While this may be a natural interpretation, it is inconsistent with dynamic economic models in which labor supply decisions are assumed to be conditioned on variables—such as income, wealth, pension incentives, the health status of oneself or one's spouse, and the employer's demand for labor—whose future values cannot be known with certainty unless, perhaps, the target date in the question is near.

Lillard and Willis (2001) propose a model of survey responses to subjective probability questions that is broadly consistent both with the existence of focal answers and with their close correspondence to objective outcomes when averaged across respondents. They assume that probability beliefs consist of a subjective prior distribution which is highly concentrated for questions such as the probability that a fair coin will come up heads and highly dispersed for questions with great deal of uncertainty. HRS participants take about 15 seconds to answer each probability question. Lillard and Willis hypothesize that respondents report the modal value of the subjective prior distribution; that is, they report that value which they believe to be the most likely among all possible probability values. They argue that the modal response is cognitively less burdensome than alternatives such as the mean or the median of the subjective prior distribution. When the degree of uncertainty is relatively low, this answer mode provides a very good estimate of the mean. Thus, reports of the mode might be construed as a "fast and frugal" algorithm of the sort that psychologists such as Gigerenzer et al. (1999) suggest often help people make complex judgments in situations in which a rapid response is called for. As uncertainty increases, Lillard and Willis show that this algorithm generates responses at "0," "50," and "100" as the median and mean of the subjective prior distribution increase from low to high values. Because of this, the average value of probability reports across people tends to track objective outcomes if people's subjective beliefs are not biased in an optimistic or pessimistic direction.

Researchers have found the HRS probability measures useful in understanding behavior. For example, Lillard and Willis (2001) argued that the propensity to heap on focal values in answering probability questions provides an indicator of the degree of imprecision of probabilistic beliefs and, further, that economic theory implies persons with more imprecise beliefs will be more risk-averse. They found evidence for this in an analysis of savings and portfolio choice. Still another use of the probability data is a book-length analysis, *The Smoking Puzzle* (Sloan, Smith, and Taylor 2003), which examines how survival expectations are affected by smoking, how smokers and nonsmokers revise their expectations as they experience health shocks, and what role expectations play in decisions to quit smoking. As a final example, Chan and Stevens (2001) study incentive effects of pensions on retirement probabilities and on actual retirement behavior.

Comparing subjective assessments

Recent methodological research in connection with the World Health Survey (Salomon, Tandon, and Murray 2001; Sadana et al. 2001; King et al. 2004) addresses a fundamental problem in survey measurement: whether all respondents use the same numeric scale in the same way when responding to questions that call for a graded response. For example, to measure negative affect, people in highly developed and less developed countries are asked, "Overall, in the last 30 days, how much difficulty did you have with feeling sad, low, or depressed?" and are given the response alternatives, "none, mild, moderate, severe, or extreme." How can we know, even after addressing language differences with careful back-translation, whether the several response categories are used similarly by individuals in such widely different circumstances? The phenomenon is essentially the same as that of differential item functioning (*dif*) in psychometric measurement, except there is no right answer to each item for all individuals.

In this context, the WHS group suggests that carefully drafted vignettes be used to calibrate self-assessments across populations. For example, each respondent is asked the self-assessment item in the domain of affect, followed by one or more vignettes of the form: "Imagine that the people described below are the same age that you are. Using the same scale that you used when talking about aspects of your own health, how would you rate the health of these people? ... Barbara feels depressed most of the time. She weeps frequently and feels hopeless about the future. She feels that she has become a burden on others and that she would be better off dead. How much of a problem does Barbara have with feeling sad, low, or depressed? (none, mild, moderate, severe, or extreme)." By making the crucial assumption that respondents use the categories in the same way in rating their own health as in rating the vignettes, it becomes possible to calibrate differences in the self-rating scale across populations.

Typically, calibration is improved by using more than one self-rating scale in each health domain and by administering several different vignettes for each health domain with corresponding rating scales. However, it is not essential that every vignette be administered to every respondent. Thus, although the vignette method requires more survey time or space than a simple rating scale, it can be made more efficient by random presentation of a subset of vignettes. In addition to other standard health measures, the WLS is administering vignette-based measures of affect and mobility in four alternate forms of a sex-specific self-administered mail instrument.

Recording full-text interviews

In developing the 2003–05 round of the Wisconsin Longitudinal Study, project staff decided to record all of the telephone interviews. The original reason for our investigation of recording technology was that two of the collaborators, Nora Cate Schaeffer and Douglas Maynard, wanted to obtain high-quality recordings of about 1,000 randomly selected interviews that could be used for intensive analysis of respondent–interviewer interaction in an older population. A second reason, which applied to parts of all interviews, was that some of the more promising protocols for cognitive assessment could not be administered reliably unless the responses were recorded, and, furthermore, recordings could be used to validate appropriate administration of the assessments.

Staff learned that almost all respondents would agree to recordings and to their retention for research purposes. This was confirmed in pretests, and a consent protocol was developed. The WLS recording technology was developed to meet four main criteria:

(1) Recordings should be digital and stored as WAV or MP3 files, thereby permitting random access for research purposes. Thus, standard or digital audio taping was eliminated as a possibility.

(2) Control of the recording process should take place automatically through the Computer Assisted Telephone Interviewing software and not require separate activation or adjustment by interviewers.

(3) The recordings should be as high in audio quality as possible, given the limited bandwidth of telephone lines.

(4) Because audio files are potentially identifiable, as well as valuable for research purposes—including at some point in the future—file storage procedures should be both secure and redundant.

The cost of the recording software and equipment is modest, less than US$250 per workstation.

Aside from the future value of the recordings for research, which will include an improved ability to edit the raw survey data, they have already proved useful in the process of instrument development in the WLS. For example, it has been efficient for researchers to listen to each instance of a pretest telephone module—for example, a family roster or employment history—in order to detect and solve problems in the logic and content of the instrument and to identify problems in interviewing that can be addressed in training sessions.

Domains and units of observation

While survey respondents are individuals, the units of observation and analysis are by no means limited to individuals. For example, the Wisconsin Longitudinal Study actually samples persons within households and their siblings, while the Health and Retirement Study samples persons in specific cohorts and their spouses, regardless of age. In the WLS, observations are also linked to high schools and geographic location in each wave of the survey. In fact, almost all household-based survey observations may be linked to geography at some level of detail in private and sometimes publicly available files. In the HRS, individuals are linked to pension plans through their employers, and in the Medicare data it is possible to link individual records to characteristics of hospitals or physicians providing treatment. Analyses based on the complex record structures resulting from such links have been facilitated by the development of new statistical software for hierarchical data.

The possibilities for useful data links continue to grow. We have already mentioned health and Medicare records, pensions, and Social Security earnings. The HRS is exploring the feasibility of links of individual survey data to characteristics of employers with the Census Research Data Center. This would map characteristics of the firm—for example, its wage policies—down to the level of the individual HRS participant, and it would also map other links, such as employer pension policies, at the level of firms. For younger cohorts, it would seem feasible to match individuals to birth records that include birth weight. For example, in Wisconsin, birth weight was not included in the birth certificates of 1939, when almost all members of the graduate cohort were born. However, for a few years following World War II, birth weight was stated on the public portion of the birth certificate. The WLS is experimenting with a self-reported birth weight item in its 2003 mail questionnaire, and for siblings of the graduates who were born during the right period, the self-reports will be validated against birth certificates.[7] In the WLS, it has already been possible to collect data on high school resources from archives in the Wisconsin State Historical Library. These are available for school districts, not individual schools, but in most of the state in the 1950s, each school district had only a single high school.

Another link in the WLS, whose construction is now in progress, is to data from high school yearbooks. The project has succeeded in borrowing and scanning the 1957 yearbooks from schools attended by about two-thirds of the graduates. Individual pictures of graduates have been extracted and used to identify African Americans in the cohort. Later, the full set of pictures will be graded for facial characteristics, such as attractiveness, obesity, and the Duchenne smile (symptomatic of muscular dystrophy), that may be associated with economic, health, and social outcomes (Hayes and Ross 1986; Hamermesh and Biddle 1994; Averett and Korenman 1996; Biddle and Hamermesh 1998; Smith 1999; Harker and Keltner 2001). In addition, although the baseline WLS survey of 1957 did not ascertain students' extracurricular activities, these data are now being coded from reports in the yearbooks.

Leadership, flexibility, and serendipity

In our discussion of institutional support, we emphasized the important role that scientific agencies such as the National Institute on Aging, the National Institute of Mental Health, and the Social Security Administration have played in supporting the development and analysis of the HRS and the WLS. Serendipity shows its hand in this arena, too. A leading example is the profound influence that Richard Suzman's arrival as a program officer at NIA in the early 1980s has had on the development of both of those surveys, among others. The idea for the HRS emerged out of a set of scientific meetings organized by Suzman early in his tenure at NIA, and the subsequent movement from idea to implementation required skill and persistence in getting both federal officials and a number of scientific constituencies to understand what was envisioned and to lend their resources to making the HRS a reality. This was not a one-off accomplishment. Suzman has been behind many other data collection initiatives, ranging from supporting international surveys such as the English Longitudinal Study of Ageing, Survey of Health, Ageing and Retirement in Europe, and Mexican Health and Aging Study, to supporting the addition of new kinds of measures, such as biomarkers, to social science surveys like the WLS (National Research Council, Committee on Population 2001). He has also been instrumental in enticing researchers of the highest caliber, from diverse disciplines and countries, many of whom were new to the field of aging, into research that exploits the data developed with the support of NIA. The effects of these investments on the growth of knowledge will be felt far into the future.

Probability samples within probability samples

At first thought, one might expect that large-scale longitudinal surveys of probability samples of well-defined populations are useful only in providing superficial descriptions and models—providing "the big picture." We think this is partly true, but large-scale observational studies also provide unusual opportunities for in-depth studies, and even experiments, in populations whose defining traits are rare. In our opinion, the major longitudinal studies should be designed to anticipate and encourage such uses of the samples, even if their exact content is unknowable at the outset. We have already mentioned the possibility of identifying, cumulating, and pooling rare observations across time, an idea that forms the basis for the ADAMS supplement to HRS, and the identification of atypical child outcomes in the WLS—developmental disability, severe mental illness, or early death.

Aside from providing a frame for intensive study of rare populations, large-scale longitudinal surveys may also provide opportunities for especially costly or intensive studies of the base population or, inversely, as ways of minimizing cost and respondent burden in segments of the base population that are not included. Current surveys provide many examples of this kind, all of which may be thought of as designs where data are deliberately missing at random, a notion that reminds us of recent advances in theory and methods for the analysis of data with missing observations (Arminger, Clogg, and Sobel 1995; Vermunt 1997; Little, Schnabel, and Baumert 2000; Little and Rubin 2002; Allison 2002).

One such example in the WLS is a plan to invite a random subsample of approximately 500 graduates to Madison for a two-day visit during which their health and psychological functioning will be assessed intensively. The protocol includes a physical examination, various psychological assessments, and functional magnetic resonance imaging (fMRI) of the brain. Richard Davidson has already established the feasibility of this project in examinations of a select subsample of about 100 WLS participants in the late 1990s (Jackson et al. 2003) and in repeated assessments of many of the same individuals in late 2002 and early 2003.

In the 2003–05 round of the WLS, there is simply too much content for all items to be administered to all eligible graduates or siblings in the telephone interviews. For that reason, the WLS has adopted a complex subsampling scheme, in which selected core items are administered to all participants, while other modules are administered to nested subsamples. This scheme is designed to provide larger numbers of observations for estimation of relationships of great interest, for example, health and access to health care, economic assets and economic transfers, and depression and alcohol use. The scheme will provide reasonable numbers of observations with complete data for analysts with typical interests and moderate statistical skill, along with richer, but incomplete data for more sophisticated analysts.

Serendipity and social change

The contingencies of economic and social change, interacting with those of the life course, imply that no longitudinal survey design will ever anticipate all uses of a study—or guarantee that planned uses of data will pay off. Indeed, we are impressed that the best research based on a given survey often explores questions or tests theories that were not contemplated by the designers of the survey. What we can do is to give our studies enough strength to hold up across time and to keep our eyes open for new opportunities to create data and add to knowledge. Such opportunities may arise through secular or cyclical change, bringing external events to bear on the lives of study participants, or they may be generated within a study population by the dynamics of the life course.

The HRS and WLS provide examples of each of these opportunities. In the HRS, successive cohorts have experienced the rise and decline in equity markets since the early 1990s. These changes appear as exogenous shocks to the economic status and plans of HRS participants and, thus, provide useful information in estimating models about individual and familial provision for retirement, about economic transfers, and about labor market behavior in older populations. In its 2002 wave, the HRS began measuring subjective expectations about the value next year at this time of a hypothetical mutual fund held in stocks. Preliminary analysis by Kézdi and Willis (2003) suggests that expectations vary greatly across respondents and are significantly related to actual investment behavior. Because the HRS was in the field from 1 April 2002 through 31 January 2003, actual variation in the recent history of stock prices at the time of interview will enable researchers to study how people alter their subjective beliefs about expected returns as market conditions change. Traditional finance theory with its emphasis on efficient markets and rational expectations has come under attack by researchers in the new field of behavioral finance, which emphasizes the heterogeneity of the beliefs of economic agents (Shleifer 2000). The HRS offers the first opportunity to address issues raised in this debate with data on a probability sample of the US population that combines information on expectations with actual behavior. Understanding of these issues is important for public policies regarding 401(k) plans and in assessing the potential benefits and pitfalls of introducing individual accounts into the Social Security system.

The WLS began, in the midst of the Cold War, as a study of the transition from high school to postsecondary schooling, military service, and the labor market. It has been sustained and increased in scientific value for two reasons: first, because the baseline measurements and survey data have survived across nearly half a century, and, second, because investigators have been willing to change direction as the sample aged. Thus, the study has now come to focus on family, health, and well-being, and the original focus on labor market outcomes is winding down. At the same time, by linking to external data the WLS has continued to expand its coverage of earlier phases of the life course, for example, using high school yearbooks, archival school district records, and, possibly, birth certificates.[8]

Epilogue

We have examined six main desiderata in a system of survey-based research: (1) representation of real populations; (2) sustained institutional support; (3) responsibility to the public; (4) innovation based on multiple disciplinary perspectives; (5) coverage of multiple domains and units of observation; and (6) opportunities for flexibility, serendipity, and scientific opportunism. Each of these points is well illustrated in the development of the Wisconsin Longitudinal Study and the Health and Retirement Study.

Scientifically useful evolution of study design and content has not been automatic and inevitable. It is easy to think of contrary examples in the recent history of survey research. Obversely, we should not become so wedded to the rich, contemporary array of data resources that we fail to keep scanning the horizon for new and unexpected scientific opportunities. With luck, the Wisconsin Longitudinal Study and the Health and Retirement Study will continue to extend their baseline measurements of aging processes and to generate novel scientific findings and innovations.

Notes

This research was supported by grants to the University of Wisconsin–Madison and to the University of Michigan from the Behavioral and Social Research Program of the National Institute on Aging. We thank Willard Rogers, Jeremy Freese, and Wes Taylor for contributions to this text and James Smith and Linda Waite for helpful advice. The order of authorship of this paper is without social or academic significance. Correspondence may be sent to Robert M. Hauser (hauser@ssc.wisc.edu) or Robert J. Willis (rjwillis@umich.edu).

1 Sewell remained active in research using the WLS until his death in 2001 at the age of 91.

2 The same goal has been achieved in the Panel Study of Income Dynamics by following all individuals who enter sample households, rather than by refreshing the sample with new cohorts (Duncan, Hofferth, and Stafford 2004).

3 In Europe, surveys like the HRS are now underway, notably, ELSA (English Longitudinal Study of Ageing) and SHARE (Survey of Health, Ageing, and Retirement in Europe). Fortunately, each of these studies will use probability sampling, thus overcoming a tradition of quota sampling in several of the participating countries.

4 Because the WLS covers siblings as well as the 1957 graduates, it is possible to carry out some intercohort comparisons within the study population. However, such comparisons necessarily pertain to differently selected populations. For example, graduates must have completed high school, but their siblings need not have done so. Graduates may be singletons, but siblings cannot be singletons.

5 For this reason, the WLS is planning special follow-up activities for low-ability graduates who do not complete the mail survey after the usual three mailings and reminders.

6 While these observations all refer to adolescent IQ test scores, differential non-response in the WLS is not solely a function of those scores. Rank in high school class has equally large effects on response. The key finding is that these cognitive/academic variables account for the association between socioeconomic variables and differential response. We thank Jeremy Freese for the tabulation of response heaping in Ryff's items.

7 Birth weights were also reported in some newspapers, and WLS staff members are exploring the feasibility of a search for such reports.

8 This parallels the evolution of the British birth cohort studies (Douglas and Blomfield 1958; Douglas 1964; Douglas, Ross, and Simpson 1968; Kerckhoff 1990; Wadsworth 1991; Kerckhoff 1993). As the cohorts have aged, scientific leadership of those studies has variously been exercised by pediatricians, developmental psychologists, education experts, demographers, sociologists, labor economists, and epidemiologists.

References

Adams, Peter, Michael D. Hurd, Daniel McFadden, Angela Merrill, and Tiago Ribeiro. 2003a. "Healthy, wealthy, and wise? Tests for direct causal paths between health and socioeconomic status," *Journal of Econometrics* 112(1): 3–56.

———. 2003b. "Response," *Journal of Econometrics* 112(1): 129–133.

Adda, Jerome, Tarani Chandola, and Michael Marmot. 2003. "Socio-economic status and health: Causality and pathways," *Journal of Econometrics* 112(1): 57–63.

Allison, Paul D. 2002. *Missing Data*. Thousand Oaks, CA: Sage Publications.

Arminger, Gerhard, Clifford C. Clogg, and Michael E. Sobel. 1995. *Handbook of Statistical Modeling for the Social and Behavioral Sciences*. New York: Plenum Press.

Averett, Susan and Sanders Korenman. 1996. "The economic reality of the beauty myth," *Journal of Human Resources* 31(2): 304–330.

Biddle, Jeff E. and Daniel S. Hamermesh. 1998. "Beauty, productivity, and discrimination: Lawyers' looks and lucre," *Journal of Labor Economics* 16(1): 172–201.

Chan, Sewin and Ann Huff Stevens. 2001. "Job loss and employment patterns of older workers," *Journal of Labor Economics* 19(2, April): 484–521.

de Bruin, W. B., B. Fischhoff, S. G. Millstein, and B. L. Halpern-Felsher. 2000. "Verbal and numerical expressions of probability: 'It's a fifty-fifty chance,'" *Organizational Behavior and Human Decision Processes* 81(1): 115–131.

Dominitz, Jeffrey and Charles F. Manski. 1999. "The several cultures of research on subjective expectations," in Robert J. Willis and James Smith (eds.), *Wealth, Work, and Health*. Ann Arbor: University of Michigan Press.

Douglas, James W. B. 1964. *The Home and the School: A Study of Ability and Attainment in the Primary School*. London: Macgibbon & Kee.

Douglas, James W. B. and J. M. Blomfield. 1958. *Children Under Five: The Results of a National Survey Made by a Joint Committee of the Institute of Child Health (University of London), the Society of Medical Officers of Health, and the Population Investigation Committee*. London: Allen & Unwin.

Douglas, James W. B., J. M. Ross, and Howard R. Simpson. 1968. *All Our Future: A Longitudinal Study of Secondary Education*. London: P. Davies.

Duncan, Greg J., Sandra L. Hofferth, and Frank Stafford. 2004. "Evolution and change in family income, wealth and health: The Panel Study of Income Dynamics, 1968–2000 and beyond," in James S. House, F. T. Juster, Robert L. Kahn, and Howard Shuman (eds.), *A Telescope on Society: Survey Research and Social Science at the University of Michigan and Beyond*. Ann Arbor, MI: Institute for Social Research, Chapter 6.

Farrell, P. and V. R. Fuchs. 1982. "Schooling and health: The cigarette connection," *Journal of Health Economics* 1(3): 217–130.

Fischhoff, Baruch and Wändi B. de Bruin. 1999. "Fifty-fifty=50%?," *Journal of Behavioral Decision Making* 12(2): 149–163.

Florens, Jean-Pierre. 2003. "Some technical issues in defining causality," *Journal of Econometrics* 112(1): 127–128.

Geweke, John. 2003. "Econometric issues in using the AHEAD panel," *Journal of Econometrics* 112(1): 115–120.

Gigerenzer, Gerd, Peter M. Todd, and ABC Research Group. 1999. *Simple Heuristics That Make Us Smart*. New York: Oxford University Press.

Granger, Clive W. J. 2003. "Some aspects of causal relationships," *Journal of Econometrics* 112(1): 69–71.

Grossman, Michael. 1972. "On the concept of health capital and the demand for health," *The Journal of Political Economy* 80(2, March–April): 223–255.

Groves, Robert M. and Mick Couper. 1998. *Nonresponse in Household Interview Surveys*. New York: Wiley.

Hamermesh, Daniel S. and Jeff E. Biddle. 1994. "Beauty and the labor market," *The American Economic Review* 84(5): 1174–1194.

Harker, L. and D. Keltner. 2001. "Expressions of positive emotion in women's college yearbook pictures and their relationship to personality and life outcomes across adulthood," *Journal of Personality and Social Psychology* 80(1): 112–124.

Hausman, Jerry A. 2003. "Triangular structural model specification and estimation with application to causality," *Journal of Econometrics* 112(1): 107–113.

Hayes, Diane and Catherine E. Ross. 1986. "Body and mind: The effect of exercise, overweight, and physical health on psychological well-being," *Journal of Health and Social Behavior* 27(4): 387–400.

Heckman, James. 2003. "Conditioning, causality and policy analysis," *Journal of Econometrics* 112(1): 73–78.

Heeringa, S. G., D. H. Hill, and D. A. Howell. 1995. "Unfolding brackets for reducing item non-response in economic surveys," HRS Working Paper 94-029. Ann Arbor: Institute for Social Research, University of Michigan.

Hill, Daniel and Robert J. Willis. 2001. "Reducing panel attrition: A search for effective policy instruments," *Journal of Human Resources* 36(3): 416–438.

Hoover, Kevin D. 2003. "Some causal lessons from macroeconomics," *Journal of Econometrics* 112(1): 121–125.

Hurd, Michael D. 1999. "Anchoring and acquiescence bias in measuring assets in household surveys," *Journal of Risk and Uncertainty* 19(1-3): 111–136.

Hurd, Michael D. and Kathleen McGarry. 1995. "Evaluation of the subjective probabilities of survival in the health and retirement study," *Journal of Human Resources* 30(Supplement): S268–S292.

Jackson, Daren C., Corrina J. Mueller, Isa Dolski, Kim M. Dalton, Jack B. Nitschke, Heather L. Urry, Melissa A. Rosenkranz, Carol D. Ryff, Burton H. Singer, and Richard J. Davidson. 2003. "Now you feel it, now you don't: Frontal EEG asymmetry and individual differences in emotion regulation," *Psychological Science* 14(6): 612–617.

Juster, F. T. 1966. "Consumer buying intentions and purchase probability: An experiment in survey design," *Journal of the American Statistical Association* 61(315): 658–696.

Juster, F. T. and James P. Smith. 1997. "Improving the quality of economic data: Lessons from the HRS and AHEAD," *Journal of the American Statistical Association* 92(440): 1268–1278.

Juster, F. T. and Richard Suzman. 1995. "The Health and Retirement Study: Data quality and early results," *Journal of Human Resources* 30(Supplement): S7–S56.

Kerckhoff, Alan C. 1990. *Getting Started: Transition to Adulthood in Great Britain*. Boulder, CO: Westview Press.

———. 1993. *Diverging Pathways: Social Structure and Career Deflections*. New York: Cambridge University Press.

Kézdi, Gábor and Robert J. Willis. 2003. "Who becomes a stockholder? Expectations, subjective uncertainty, and asset allocation," presented at the Fifth Annual Joint Conference for the Retirement Research Consortium, 15–16 May 2003, Washington, DC.

King, Gary, Christopher J. L. Murray, Joshua A. Salomon, and Ajay Tandon. 2004. "Enhancing the validity and cross-cultural comparability of survey research," *American Political Science Review* 98(1): 191–207.

Lillard, Lee A. 1977. "Inequality: Earnings vs. human wealth," *The American Economic Review* 67(2): 42–53.

Lillard, Lee A. and Robert J. Willis. 2001. "Cognition and wealth: The importance of probabilistic thinking," Michigan Retirement Research Center Working Paper UM00-04, University of Michigan, Ann Arbor.

Little, Roderick J. A. and Donald B. Rubin. 2002. *Statistical Analysis With Missing Data*. 2nd ed. Hoboken, NJ: Wiley-Interscience.

Little, Todd D., Kai U. Schnabel, and Jürgen Baumert. 2000. *Modeling Longitudinal and Multilevel Data Practical Issues, Applied Approaches, and Specific Examples*. Mahwah, NJ; London: Lawrence Erlbaum.

Manski, Charles F. 1990. "The use of intentions data to predict behavior: A best-case analysis," *Journal of the American Statistical Association* 85(412): 934–940.

Mealli, Fabrizia and Donald B. Rubin. 2003. "Assumptions allowing the estimation of direct causal effects," *Journal of Econometrics* 112(1): 79–87.

National Academy of Sciences (US), Science, Technology, and Law Panel, National Academy of Sciences (US), Policy and Global Affairs, and National Research Council (U.S.). 2002. *Access to Research Data in the 21st Century: An Ongoing Dialogue Among Interested Parties: Report of a Workshop*. Washington, DC: National Academy Press.

National Research Council, Panel on Institutional Review Boards, Surveys, and Social Science Research. 2003. *Protecting Participants and Facilitating Social and Behavioral Sciences Research*, Constance F. Citro, Daniel R. Ilgen, and Cora B. Marret (eds.). Washington, DC: National Academies Press.

National Research Council (US) and Panel on a Research Agenda and New Data for an Aging World. 2001. *Preparing for an Aging World the Case for Cross-National Research*. Washington, DC: National Academy Press.

National Research Council (US), Committee on Population. 2001. *Cells and Surveys Should Biological Measures Be Included in Social Science Research?*, Caleb E. Finch, James W. Vaupel, and Kevin G. Kinsella (eds.). Washington, DC: National Academy Press.

Poterba, James M. 2003. "Some observations on health status and economic status," *Journal of Econometrics* 112(1): 65–67.

Robins, James M. 2003. "General methodological considerations," *Journal of Econometrics* 112(1): 89–106.

Rodgers, Willard L. 2002. "Size of incentive effects in a longitudinal study," presented at the 57th Annual Meeting of the American Association for Public Opinion Research, St. Pete Beach, FL.

Ryff, Carol D. 1989. "Happiness is everything, or is it? Explorations on the meaning of psychological well-being," *Journal of Personality and Social Psychology* 57(6): 1069–1081.

Ryff, Carol D. and Corey L. Keyes. 1995. "The structure of psychological well-being revisited," *Journal of Personality and Social Psychology* 69(4): 719–727.

Sadana, Ritu, Ajay Tandon, Christopher J. Murray, Irina Serdobova, Yang Cao, Wanjun Xie, Bedirhan Ustun, and Somnath Chatterji. 2001. "Describing population health in six domains: Comparable results from 66 household surveys," *The Global Burden of Disease 2000 in Aging Populations*. Research Paper No. 01.16. Cambridge, MA: Harvard Burden of Disease Unit, Center for Population and Development Studies.

Salomon, Joshua A., Ajay Tandon, and Christopher J. Murray. 2001. "Using vignettes to improve cross-population comparability of health surveys: Concepts, design, and evaluation techniques," Discussion Paper No. 41. Geneva, Switzerland: World Health Organization.

Sewell, William H., Robert M. Hauser, Kristen W. Springer, and Taissa S. Hauser. 2003. "As we age: The Wisconsin Longitudinal Study, 1957–2001," in Kevin Leicht (ed.), *Research in Social Stratification and Mobility*, vol. 20. London: Elsevier, pp. 3–111.

Shleifer, Andrei. 2000. *Inefficient Markets an Introduction to Behavioral Finance*. Oxford; New York: Oxford University Press.

Sloan, Frank A., V. K. Smith, and Donald H. Taylor, Jr. 2003. *The Smoking Puzzle: Information, Risk Perception, and Choice*. Cambridge, MA: Harvard University Press.

Smith, James P. 1999. "Healthy bodies and thick wallets: The dual relation between health and economic status," *The Journal of Economic Perspectives* 13(2): 145–166.

Smith, P. M. and B. B. Torrey. 1996. "The future of the behavioral and social sciences," *Science* 271(5249): 611–612.

Snowdon, D. A., S. J. Kemper, J. A. Mortimer, L. H. Greiner, D. R. Wekstein, and W. R. Markesbery. 1996. "Linguistic ability in early life and cognitive function and Alzheimer's disease in late life: Findings from the Nun Study," *Journal of the American Medical Association* 275(7): 528–532.

Snowdon, David. 2001. *Aging With Grace: What the Nun Study Teaches Us About Leading Longer, Healthier, and More Meaningful Lives*. New York: Bantam Books.

Soldo, B. J., M. D. Hurd, W. L. Rodgers, and R. B. Wallace. 1997. "Asset and health dynamics among the oldest old: An overview of the AHEAD study," *Journals of Gerontology, Series B, Psychological Sciences and Social Sciences* 52 Spec No: 1–20.

Taubman, Paul J. and Terence J. Wales. 1973. "Higher education, mental ability, and screening," *Journal of Political Economy* 81(1, January–February): 28–55.

Thorndike, Robert L. and Elizabeth Hagen. 1959. *Ten Thousand Careers*. New York: Wiley.

Tversky, Amos and Daniel Kahneman. 1974. "Judgment under uncertainty: Heuristics and biases," *Science* 185:1124–131.

Vermunt, Jeroen K. 1997. *Log-Linear Models for Event Histories*. Thousand Oaks, CA: Sage Publications.

Wadsworth, M. E. J. 1991. *The Imprint of Time: Childhood, History, and Adult Life*. Oxford: Clarendon Press.

Willis, Robert J. 1999. "Theory confronts data: How the HRS is shaped by the economics of aging and how the economics of aging will be shaped by the HRS," *Labour Economics* 6(2, June): 119–145.

Willis, Robert J. and Sherwin Rosen. 1979. "Education and self-selection," *The Journal of Political Economy* 87(5, Part 2: Education and Income Distribution): S7–S36.

EPILOGUE

Research on Population Aging at NIA: Retrospect and Prospect

Richard Suzman

The National Institute on Aging (NIA), one of the 27 institutes and centers of the National Institutes of Health (NIH), was established by Congress in 1974 with the primary mission "to improve the health and well-being of older Americans through research." Subsequent amendments to this legislation designated NIA as the primary federal agency on Alzheimer's disease research. Today NIA is one of the mid-sized NIH institutes, with an annual budget of just over $1 billion. NIA leads a broad scientific effort to understand the nature of aging and to extend the healthy, active years of life. It supports and conducts research on aging processes, age-related diseases, and the special problems and needs of the aged. An interest in demographic and economic aspects of population aging was present from NIA's inception.

The Behavioral and Social Research (BSR) program was one of the two original extramural NIA research programs within NIA set up under the institute's broad mandate.[1] An early report, *Our Future Selves* (National Institute on Aging 1978), drafted by panels reporting to NIA's National Advisory Council, provided the blueprint for NIA's early research directions. The panel on the behavioral and social sciences, co-chaired by Bernice Neugarten and George Maddox, that laid the foundation for the modern-day BSR, was heavily dominated by psychologists, sociologists, and social psychologists, with minimal input from economists and demographers.[2] The first head of BSR, Matilda Riley, joined the NIA as associate director in 1979. With the encouragement of Robert Butler, NIA's founding director, and relying heavily on *Our Future Selves*, Riley developed a broad blueprint for the program. The blueprint called for research on aging at the individual, cultural, and societal levels, drawing on the disciplines of psychology, sociology, anthropology, and economics.

In 1983, the year I formally joined the program,[3] BSR had a tripartite structure with separate "clusters,"[4] concerned with social science, social psychology, and cognitive psychology (see Figure 1). The social science cluster,

FIGURE 1   Organization of the Behavioral and Social Research program, 1982–2004

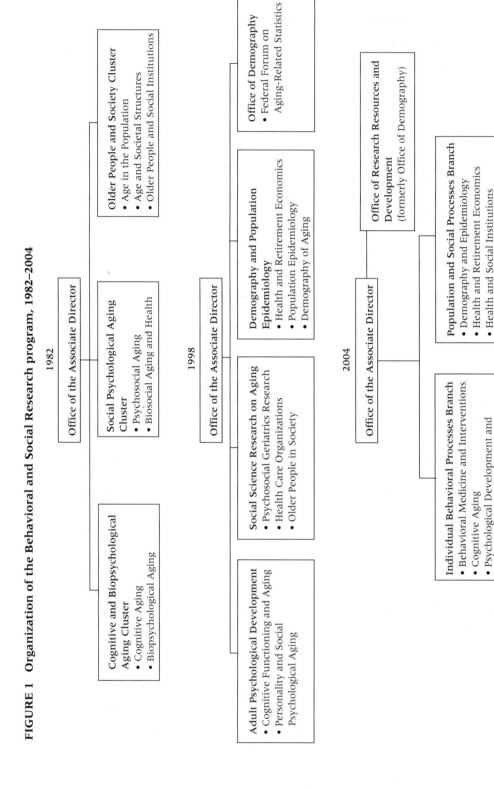

Older People and Society, was composed of three sections, focusing on population, social structure, and social institutions. Most of the research grants in economics and demography were housed in the first two of these sections, called Age in the Population and Age and Societal Structures.

Organizational structures in bureaucratic organizations such as NIH provide important cues to the extramural research community, and to the organization itself, on how research is to be organized and how its importance is gauged. This particular formal structure affected the development of population research at NIA in fundamental ways. The field of demographic and economic research on aging, because it initially did not have a unit specifically designated for it, was put at a disadvantage both within NIA and in the larger social science research community. This was one of several hurdles that the field needed to overcome.

As a further instance of organizational influence on research, the unit Age and Societal Structures originally operated as two distinct disciplinary components, with grants in economics and sociology assigned to staff members who had different views on research priorities. This made collaboration on scientific initiatives difficult. As a consequence, NIA-sponsored sociological and psychological research on the family and work was separated for many years from demographic and economic analyses, perhaps affecting how the field developed. The lesson here is that while there is sometimes a strong internal logic of discovery in the scientific community that guides the development of a scientific area, almost random variations in the funding environment, including the interpersonal dynamics among program staff, may have a substantial effect on the actual course of development. Where the internal logic of the field is relatively weak, essentially random dynamics within a funding agency presumably become even more influential.

The NIA extramural portfolio in demography and economics has shown tremendous growth. In 1982 the Older People and Society cluster contained some 53 grants totaling $4.6 million, with the largely demographic subunit, Age in the Population, having just 14 grants and $1.2 million in funding. There were about seven or eight demographic grants and three or four economic ones in the portfolio.[5] A research infrastructure for work in the demography of aging and in health and retirement economics was virtually absent: one minuscule training grant, fragmentary databases, and little in the way of a community of researchers. Evidence of this state of affairs was the scant attention the field received at the Population Association of America's annual meeting that year. The Older People and Society cluster was largely dominated by sociologists and social psychologists.

By 1987 the cluster had been renamed Demography and Population Epidemiology and reorganized into something close to the present structure (see Figure 1), with separate sections on demography, health and retirement economics, and population epidemiology. (This last-mentioned anomalous descriptor resulted from the fact that much of psychosocial epi-

FIGURE 2 Growth of funding of population aging research supported by NIA's Behavioral and Social Research program, 1982–2004

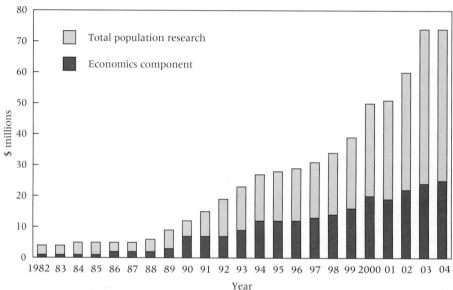

SOURCE: Data for 1982–87 have been estimated from BSR records rather than official records.

demiology was located in another cluster.) The cluster's portfolio (see Figure 2) by then had 45 grants totaling $3.6 million; about half were devoted to demography (22 grants and $1.7 million), with a substantial portion of the remainder focused on economics (7 grants and $1.1 million). By 1989 the population portfolio had risen to $9 million, with the economics and demographic units totaling about $3 million each. By 2004 the grant and contract portfolio of the population branch had grown to about $75 million. Dividing the population portfolio into demographic, economic, and epidemiologic sections had become increasingly difficult as a result of the growth of multidisciplinary and interdisciplinary research.

Databases and statistics for research on aging

The existence of strong reciprocal interactions between the development of sample survey databases and the development of social scientific knowledge is now well recognized. In the early days of the BSR program, the absence of both longitudinal and cross-sectional data severely constrained research on population aging. The field of economics seemed to be especially passive and accepting of major deficiencies in data. Rather than seeking to create new and more appropriate datasets, researchers' efforts went instead into finding ingenious methodological approaches to circumvent obvious data limitations. A major goal of NIA's population program has been to remedy the lack of data by designing, funding, and creating the rationale for a number of large-scale longitudinal surveys (see Table 1). The creation of these publicly available datasets, in turn, has been a major engine driving the program's growth.

In 1979 the main longitudinal social surveys potentially available for use by BSR grantees were the Panel Study of Income Dynamics (PSID), the Social Security Administration's Retirement History Survey (RHS), and the

TABLE 1 Major surveys and databases funded by NIA's Behavioral and Social Research program[a]

Year of initial NIA funding	Name of survey	Year(s) of data collection
None	Retirement History Survey (RHS)[b]	1969–79
1989	National Long Term Care Survey (NLTCS)	1982–
1986	National Health Interview Survey Supplement on Aging (SOA)[c]	1984
1986	Longitudinal Study on Aging (LSOA) based on SOA	1984–90
1989	Panel Study of Income Dynamics (PSID) modules	1968–
1988	Second Malaysian Family Life Survey (MFLS)[d]	1976–89
1991	Early Indicators of Later Work Levels, Disease and Death	1850–1910
1992	Health and Retirement Study (HRS)[e]	1992–
1992	National Survey of Families and Households (NSFH)[f]	1987–2003
1992	Wisconsin Longitudinal Study (WLS)	1957–
1993	Human Mortality Database (HMD)	1750–
1997	Indonesian Family Life Survey (IFLS)[g]	1993–2004
1999	Mexican Health and Aging Study (MHAS)	2001–
1999	Social Environment and Biomarkers of Aging Study (SEBA)	1999–
2000	Puerto Rican Elderly Health Study (PRECO)	2000–
2000	New Immigrant Survey (NIS)[h]	1998–
2001	Longitudinal Employer Household Dynamics (LEHD)[i]	1973–99
2002	MacArthur Midlife Study in the US (MIDUS)[j]	1995–
2002	English Longitudinal Study of Ageing (ELSA)[k]	1998–
2002	Survey of Health, Ageing and Retirement in Europe (SHARE)[l]	2004–
2002	National Longitudinal Mortality Study (NLMS)[m]	1973–98
2003	National Social Life, Health, and Aging Project (NSHAP)	2005
2003	WHO Survey on Global Aging (SAGE)	2005

[a]See BSR Inventory of Publicly Available Databases at «http://www.nia.nih.gov/ResearchInformation/ExtramuralPrograms/BehavioralAndSocialResearch» for descriptions and a more complete listing of over 50 BSR-funded databases. These are also generally available from a BSR-funded center, the National Archive of Computerized Data on Aging (NACDA).
[b]Survey funded by Social Security Administration. NIA provided modest funds to obtain death certificates that were discarded because of Title 13 concerns.
[c]This became the basis for the LSOA.
[d]Co-funded with NICHD.
[e]Co-funded by Social Security Administration.
[f]Co-funded by NICHD.
[g]Co-funded by NICHD.
[h]Funded by NICHD and multiple federal agencies.
[i]Multiple co-funders, including Census.
[j]Multiple co-funders, including Census.
[k]Co-funded by UK government.
[l]Major funding agency: European Union.
[m]Co-funded with multiple agencies.

Bureau of Labor Statistics' National Longitudinal Survey (NLS) on Older Men. Given their sampling designs, neither the RHS nor the PSID was usable for research on the older segment of the elderly population, and the RHS had ended in 1979. At that time none of the surveys collected fully adequate data on income and assets, and datasets generated within NIA were not being routinely archived for use by grantees. No national longitudinal data on the health of the elderly existed, and given the small number of elderly in the PSID, the same was more or less true for economic status. No survey sought to combine both health and economic information. By the mid-1980s the situation had improved only a little. Data from the National Long Term Care Survey (NLTCS),[6] which sampled from the 65+ Medicare files, were available to researchers, but were poorly documented and difficult to use. Additionally, surveys that used sampling based on the decennial census, as did the RHS and the NLS, encountered increasingly stringent Title 13 privacy restrictions.[7] Linked administrative data, such as death records and Social Security earnings, could no longer be used, and in some cases these datasets were actually recalled. It was clear that the lack of high-quality longitudinal (or, in some cases, even cross-sectional) data in the public domain was a major obstacle to the development of the field.

BSR's effort to remedy the inadequate data infrastructure resulted in a large increase in our investment in major surveys and databases (Table 1). By 2003 BSR's investment in surveys and databases relevant to the study of population aging had grown from a single survey in 1982 to 18 surveys and 12 database construction and archiving efforts and an expenditure of more than $20 million. In some cases BSR provided support for continuing surveys started by other agencies or co-funded studies with partners such as the National Institute for Child Health and Human Development (NICHD). In other cases BSR provided the rationale and impetus for the study, with other sources providing the major funding.

The first efforts focused on improving the data on health and functioning. In 1986, BSR began funding three follow-up waves of interviews of those aged 70+ who had previously been interviewed in the National Center for Health Statistics' (NCHS) National Health Interview Survey's 1984 Supplement on Aging. Intended primarily to document transitions in health, this became the heavily used 1984–90 Longitudinal Study on Aging. BSR then funded the third (1989) wave of the NLTCS under the direction of Kenneth Manton.

The state of survey data on the retirement and the economic status of the elderly had shown no improvement in the decade since the RHS ended in 1979—indeed, arguably there had been a deterioration. To rectify this state of affairs, in late 1987 BSR organized an Ad Hoc Panel on the Data Needs for Research in Health and Retirement, chaired by James Smith. In its seminal report the panel identified a pressing need for high-quality, publicly available, longitudinal data that included good measures of both health and economic status. It stressed the value of linked administrative data and soundly rejected the notion, advanced by the Census Bureau and other federal statistical agencies, that analyses could be fruitfully conducted only within the confines of highly regulated enclaves in these agencies. In arguing for the value of combining high-quality health and economic data in the same survey, the report helped sow the seeds of BSR's current multi-disciplinary approach to data collection. Specifically, the report led to the development of the Health and Retirement Study (HRS).

The Health and Retirement Study

The HRS is now the principal statistical resource for investigating retirement issues as well as the co-evolution of health and economic status over the second half of the life course. It has been described as "one of the largest and most ambitious academic social science projects ever undertaken" (Juster and Suzman 1995).

The need for such a study was so evident at the time that some sort of retirement study would likely have started at some agency, such as the Social Security Administration, the Bureau of Labor Statistics, the Health Care Financing Administration, or the Census Bureau. Arguably, however, it would have been less innovative and multidisciplinary than NIA's initiative: the statistical and mission-oriented agencies focus on policy questions and do not always share NIA's level of commitment to more basic social and behavioral science research. What prevented one of those agencies from taking the lead was that many of the social science units within them had been radically downsized during the 1980s—with several surveys, such as the NLTCS, discontinued. These cuts left a space for NIA's entry into large-scale data collection in its areas of interest.

Although initially conceived as a successor to the Retirement History Survey, which had a largely economic focus, the HRS from its inception in 1990 was designed as a broader social science project. It was to include the participation of demographers, epidemiologists, and psychologists as well as economists. Despite that avowed intention, it was still perceived by many as essentially an economic study—perhaps understandably so given the dominance of economists in its early phase. The baseline HRS survey included only limited cognitive and psychosocial measures: the measures then available in those areas were judged to be problematic, and there was no time to undertake needed development work on them. The separation of disciplines within the structure of NIA may have been an additional factor hindering wider participation in the HRS. Despite representation of a broad range of disciplines among the principal investigators and members of steering and monitoring committees, it took about ten years of frequent meetings for some of those disciplinary strands to become interwoven in an area such as intergenerational exchanges within the family.

The first wave of the HRS interviewed persons aged 51–61 and their spouses of any age. Recognizing the paucity of good economic and health data on older individuals, in the next wave a cohort consisting of those aged 70+ was added. This was known as the Asset and Health Dynamics among the Oldest Old (AHEAD) study (Myers, Juster, and Suzman 1997). Given the mandated role of NIA in studying Alzheimer's disease, it was natural that AHEAD should include a dementia sub-study in which elements of cognition would be more intensively assessed. Beyond its intrinsic scientific value, such a sub-study made the HRS more relevant to NIA staff outside of BSR, thus helping safeguard the future of this very expensive enterprise— one that by the end of 2005 will have cost about $112 million and will have resulted in well over 1,000 publications.[8] The HRS has had a major impact on survey research, with many other surveys adopting its innovations. It has also spawned a number of analogs, including the English Longitudinal Study of Ageing (ELSA) and the Survey of Health, Ageing and Retirement in Europe (SHARE), that have led to the creation of a powerful cross-national database (see below).

As a research instrument for the study of aging, the HRS is analogous to a powerful accelerator for particle physics or the Hubble telescope for astronomy. The availability of large amounts of new data and the ability to propose new experimental modules for the HRS (equivalent to Hubble payloads) have influenced career paths of researchers and contributed to interdisciplinary thinking in areas such as cognition and economic behavior.

The Federal Forum

A milestone in the development of a statistical infrastructure for research on aging was the establishment in 1986, following Senate hearings on the state of data on aging, of the Federal Interagency Forum on Aging-Related Statistics. The forum brought together more than 15 federal agencies under the tripartite leadership of the directors of the Bureau of the Census, National Center for Health Statistics, and NIA. Its purpose was to assist in the exchange and coordination among federal agencies of information relevant to the older population. The Senate Appropriations Committee provided NIA with special funding to support the forum, along with parallel funding for offices devoted to aging-related statistics at the Census Bureau and NCHS. Despite their own distinguished records of demographic, statistical, and economic innovation, many of the federal statistical agencies had little contact with the leading extramural researchers on the demography and economics of aging, and the Federal Forum provided an opportunity to introduce these researchers to their counterparts in the agencies.

Within BSR, the forum also gave a stimulus and rationale for the 1991 establishment of an Office of Demography, thereby helping to boost the visibility of population studies within NIA. The Office of Demography (see Figure 1) became the focal point for efforts to fund data collection activities in other agencies. It commissioned a series of publications from the Census Bureau and NCHS. Over time its contacts expanded to include other federal agencies and multilateral organizations such as the World Health Organization (WHO), Organisation for Economic Co-operation and Development (OECD), the UN Economic Commission for Europe's (ECE) Population Activities Unit, and the UN Population Division, all with the aim of collecting, refining, and publishing statistical data on the older population. Among the publications resulting from these collaborations were *65+ in the United States* (US Bureau of the Census 1996), *An Aging World* (Kinsella and Velkoff 2001), and "Trends in the Health of Older Americans, United States, 1994" (Cohen and Van Nostrand 1995). The more recent *Older Americans 2001: Key Indices of Well-Being* and *Older Americans 2004: Key Indicators of Well-Being* were also supported by the forum (Federal Interagency Forum on Aging-Related Statistics 2000, 2004).

A strong principle of NIA's population program has always been that data should be made rapidly available to interested users. The assumption is that it is easier to justify large investments when the use in effect is amortized over a large number of researchers, especially researchers with NIA funding. Unfortunately, since this perspective was not widely shared within epidemiology, extramural researchers had little free access during the 1980s and most of the 1990s to a number of important studies, including the Framingham study and epidemiologic studies of elderly populations. More recently NIH as a whole has encouraged data sharing for all population studies including epidemiology.

The oldest old and the biodemography of aging

The population aged 85 and older is commonly referred to as the oldest old. In the 1980s this was a largely obscure segment of the US population, one on which data collection was fragmentary and data quality, including age reporting, very poor. The segment was also fast-growing—faster, in fact, than had been forecast by the Census Bureau.

Intrigued by this latter observation, Matilda Riley and I organized a session on the 85+ population (there for the first time designated the "oldest old") at the 1984 American Association for the Advancement of Science (AAAS) annual meeting and subsequently edited a special issue of the *Milbank Memorial Fund Quarterly* on the topic (Suzman and Riley 1985). These activities brought the economic and demographic consequences of the growth of the 85+ population to the attention of the media. The *New York*

Times front-page articles on the rapid growth of the 85+ population and its consequences caught the attention of both policymakers and the NIA leadership, giving support to development of an NIA initiative on the Oldest Old. That initiative became the major vehicle for developing and financing the demography of aging at NIA. Two of the articles in the special issue, jointly authored by Kenneth Manton and Beth Soldo (1985; Soldo and Manton 1985), were an important foundation for subsequent research on disability in the older population.[9]

The apparent conservatism of the Census Bureau's projections of mortality decline at older ages raised more general questions about forecasting health and mortality at those ages. These were explored in a BSR-sponsored edited volume (Manton, Singer, and Suzman 1993). A specific issue that became the topic of vigorous debate was whether there was an upper limit on human life expectancy—and, if so, how high it might be. A 1988 Berkeley workshop on this subject concluded that there was then no evidence that life expectancy in the United States was approaching any such maximum; moreover, there was no clear evidence that a maximum human life expectancy even existed. This contrasted sharply with the dominant paradigm at that time, espoused by James Fries (1980) and later by Jay Olshansky (Olshansky, Carnes, and Cassel 1990), that human life expectancy could not exceed a level of about 85 years without a radical alteration in the underlying biology of the aging process. Demographers now seemed to be asserting, as one well-known biologist was heard to remark, that humans could live forever. Not surprisingly, the debate between the proponents of 85 years as the maximum attainable human life expectancy and those who asserted that no limit was in sight captured the interest of the press.

A conversation at the Berkeley workshop between the demographer James Vaupel and the entomologist James Carey gave rise to an innovative demographic experiment to explore the shape of the upper tail of the mortality distribution. The subjects of this experiment were to be fruit flies. The resulting study of age patterns of mortality in a very large medfly population, published in *Science* in 1992 (Carey et al.), was a landmark in the biodemography of aging. It also marked the origin of experimental demography. The seminal finding of this project and of those it spawned was that, rather than increasing exponentially with age, the force of mortality, at least in medfly populations, flattened at older ages. This striking finding led to a series of experiments that demonstrated the essential plasticity of the aging process. It also helped put demography "on the map" at NIA as a dynamic scientific area rather than a policy-oriented descriptive discipline.

Following the thread of biodemography a little further, BSR eventually commissioned the Committee on Population at the National Academy of Sciences, then chaired by Samuel Preston, to conduct a workshop on biodemography. The workshop's 1997 report, entitled *Between Zeus and the Salmon: The Biodemography of Longevity*, edited by Kenneth Wachter and Caleb Finch (National Research Council 1997), helped establish biodemography as a new subfield within demography. The report also helped reinforce the trend in BSR toward the integration of behavioral science with biology. Surprisingly, when the workshop was first proposed to the Committee on Population, the idea met with considerable skepticism. It was felt that the topic offered no near-term scientific opportunity.[10]

Disability transitions and trends

Several chapters in the 1985 *Milbank* special issue and a subsequent edited volume on the oldest old (Suzman, Willis, and Manton 1992) focused on the burden of disability and the transitions from health into various states of disability and, ultimately, death. Characterizing these changes in disability and, in turn, the associated changes into and out of long-term care settings such as nursing homes, had obvious public policy significance and relevance to NIA's agenda. The need to describe these transitions, including the varying degrees of recovery from disability, led both to methodological advances in demography and to development of longitudinal surveys on health and functioning. Notable among the latter were the Longitudinal Study on Aging (one of the first longitudinal studies fielded by NCHS) and the "revived" National Long Term Care Survey.

A major event in the development of the population program at BSR was the discovery by Kenneth Manton of a declining trend in disability among the aged. The dominant view in gerontology and epidemiology during the 1980s and 1990s was that described by Ernest Gruenberg's phrase, "failures of success." Gruenberg (1977) argued that modern medicine could save people from dying, but could not cure or prevent chronic degenerative diseases such as arthritis, cancer, and cardiovascular disease. Renal dialysis was the archetype: more and more patients would survive renal failure but remain dependent on dialysis machines, with a consequent poor quality of life. Visions of a mounting pandemic of chronic disease and associated disability dominated the literature on the health consequences of population aging. Not until the 1995 edition of *The Oldest Old* (Suzman, Willis, and Manton 1995) was there even a mention of a more optimistic perspective— that medicine and other forces might not inevitably extend years of disabled rather than healthy life.

Manton's analysis of the 1989 wave of the NLTCS showed that the prevalence rate of disability seemed to be declining, at least since 1982 (Manton, Stallard, and Corder 1995). The publication of his results in the *Journal of Gerontology* elicited widespread disbelief. The findings were described as a "flash in the pan," probably due to bad data or errors in analysis of the complicated NLTCS dataset. An even stronger reaction greeted the results of the 1994 wave, which indicated that the decline had accelerated between 1989 and 1994. To be sure of the results, BSR commissioned a number of researchers to examine the findings and analyses and to replicate some of Manton's findings. (Some support for the finding even came from historical demography: when Robert Fogel and Dora Costa (1997) compared the health of Union Army Civil War pensioners with the health of later cohorts, they found substantial evidence that the prevalence of chronic diseases measured in their study had declined, potentially extending the disability decline as far back as the late nineteenth century.) A 1996 front-page article by Gina Kolata in *The New York Times* brought the declining trend in disability to the attention of NIH's leaders and Congress. To some of those arguing for a much higher NIH budget, the trend was taken to represent the positive impact of NIH's research on health and disability. Those advocates tended to ignore cohort effects— for example, improvements in the education and general health of successive birth cohorts, both of them powerful factors in accounting for the lessening of disability. Rather they focused on the positive impact of modern medicine.

Many research questions about the disability decline remain open. Still to be determined is whether similar declines are occurring in other countries. Within the United States, a major unanswered question is whether the declining trend will continue, or halt as cohort improvements in education and health level off, or worsen because of factors such as obesity. Also needing investigation is the issue of how to calculate the economic impact of changes in disability.

Economics of aging

So far I have focused largely on the demography side of the BSR program rather than on the areas of health and retirement economics, in part because for a long time the two sides had developed as separate research communities. Although economics had been included in the original BSR blueprint, many in BSR—and more widely in NIA and NIH—were cautious about funding economic research, despite the mathematical rigor of the discipline. A primary concern seemed to stem from the fear that economics was prescriptive, more policy oriented than scientific. By comparison, sociology was seen as more legitimate.

NIA's altered stance on the economics of aging followed a request from the National Bureau of Economic Research (NBER) to support research in this area.[11] An NBER proposal to NIA to fund such a program was successful. The program, directed by David Wise, brought a number of talented labor and health economists into the field and has continued to entice top graduate students and young faculty to make careers in the economics of aging. Significant numbers of the investigators and fellows supported by the NBER's training grant have subsequently served in high positions in the US Treasury Department and the White House and in other federal agencies. Two of the three BSR grantees who have won Nobel prizes in economics (Robert Fogel and Daniel McFadden) were part of the initial NBER program proposal.

Researchers on BSR-supported NBER projects have transformed our understanding of the role of public and private pensions in retirement, the process of saving for retirement, the value of new medical technology, and the value of comparative international research (notwithstanding NBER's initial reluctance to include an international dimension in the program). In this last area, work by Jonathan Gruber and David Wise (1998) showing the very strong effects of the provision of public pensions on the labor force participation of older workers has been a factor in the decisions of several European countries to seek to increase their retirement ages.

Comparative international research

In the early years of BSR, international research was limited and fragmentary in scope, in part because the NIH mandate for international research focused on its domestic value rather than its global significance. Studies such as RAND's Malaysian Family Life Survey (MFLS), jointly funded by NIA and NICHD, attracted questions by Congress about the relevance of the research to aging in the United States. Such reservations applied especially to studies in low-income countries, since the issue of health disparities had not yet become prominent. BSR did not highlight the results of the MFLS (or the later Indonesian Family Life Survey), and it generally kept a low profile in the international arena. Nonetheless, it gradually built a portfolio of international population studies and developed working relationships with networks such as REVES (an international network devoted to exchanges on active life expectancy) and agencies such as the International Division of the US Census Bureau, WHO, the Economic Commission for Europe, and OECD. The Census Bureau's 1987 publication *An Aging World* (Torrey, Kinsella, and Taueber) received significant press publicity both in the United States and internationally.

The global AIDS epidemic was a major factor leading NIH to adopt a more comprehensive and global perspective on international health. Harold Varmus, who became the NIH director in 1993, took an active role in international health in areas such as malaria vaccine development and in strengthening the economic rationale for improving health. The international collaboration on the sequencing of the human genome probably added to the respectability of international collaborative research.

An NBER international project led by David Wise and Jonathan Gruber yielded what many consider to be a seminal paper in comparative social and economic research on aging (Gruber and Wise 1998; originally published as an NBER Working Paper in 1997). In a cross-national study of 11 industrialized countries, the authors found a remarkably powerful relationship between the way that public pensions reward or penalize work at older ages and the fraction of older people who remain in the labor force. The study has had a significant impact on the thinking of numerous European countries. It was probably a stimulus for the development of ELSA and SHARE as well as in the creation of an energetic trans-Atlantic research community on population aging.

The findings from the NBER project on Social Security Programs and Retirement Around the World, were important influences on the discussion of aging at the Denver G-7/8 Summit in June 1997. BSR had been invited to organize a pre-Summit working group to develop a statement on aging, along with talking points and draft Communiqué language. The Denver Summit Communiqué included a strong statement entitled "The Opportunities and Challenges of Aging Populations" that acknowledged the declines in disability and the pressures on retirement systems in some countries. The statement ended with a call to identify comparable cross-national data. Following the Denver Summit, BSR commissioned the National Academy of Sciences to develop an agenda for cross-national research on population aging, resulting in the NAS report entitled *Preparing for an Aging World: The Case for Cross-National Research* (National Research Council 2001).

Although an envisaged international White Paper on the topic drawing on the combined efforts of a number of national academies was never produced, interactions fostered by these activities continued. Most recently, NIA has contracted with WHO to field the Survey on Global Aging (SAGE) as part of the World Health Survey (WHS). SHARE and the HRS have influenced the development of SAGE, while the WHS anchoring vignettes,[12] developed to calibrate responses across national and other groups, have been imported into SHARE (see Salomon, Tandon, and Murray 2004).

Administration of population aging research

Expertise in aging research in the United States in the 1970s and 1980s was scattered across many campuses, but in nearly every place lacking a critical mass. In some, such as Duke University and the University of Southern California, there were formal connections with gerontology. But in most, the field was heavily balkanized, with researchers generally unaware of relevant research in allied disciplines. Even in the 1990s, demography, economics, and epidemiology were relatively isolated from each other—much more so than they are today. Thus despite the significant parallels between them, the demography and epidemiology communities rarely interacted; researchers in demography and in retirement economics were largely unfamiliar with each other's work. Similarly, interaction between long-time researchers on the economics of aging and new entrants to the field was limited. Training grants in demography and economics reflected these fragmented conditions, and the training that students received was consequently narrow.

The long-established population program at NIH, located within NICHD's Demographic and Behavioral Science Branch, had for years provided much of the central infrastructure for demographic research at US universities and research institutes.[13] NIA was able to add components to NICHD training grants in demography and also to NICHD-funded population centers. Many of the training and center programs that received those NIA administrative supplements later competed successfully for their own NIA training and center grants. Indeed, nearly half of the current NIA demography centers received their initial funding through this administrative supplement program.

It took until 1994 for BSR to obtain Congressional support and NIA funding to establish a modest stand-alone center program in the demography and economics of aging. Given that expertise in population aging was scarce at most interested institutions (and their level of interest in the subject fairly modest), we opted for a program of small exploratory centers rather than a few larger ones. In 1995 we funded nine exploratory centers, most of which were a small fraction of the size of NICHD's. This reflected the fragmentary nature of the population aging research community and the fact that no institution then seemed to be strong in both the economics and the demography of aging. To compensate for the lack of a critical mass at any single center, we strongly encouraged collaboration among centers, with Michigan, led by Albert Hermalin, as the coordinator.[14] We avoided investing in large computing cores, which was the NICHD model, preferring to provide needed computational resources through research grants. Rather, we strongly emphasized pilot cores that provided seed funding for innovative ideas and special funds for projects involving multi-center collaboration.

In 1999–2000 the exploratory center program, having been deemed a success, was replaced by regular core centers. Eleven centers were funded; seven of the initial nine successfully recompeted, and four new ones were added. Pilot cores to support innovation continued to be emphasized. Collaboration among the centers was encouraged and rewarded. On the basis of our experience with biodemography and the Health and Retirement Study, we now had a strong hunch that a new era of large-team social science was dawning. This new way of structuring research required the collaboration of multiple institutions and disciplines around a strong infrastructure.[15] In the 2004 competition, the number of centers was increased to 13, including four new centers. The demography centers along with the databases, training grants, program projects, MERIT awards, Academic Leadership career awards, and the RAND Summer Institute constitute the essential infrastructure of the new field.[16]

BSR's own funding, and more generally that of NIA, depend on a variety of factors and considerations that influence decisionmaking at NIH. These include scientific opportunities, public health priorities such as those based on measures of the burden of disease (Varmus 1999), and pressures from Congress and the general public. Especially for the social sciences, areas regarded as particularly deserving of attention are those where there is a clear scientific debate with evident significance for social and economic policy (such as the timing of when the Social Security program will enter into deficit). Those areas have an advantage in the competition within NIH to obtain special "set-aside" funding for developing new areas. For example, following publicity about the declining trend in old-age disability, set-aside funds were allocated to the Oldest Old initiative. This funding led to growth in the demography portfolio of BSR and indirectly to expanded interest by demographers in the demography of aging.

NIH is something of a "momentum investor" in that it is often easiest to get priority funding for areas showing rapid progress. One indicator of progress is a cluster or series of articles on the same topic appearing in high-impact journals. A factor perhaps not fully appreciated is that the sometimes glacial publication process in the social sciences, especially in economics, is one of the barriers at NIH to getting a more equal footing with the life sciences. Articles published in the top general science and medical journals, including *Science, Nature, Journal of the American Medical Association,* and *New England Journal of Medicine,* generally count for far more at NIH than those published in top disciplinary journals in the social sciences, especially if publication is accompanied by press attention to the article in a major newspaper. The biomedical world seems to have trouble evaluating social science publications. With reference to the disability decline, a senior NIH official asked why—if the finding was so important—the report had been published in a gerontology journal rather than in a major science or medical journal. Arguably, what is needed is a social and behavioral science equivalent of *Nature Medicine* or *Nature Genetics,* in which brief, high-profile articles could be rapidly published.

Fostering multidisciplinary and interdisciplinary aging research

Over the years BSR had accumulated an astonishing number—more than 50—of "priorities." In a radical simplification, these were reduced to the present seven broad areas of emphasis, designed to cut across the program's two branches and offset the tendency for units to become insulated "silos" or "stove pipes." They are complemented with a set of five principles (or perhaps more accurately, descriptors), some of which had been guiding BSR since its inception (see Table 2). The seven areas cover what are currently seen as the major issues in population aging, such as understanding the determinants of retirement, the large differences in health between those with high and low education, how aging-related cognitive impairment (including Alzheimer's) affects individual decisions about finances—or even how impairment affects answers to survey questions—and how to measure the value of good health and well-being. In each of the areas, it seems apparent that progress will require the efforts of multiple disciplines.

The dynamics of the interplay among the disciplines central to BSR have been complex. The program has encouraged multidisciplinary research from its earliest days, though perhaps with variable success. From the standpoint of demography, the main tasks have been to bring in expertise in economics, biology, and psychology.

The Population Association of America had always included economists working on population issues, but most of the economists working on pensions, retirement, and health had few or no connections to those researchers or to any demographers. Both the RAND Summer Institute and the NIA-funded demography centers have helped bridge these gaps. Participation in the HRS and its subcommittees (and in the surveys spawned by the HRS, such as ELSA and SHARE) was probably a more important avenue for collaboration and integration, though it has often seemed as if groups were on the verge of disciplinary warfare as they competed for scarce interview time on the survey.

TABLE 2 Priorities and principles of the NIA's Behavioral and Social Research program

Areas of emphasis
—Health disparities
—Aging minds
—Increasing health expectancy
—Health, work, and retirement
—Interventions and behavior change
—Genetics, behavior, and the social environment
—Burden of illness and efficiency of health systems

Cross-cutting principles
—Aging from birth to death—a life course perspective
—Biobehavioral linkages and collaboration with other NIA programs
—Integration and synthesis—multilevel interactions among psychological, physiological, social, and cultural levels
—Development of improved methodologies and measurement
—Translation and application of findings

In the forefront of integrating biology with the demography of aging were the teams led by Kenneth Manton and James Vaupel (e.g., Vaupel et al. 1988). Members of Vaupel's team, including Kaare Christensen who worked with the Danish Twins study, were among the first to work at the intersection of demography and genetics. The link with genetics was also forged with the publication of the two NAS volumes, *Between Zeus and the Salmon* and *Cells and Surveys*. Important too has been collaboration with other NIA programs in biology, neuroscience, and clinical geriatrics. The sequencing of the human genome has potentially large implications for aging research. Interest in those developments in the demography-of-aging community has been keen. Several studies, including ELSA, have collected physiological data and bio-specimens, including DNA. Surprisingly, many of the psychologists that BSR traditionally supported felt threatened by the emphasis on the interface with physiology—fearing that the purely psychological level of analysis was being abandoned.

Integration of psychology into population research on aging has taken longer than in the cases of physiology and genetics. The reasons for this include both BSR's formal organizational structure and the dynamics within the field. The design and analysis of the cognitive components in the HRS have proven to be an important avenue for interactions with psychologists, at both the cognitive and psychosocial levels. Bringing consideration of psychological factors—attitudes, emotions, values, beliefs, ways of thinking and deciding—into research on aging has proven more difficult than adding cognitive measures to the HRS, and progress is just beginning. The growth in the influence of behavioral economics has made the task somewhat easier. A long-range goal is the development of better measures of individual self-rated well-being.

In many respects BSR's encouragement of interdisciplinary research foreshadowed a key component of the NIH Road Map initiative that was instituted by Elias Zerhouni when he became NIH director in 2002. Quite early in my tenure as associate director we funded four highly interdisciplinary and multidisciplinary program projects at Chicago (John Cacioppo), Wisconsin (Robert Hauser and Carol Ryff), and Berkeley-Davis-Stanford (James Carey), which are forging new areas of interaction among the social and behavioral sciences. Other BSR activities have aimed to spur the development of behavioral genetics, which at some distant time may be ready for integration into the population sciences, and supported an initial effort (by David Laibson at the NBER demography center) seeking to integrate genetics with economics. The program project on loneliness directed by John Cacioppo runs the gamut from pheromones to an analysis of HRS data. The program projects centered around the Wisconsin Longitudinal Study (WLS) and the MacArthur Midlife Study in the US (MIDUS) include projects ranging from sociology to physiological psychology and now potentially genetics, and aim at achieving significant integration across the physiological, psychological, and social levels. The most recent advance in the creation of hybrid disciplines is the development of a new field of neuroeconomics (McClure et al. 2004).

Gauging progress

Over 30 years ago, Karl Deutsch et al. (1971) explored the conditions favoring major advances in the social sciences, including the achievements of teams versus individuals, geographical clustering, the roles of funding and infrastructure, whether or not quantification was involved, and delays in impact. In the course of their study, they developed a list of 62 advances occurring from 1900 to 1965 that they ranked as the most important. While several of the "advances" that made their list would be unlikely to be included in anyone's list today, their approach did pick several economists who were subsequently Nobel prizewinners. But the point to be made here is the difficulty of deciding what is a major advance or discovery in the social and behavioral sciences. Several of the advances reported at the RAND Tenth Anniversary Summer Institute would seem to be plausible candidates for the top 200 of the last century. Making any such a list does, however, raise a vexing issue that has long troubled BSR. While the life sciences and physical sciences are hardly free from controversy in this respect, the social and behavioral sciences seem to have less agreement on the canons of excellence or even on what constitutes a major discovery. It is as if there are many local markets for research findings without any widely agreed upon standards for judging.

Throughout BSR's history there have been disciplinary disagreements among staff and advisers over just this issue. Does one measure advances and their importance by citation counts, awards, election to the Institute of Medicine and NAS, press coverage, implementation, or what? The answer is critical both for funding and for development strategies. As a step forward, we commissioned the NAS to establish a panel to determine how best to measure progress in the social and behavioral sciences, and have also asked the Social Science Research Council to consider the issue from the perspective of the history of science. Each of the proposed measures encounters significant methodological problems. One approach, however, seems to hold significant promise: the construction of stories of discovery that trace the evolution of topics such as the decline in disability or the determinants of retirement in reference to grantee research findings and staff activities. These stories are potentially an excellent way to assess both the significance of a problem and the power of the solution. However, to avoid programmatic self-aggrandizement they should ideally be constructed by independent historians of social science.

It is probably too early in BSR's history to evaluate how a funding agency can increase the rate of progress and innovation in social and behavioral science. To do so would require disentangling the separate but interconnected roles of increases in funding, recruitment of first-rate researchers, new ideas, infrastructure, the peer review system, funding agency staff actions, and the tractability of the problem to empirical solutions.

Prospects

In preparation for the 2004 quadrennial review by NIA's National Advisory Council, BSR laid out a plan for the near to mid-term future. The plan proposed to continue several long-standing initiatives in areas such as cognitive aging, interventions to improve cognitive functioning, behavioral genetics, psychological development, and understanding health disparities. In the population area the plan continued the focus on retirement, including developing international analogs of the HRS for comparative analyses and pursuing more integrative models of the determinants of retirement. BSR's plan also called for going beyond tracking and understanding the trend of declining mortality and disability, toward finding ways to maintain and accelerate the disability decline through multi-level interventions at the community or population level. The emphasis on moving from observation to intervention, together with developing new approaches to improve behavioral interventions, is a new track, especially for the demography of aging, which has traditionally focused on observation and analysis.

Other proposed new directions in the BSR plan included:

—The cognitive aspects of economic and health decisionmaking and the emerging field of neuroeconomics. These would further consolidate the integration of economics, psychology, and neurosciences within NIA.

—Development of methodology and data for experimental National Health Accounts and National Well-being Accounts that could be used to chart the impact of interventions and systems on the older population.[17]

—Expansion of macroeconomic–demographic approaches to population aging beyond Ronald Lee's work on intergenerational exchanges and the projection of the Social Security Trust Fund's solvency. Specifically, there is a need to consider the impact of population aging more generally on Medicare and the health system, public and private pensions, the labor force, competitiveness among firms and even countries, and on immigration demand.

—A follow-on panel to the 1987 panel on data needs in health and retirement economics, recognizing this enormous growth in NIA's investment in data and the many changes in this field's long-term data needs in the intervening years.

The report to the National Advisory Council on Aging (one of the periodic reviews of NIA programs) by a committee chaired by Ronald Lee endorsed in large measure the directions proposed by BSR. It also recommended additional attention to formal demography, new analytic methods, and areas in behavioral genetics. The report remarked that an interdisciplinary focus was a defining feature of BSR.

In the early days of BSR the divisions within NIA between BSR and the biomedical and biological research programs were sharply defined. This has changed significantly and BSR has become far more central and more integrated with the other programs. Several evolving forces should continue fostering this trend toward closer integration. These include an increasing focus in the social and behavioral sciences on the physiological pathways that connect the social and physical environments with health and functional outcomes: the emerging field of social and behavioral neuroscience. But the life sciences are not static: there is a radical transformation underway in medicine and biology resulting in part from the sequencing of the human genome and its sequelae, such as the nearly completed haplotype map (Collins 2004). Just how these trends will play out in relation to social and behavioral science remains in the far-off realm of speculation.

We do not yet know how many genes operate to regulate the speed of individual aging or survival, or the force with which they operate. We have just begun to understand how complex the interplay can be between genes and the social and physical environments (Harris, in press). It is not impossible that the genomic revolution will become a major force leading to a thorough transformation of social and behavioral science as some of the more basic underlying features of human biology and the human mind are described. Certainly, as argued by Kenneth Wachter in *Between Zeus and the Salmon* (National Research Council 1997), having the genetic knowledge that enables social scientists to control for what hitherto has been considered unobserved heterogeneity should permit a more accurate picture of the social forces in play. It is also unclear how the social sciences will change over the next decades. Will disciplines lose some of their individual distinctiveness and perhaps be replaced by a broader quantitative social science with shared methods and blurred disciplinary boundaries?

It would be hubris to suggest that we are on the verge of a more unified social and behavioral science that rests on physiological, neuroscientific, and genetic bases, but several of the needed building blocks and methodologies are becoming more readily available. This is not a prediction of molecular reductionism in which macroeconomic–demographic analyses are replaced by more molecular approaches (since each level from micro to macro explains phenomena that cannot be explained at more molecular levels), but rather of increasing integration across some levels. As these developments play out, the NIA demography centers, working in concert with the RAND Summer Institute and program projects, are well-positioned to be at the research frontier.

Appendix

National Academy of Sciences reports commissioned by NIA's Behavioral and Social Research program[a]

Forecasting Survival, Health and Disability. 1993. Michael J. Stoto and Jane S. Durch, editors. Committee on National Statistics.

Trends in Disability at Older Ages. 1994. Vicki A. Freedman and Beth J. Soldo, editors. Committee on National Statistics.

Demography of Aging. 1994. Linda G. Martin and Samuel H. Preston, editors. Committee on Population.

Improving Data on America's Aging Population: Summary of a Workshop. 1996. Deborah Carr, Anu Pammarazu, and Dorothy P. Rice, editors. Workshop on Priorities for Data on the Aging Population, Committee on National Statistics.

Assessing Knowledge of Retirement Behavior. 1996. Eric A. Hanushek and Nancy L. Maritato, editors. Panel on Retirement Income Modeling, Committee on National Statistics.

Racial and Ethnic Differences in the Health of Older Americans. 1997. Linda G. Martin and Beth J. Soldo, editors. Committee on Population.

Between Zeus and the Salmon: The Biodemography of Longevity. 1997. Kenneth W. Wachter and Caleb E. Finch, editors. Committee on Population.

Assessing Policies for Retirement Income: Needs for Data, Research and Models. 1997. Constance E. Citro and Eric A. Hanushek, editors. Panel on Retirement Income Modeling, Committee on National Statistics.

Improving Access to and Confidentiality of Research Data: Report of a Workshop. 2000. Christopher Mackie and Norman Bradburn, editors. Workshop on Confidentiality of and Access to Research Data, Committee on National Statistics.

The Aging Mind: Opportunities in Cognitive Research. 2002. Paul C. Stern and Laura L. Carstensen, editors. Committee on Future Directions for Cognitive Research on Aging, Board on Behavioral, Cognitive, and Sensory Sciences.

Preparing for an Aging World: The Case for Cross-National Research. 2001. Panel on a Research Agenda and New Data for an Aging World, Committee on Population and Committee on National Statistics.

New Horizons in Health: An Integrative Approach. 2001. Burton H. Singer and Carol D. Ryff, editors. Committee on Future Directions for Behavioral and Social Sciences Research at the National Institutes of Health, Board on Behavioral, Cognitive, and Sensory Sciences.[b]

Cells and Surveys: Should Biological Measures Be Included in Social Science Research? 2000. Caleb E. Finch, James W. Vaupel, and Kevin Kinsella, editors. Workshop on Collecting Biological Indicators and Genetic Information in Household Surveys, Committee on Population.

Elder Mistreatment: Abuse, Neglect and Exploitation in an Aging America. 2003. Richard J. Bonnie and Robert B. Wallace, editors. Panel to Review Risk and Prevalence of Elder Abuse and Neglect, Committee on National Statistics.

Technology for Adaptive Aging. 2003. Richard W. Pew and Susan B. Van Hemel, editors. Steering Committee for the Workshop on Technology for Adaptive Aging, Board on Behavioral, Cognitive, and Sensory Sciences.

---

[a]All reports were issued by the Division of Behavioral and Social Sciences and Education.
[b] Funded by the NIH Office of Behavioral and Social Science Research, but many of the panel members were BSR grantees.

Health and Safety Needs of Older Workers. 2004. David H. Wegman and James P. McGee, editors. Committee on the Health and Safety Needs of Older Workers, Board on Behavioral, Cognitive, and Sensory Sciences.

Critical Perspectives on Racial and Ethnic Differences in Health in Late Life. 2004. Norman B. Anderson, Rodolfo A. Bulatao, and Barney Cohen, editors. Panel on Race, Ethnicity, and Health in Later Life, Committee on Population.

Understanding Racial and Ethnic Differences in Health in Late Life: A Research Agenda. 2004. Rodolfo A. Bulatao and Norman B. Anderson, editors. Panel on Race, Ethnicity, and Health in Later Life, Committee on Population.

Notes

All views expressed in this chapter are my own and do not necessarily reflect those of NIA or NIH. Angie Chon-Lee, Elayne Heisler, Linda Ingram, and Lyn Neil assisted in the preparation of the chapter.

1 Originally called the Social and Behavioral Research Program, it was renamed in the early 1980s at a time when the Washington, DC environment had turned hostile to social science. Over the intervening years the other original extramural program was subdivided into the three present-day extramural programs covering roughly geriatric medicine, biology of aging, and neuroscience and neuropsychology with a strong emphasis on Alzheimer's disease. This chapter discusses only extramural research and does not discuss the intramural Laboratory of Epidemiology, Demography and Biometry since it has focused largely on epidemiology, and dropped economics nearly 15 years ago.

2 Among the 60 contributors to the panel, and commentators, I recognized only two economists, James Schulz and Juanita Kreps, and one demographer, Philip Hauser (uncle of Robert Hauser). The report included sections on life expectancy, population forecasting, assessing economic status, work and retirement, and the impact of aging on the economy. Robert Butler, NIA's first director, told me that he had also consulted Arthur Okun, a former chairman of the Council of Economic Advisers.

3 Between 1980 and 1981 I had been seconded from the University of California Medical School in San Francisco to help develop BSR's program in behavioral medicine.

4 At that time these units were not considered large enough to be described as formal branches, a status that brought additional prestige and staffing benefits. They became branches, at least informally, around 1999.

5 Among grantees, demographers included Kenneth Manton, Eileen Crimmins, Ira Rosenwaike, Charles Longino, and Fred Pampel; economists, Paul Taubman, Marc Nerlove, and Gary Fields.

6 The NLTCS was initially located in the Health, Education, and Welfare Department; a follow-up survey was funded by the Health Care Financing Agency (which administered Medicare). Its continuation was vetoed by the Office of Management and Budget.

7 Title 13 is the US law that established the decennial census.

8 With over 900 articles, books, chapters, monographs, and reports the HRS's rate of publication has been very high compared with other surveys.

9 The special *Milbank Quarterly* issue also included articles on economics (Barbara Torrey), clinical perspectives (Kenneth Minaker and John Rowe), and demography (Ira Rosenwaike).

10 More than a decade of BSR collaboration with the National Academy of Sciences has yielded numerous commissioned reports from this and other National Research Council committees and panels. A listing of these is given in the Appendix.

11 The director of NIA was approached by NBER economists Martin Feldstein and David Wise. Feldstein had been chairman of the Council of Economic Advisers in the Reagan administration.

12 "Anchoring vignettes" are standardized concrete descriptions that are rated by respon-

dents along the dimensions of interest. Country-level differences in how the same vignette is rated can then be used to calibrate self-rated health and mobility levels in cross-national contexts.

13 In 1975 the Adult Development and Aging Branch at NICHD had been transferred to NIA, and several of BSR's earliest grants had received initial funding from NICHD. It is interesting to speculate how this division affected birth-to-death life course studies.

14 The RAND Summer Institute and the RAND Mini-Med School provided informal forums for interaction and collaboration among researchers on aging across disciplines and centers.

15 The productivity of the centers is impressive by any standard. For example, between 1999 and 2003 the combined 11 centers funded 220 pilot projects (60 of which have already led to funded projects), sponsored 60 workshops and mini-conferences, and funded or co-funded over 1,200 peer-reviewed articles. The centers also play a critical role in recruiting junior and senior researchers to the field.

16 Program projects are composed of multiple thematically related research projects clustered around a set of common cores. They have included the ones directed by David Wise at NBER, James Vaupel at Minnesota and Duke, Robert Fogel at NBER and Chicago, Christopher Murray at Harvard and WHO, and Michael Hurd at RAND. MERIT awards are special grants that can be awarded for up to ten years to exceptional researchers who are leaders in the field. NIA's MERIT awardees in demography and economics have included Albert Hermalin, Ronald Lee, Lee Lillard, Kenneth Manton, Michael Marmot, Samuel Preston, James Smith, James Vaupel, David Wise, and Max Woodbury. Academic Leadership awards are for organizing research at an institution; recipients have included David Blau, Richard Burkhauser, Paul Gertler, Kenneth Land, Kenneth Wachter, Linda Waite, and David Wise.

17 BSR has separately commissioned David Cutler at NBER and the NAS to begin the development of National Health Accounts, and work by Daniel Kahneman, Alan Kruger, and a large team has already made some progress on improving the measurement of well-being (Kahneman et al. 2004).

References

Carey, J. R., P. Liedo, D. Orozco, and J. W. Vaupel. 1992. "Slowing of mortality rates at older ages in large medfly cohorts," *Science* 258 (October 16): 457–461.

Cohen, R. A. and J. F. Van Nostrand. 1995. "Trends in the Health of Older Americans: United States, 1994." National Center for Health Statistics. *Vital Health Statistics* 3(30).

Collins, F. S. 2004 "The case for a US prospective cohort study of genes and environment," *Nature.* 429: 475–477.

Deutsch, K. W., J. Platt, and D. Senghaas. 1971. "Conditions favoring major advances in social science," *Science* 171: 450–459.

Federal Interagency Forum on Aging-Related Statistics. 2004. *Older Americans 2004: Key Indicators of Well-Being.* Federal Interagency Forum on Aging-Related Statistics. Washington, DC: USGPO.

———. 2000. *Older Americans 2000: Key Indicators of Well-Being.* Federal Interagency Forum on Aging-Related Statistics. Washington, DC: USGPO.

Fogel, R. W. and D. L. Costa. 1997. "A theory of technophysio evolution, with some implications for forecasting population, health care costs, and pension costs," *Demography* 34(1): 49–66.

Fries, J. F. 1980. "Aging, natural death, and the compression of morbidity," *New England Journal of Medicine* 303(3): 130–135.

Gruber, J. and D. Wise. 1998. "Social security and retirement: An international comparison," *American Economic Review* 88(2): 158–163.

Gruenberg, E. 1977. "The failures of success," *Milbank Memorial Fund Quarterly/Health and Society* (55): 3–24.

Harris, J. R. 2005, in press. "Introduction to special issue on gene by environment interactions in aging," *Journal of Gerontology: Social Sciences* (60B).

Juster, T. F. and R. Suzman. 1995. "An overview of the Health and Retirement Study," *Journal of Human Resources* 30 (5): S7–S56.

Kahneman, D., A. B. Krueger, D. A. Schkade, N. Schwarz, and A. A. Stone. 2004 "A survey method for characterizing daily life experience: The day reconstruction method" *Science* 306: 1776–1780

Kinsella, K. and V. A. Velkoff. 2001. US Census Bureau, Series P95/01-1, *An Aging World: 2001.* Washington, DC: USGPO.

Manton, K. G. and B. J. Soldo. 1985. "Dynamics of health changes in the oldest old: New perspectives and evidence," *Milbank Memorial Fund Quarterly* 63(2): 206–285.

Manton, K. G., E. Stallard, and L. Corder. 1995. "Changes in morbidity and chronic disability in the US elderly population: Evidence from the 1982, 1984, and 1989 National Long Term Care Surveys," *Journal of Gerontology B. Psychology Sciences and Social Sciences* 50(4): S194–S204.

Manton, K. G., B. Singer, and R. Suzman. 1993. "The scientific and policy needs for improved health forecasting models for elderly populations," in K. G. Manton, B. Singer, and R. Suzman (eds.), *Forecasting the Health of Elderly Populations.* New York: Springer Verlag, pp. 3–35.

McClure, S. M., D. I. Laibson, G. Loewenstein, and J. D. Cohen. 2004. "Separate neural systems value immediate and delayed monetary rewards," *Science* 306: 503–507.

Minaker, K. L. and J. Rowe. 1985. "Health and disease among the oldest old: A clinical perspective," *Milbank Memorial Fund Quarterly* 63(2): 324–349.

Myers, G. C., F. T. Juster, and R. Suzman. 1997. "Asset and health dynamics among the oldest old (AHEAD): Initial results from the longitudinal study." Introduction, *Journal of Gerontology B. Psychology Sciences and Social Sciences* 52 (May): v–viii.

National Institute on Aging. 1978. *Our Future Selves.* Bethesda, MD: USGPO.

National Research Council. 1997. *Between Zeus and the Salmon: The Biodemography of Longevity.* Kenneth W. Wachter and Caleb E. Finch (eds.). Committee on Population, Commission on Behavioral and Social Sciences and Education. Washington, DC: National Academy Press.

———. 2001. *Preparing for an Aging World: The Case for Cross-National Research.* Panel on a Research Agenda and New Data for an Aging World. Committee on Population and Committee on National Statistics. Division of Behavioral and Social Sciences and Education. Washington, DC: National Academy Press.

Olshansky, S. J., B. A. Carnes, and C. Cassel. 1990. "In search of Methuselah: Estimating the upper limits to human longevity," *Science* 250 (4981): 634–640.

Rosenwaike, I. 1985. "A demographic portrait of the oldest old," *Milbank Memorial Fund Quarterly* 63(2): 187–205.

Salomon, M. J., A. Tandon, and C. J. L. Murray. 2004. "Comparability of self-rated health: Cross-sectional multi-country survey using anchoring vignettes," *British Medical Journal*, doi:10.1136/bmj.37963.691632.44.

Soldo, B. J. and K. G. Manton. 1985. "Health status and service needs of the oldest old: Current patterns and future trend," *Milbank Memorial Fund Quarterly* 63(2): 286–319.

Suzman, R. and M. W. Riley. 1985. "Introducing the "oldest old," *Milbank Memorial Fund Quarterly* 63(2): 177–186.

Suzman, R., D. P. Willis, and K. G. Manton (eds.). 1992. *The Oldest Old.* New York: Oxford University Press.

———. 1995. *The Oldest Old.* New York: Oxford University Press.

Torrey, B. B. 1985. "Sharing increasing costs on declining income: The invisible dilemma of the invisible aged," *Milbank Memorial Fund Quarterly* 63(2): 377–394.

Torrey, B. B., K. Kinsella, and C. M. Taueber. 1987. US Census Bureau, International Population Reports, Series P-95, No. 78. *An Aging World*. Washington, DC: USGPO.

US Bureau of the Census. 1996. Current Population Reports, Special Studies, P23-190, *65+ in the United States*. Washington, DC: USGPO.

Varmus, H. 1999. "Evaluating the burden of disease and spending the research dollars of the National Institutes of Health," *New England Journal of Medicine* 340(24): 1914–1915.

Vaupel, J. W., J. R. Carey, K. Christesen, T. Johnson, A. I. Yashin, N. V. Holm, I. A. Iachiane, V. Kannisto, A. A. Khazaeli, P. Liedo, V. D. Longo, Y. Zeng, K. Manton, K. and J. W. Curtsinger. 1998. "Biodemographic trajectories of longevity," *Science* 280: 855–860.

EILEEN M. CRIMMINS is Edna M. Jones Professor of Gerontology, University of Southern California.

DOUGLAS EWBANK is Research Professor, Population Studies Center, University of Pennsylvania.

ROBERT WILLIAM FOGEL is Charles R. Walgreen Distinguished Service Professor of American Institutions, and Director, Center for Population Economics, Graduate School of Business, University of Chicago.

ROBERT M. HAUSER is Vilas Research Professor of Sociology, and Director, Center for Demography of Health and Aging, University of Wisconsin-Madison.

RONALD LEE is Professor of Demography and Economics, Jordan Family Chair in Economics, University of California at Berkeley.

MICHAEL MARMOT is Medical Research Foundation Professor of Epidemiology, Department of Epidemiology and Public Health, University College London.

TERESA E. SEEMAN is Professor of Medicine, Division of Geriatrics, Geffen School of Medicine, University of California, Los Angeles.

JAMES P. SMITH holds the RAND Chair in Labor Market and Demographic Studies.

ANDREW STEPTOE is British Heart Foundation Professor of Psychology, Department of Epidemiology and Public Health, University College London.

RICHARD SUZMAN is Associate Director for Behavioral and Social Research, National Institute on Aging, National Institutes of Health.

JAMES W. VAUPEL is Founding Director, Max Planck Institute for Demographic Research, Rostock, Germany.

LINDA J. WAITE is Director, Center on Aging, and Lucy Flower Professor of Sociology, NORC and University of Chicago.

ROBERT J. WILLIS is Research Professor, Institute for Social Research, and Professor of Economics, University of Michigan.

DAVID A. WISE is John F. Stambaugh Professor of Political Economy, John F. Kennedy School of Government, Harvard University, and Area Director of Aging and Retirement Programs, National Bureau of Economic Research.